Texinfo

Texinfo

The GNU Documentation Format
for Texinfo version 4.0, 28 September 1999

Happy Hacking

Richard Stallman

Robert J. Chassell
Richard M. Stallman

Cover art by Etienne Suvasa.

Short Contents

Table of Contents

Documentation is like sex: when it is good, it is very, very good; and when it is bad, it is better than nothing. —Dick Brandon

Texinfo Copying Conditions

The programs currently being distributed that relate to Texinfo include portions of GNU Emacs, plus other separate programs (including `makeinfo`, `info`, `texindex`, and '`texinfo.tex`'). These programs are *free*; this means that everyone is free to use them and free to redistribute them on a free basis. The Texinfo-related programs are not in the public domain; they are copyrighted and there are restrictions on their distribution, but these restrictions are designed to permit everything that a good cooperating citizen would want to do. What is not allowed is to try to prevent others from further sharing any version of these programs that they might get from you.

Specifically, we want to make sure that you have the right to give away copies of the programs that relate to Texinfo, that you receive source code or else can get it if you want it, that you can change these programs or use pieces of them in new free programs, and that you know you can do these things.

To make sure that everyone has such rights, we have to forbid you to deprive anyone else of these rights. For example, if you distribute copies of the Texinfo related programs, you must give the recipients all the rights that you have. You must make sure that they, too, receive or can get the source code. And you must tell them their rights.

Also, for our own protection, we must make certain that everyone finds out that there is no warranty for the programs that relate to Texinfo. If these programs are modified by someone else and passed on, we want their recipients to know that what they have is not what we distributed, so that any problems introduced by others will not reflect on our reputation.

The precise conditions of the licenses for the programs currently being distributed that relate to Texinfo are found in the General Public Licenses that accompany them.

1 Overview of Texinfo

Texinfo[1] is a documentation system that uses a single source file to produce both online information and printed output. This means that instead of writing two different documents, one for the online information and the other for a printed work, you need write only one document. Therefore, when the work is revised, you need revise only that one document.

1.1 Reporting Bugs

We welcome bug reports or suggestions for the Texinfo system, both programs and documentation. Please email them to `bug-texinfo@gnu.org`. You can get the latest version of Texinfo from `ftp://ftp.gnu.org/gnu/texinfo/` and its mirrors worldwide.

For bug reports, please include enough information for the maintainers to reproduce the problem. Generally speaking, that means:

- the version number of Texinfo and the program(s) or manual(s) involved.
- hardware, operating system, and compiler versions.
- any unusual options you gave to `configure`.
- the contents of any input files necessary to reproduce the bug.
- a description of the problem and samples of any erroneous output.
- anything else that you think would be helpful.

When in doubt whether something is needed or not, include it. It's better to include too much than to leave out something important.

Patches are most welcome; if possible, please make them with '`diff -c`' (see section "Overview" in *Comparing and Merging Files*) and include '`ChangeLog`' entries (see section "Change Log" in *The GNU Emacs Manual*).

When sending email, please do not encode or split the messages in any way if possible; it's much easier to deal with one plain text message, however large, than many small ones. GNU shar (`ftp://ftp.gnu.org/gnu/sharutils/`) is a convenient way of packaging multiple and/or binary files for email.

---

[1] The first syllable of "Texinfo" is pronounced like "speck", not "hex". This odd pronunciation is derived from, but is not the same as, the pronunciation of TeX. In the word TeX, the 'X' is actually the Greek letter "chi" rather than the English letter "ex". Pronounce TeX as if the 'X' were the last sound in the name 'Bach'; but pronounce Texinfo as if the 'x' were a 'k'. Spell "Texinfo" with a capital "T" and the other letters in lower case.

1.2 Using Texinfo

Using Texinfo, you can create a printed document with the normal features of a book, including chapters, sections, cross references, and indices. From the same Texinfo source file, you can create a menu-driven, online Info file with nodes, menus, cross references, and indices. You can also create from that same source file an HTML output file suitable for use with a web browser. *The GNU Emacs Manual* is a good example of a Texinfo file, as is this manual.

To make a printed document, you process a Texinfo source file with the TEX typesetting program (but the Texinfo language is very different from TEX's usual language, plain TEX). This creates a DVI file that you can typeset and print as a book or report (see Chapter 19 [Hardcopy], page 153).

To output an Info file, process your Texinfo source with the `makeinfo` utility or Emacs's `texinfo-format-buffer` command. You can install the result in your Info tree (see Section 20.2 [Install an Info File], page 173).

To output an HTML file, process your Texinfo source with `makeinfo` using the '`--html`' option. You can (for example) install the result on your web site.

If you are a programmer and would like to contribute to the GNU project by implementing additional output formats for Texinfo, that would be excellent. But please do not write a separate translator texi2foo for your favorite format foo! That is the hard way to do the job, and makes extra work in subsequent maintenance, since the Texinfo language is continually being enhanced and updated. Instead, the best approach is modify `makeinfo` to generate the new format, as it does now for Info and HTML.

TEX works with virtually all printers; Info works with virtually all computer terminals; the HTML output works with virtually all web browsers. Thus Texinfo can be used by almost any computer user.

A Texinfo source file is a plain ASCII file containing text and @-*commands* (words preceded by an '@') that tell the typesetting and formatting programs what to do. You may edit a Texinfo file with any text editor; but it is especially convenient to use GNU Emacs since that editor has a special mode, called Texinfo mode, that provides various Texinfo-related features. (See Chapter 2 [Texinfo Mode], page 16.)

Before writing a Texinfo source file, you should learn about nodes, menus, cross references, and the rest, for example by reading this manual.

You can use Texinfo to create both online help and printed manuals; moreover, Texinfo is freely redistributable. For these reasons, Texinfo is the official documentation format of the GNU project. More information is available at the GNU documentation web page (`http://www.gnu.org/doc/`).

From time to time, proposals are made to generate traditional Unix man pages from Texinfo source. This is not likely to ever be supported, because man pages have a very strict conventional format. Merely enhancing `makeinfo` to output troff format would be insufficient. Generating a good man page therefore requires a completely different source than the typical Texinfo applications of generating a good user manual or a good reference manual. This makes generating man pages incompatible with the Texinfo design goal of not having to document the same information in different ways for different output formats. You might as well just write the man page directly.

If you wish to support man pages, the program `help2man` may be useful; it generates a traditional man page from the '`--help`' output of a program. In fact, this is currently used to generate man pages for the Texinfo programs themselves. It is free software written by Brendan O'Dea, available from `http://www.ozemail.com.au/~bod/help2man.tar.gz`.

1.3 Info files

An Info file is a Texinfo file formatted so that the Info documentation reading program can operate on it. (`makeinfo` and `texinfo-format-buffer` are two commands that convert a Texinfo file into an Info file.)

Info files are divided into pieces called *nodes*, each of which contains the discussion of one topic. Each node has a name, and contains both text for the user to read and pointers to other nodes, which are identified by their names. The Info program displays one node at a time, and provides commands with which the user can move to other related nodes.

Each node of an Info file may have any number of child nodes that describe subtopics of the node's topic. The names of child nodes are listed in a *menu* within the parent node; this allows you to use certain Info commands to move to one of the child nodes. Generally, an Info file is organized like a book. If a node is at the logical level of a chapter, its child nodes are at the level of sections; likewise, the child nodes of sections are at the level of subsections.

All the children of any one parent are linked together in a bidirectional chain of 'Next' and 'Previous' pointers. The 'Next' pointer provides a link to the next section, and the 'Previous' pointer provides a link to the previous section. This means that all the nodes that are at the level of sections within a chapter are linked together. Normally the order in this chain is the same as the order of the children in the parent's menu. Each child node records the parent node name as its 'Up' pointer. The last child has no 'Next' pointer, and the first child has the parent both as its 'Previous' and as its 'Up' pointer.[2]

The book-like structuring of an Info file into nodes that correspond to chapters, sections, and the like is a matter of convention, not a requirement. The 'Up', 'Previous', and 'Next' pointers of a node can point to any other

---

[2] In some documents, the first child has no 'Previous' pointer. Occasionally, the last child has the node name of the next following higher level node as its 'Next' pointer.

nodes, and a menu can contain any other nodes. Thus, the node structure can be any directed graph. But it is usually more comprehensible to follow a structure that corresponds to the structure of chapters and sections in a printed book or report.

In addition to menus and to 'Next', 'Previous', and 'Up' pointers, Info provides pointers of another kind, called references, that can be sprinkled throughout the text. This is usually the best way to represent links that do not fit a hierarchical structure.

Usually, you will design a document so that its nodes match the structure of chapters and sections in the printed output. But occasionally there are times when this is not right for the material being discussed. Therefore, Texinfo uses separate commands to specify the node structure for the Info file and the section structure for the printed output.

Generally, you enter an Info file through a node that by convention is named 'Top'. This node normally contains just a brief summary of the file's purpose, and a large menu through which the rest of the file is reached. From this node, you can either traverse the file systematically by going from node to node, or you can go to a specific node listed in the main menu, or you can search the index menus and then go directly to the node that has the information you want. Alternatively, with the standalone Info program, you can specify specific menu items on the command line (see section "Top" in Info).

If you want to read through an Info file in sequence, as if it were a printed manual, you can hit (SPC) repeatedly, or you get the whole file with the advanced Info command g *. (See Info file 'info', node 'Expert'.)

The 'dir' file in the 'info' directory serves as the departure point for the whole Info system. From it, you can reach the 'Top' nodes of each of the documents in a complete Info system.

If you wish to refer to an Info file in a URI, you can use the (unofficial) syntax exemplified in the following. This works with Emacs/W3, for example:

```
info:///usr/info/emacs#Dissociated%20Press
info:emacs#Dissociated%20Press
info://localhost/usr/info/emacs#Dissociated%20Press
```

The info program itself does not follow URI's of any kind.

1.4 Printed Books

A Texinfo file can be formatted and typeset as a printed book or manual. To do this, you need TEX, a powerful, sophisticated typesetting program written by Donald Knuth.[3]

---

[3] You can also use the texi2roff (ftp://tug.org/texi2roff.tar.gz) program if you do not have TEX; since Texinfo is designed for use with TEX, texi2roff is not

A Texinfo-based book is similar to any other typeset, printed work: it can have a title page, copyright page, table of contents, and preface, as well as chapters, numbered or unnumbered sections and subsections, page headers, cross references, footnotes, and indices.

You can use Texinfo to write a book without ever having the intention of converting it into online information. You can use Texinfo for writing a printed novel, and even to write a printed memo, although this latter application is not recommended since electronic mail is so much easier.

TeX is a general purpose typesetting program. Texinfo provides a file 'texinfo.tex' that contains information (definitions or *macros*) that TeX uses when it typesets a Texinfo file. ('texinfo.tex' tells TeX how to convert the Texinfo @-commands to TeX commands, which TeX can then process to create the typeset document.) 'texinfo.tex' contains the specifications for printing a document. You can get the latest version of 'texinfo.tex' from ftp://ftp.gnu.org/gnu/texinfo.tex.

Most often, documents are printed on 8.5 inch by 11 inch pages (216 mm by 280 mm; this is the default size), but you can also print for 7 inch by 9.25 inch pages (178 mm by 235 mm; the @smallbook size) or on European A4 size paper (@afourpaper). (See Section 19.11 [Printing "Small" Books], page 161. Also, see Section 19.12 [Printing on A4 Paper], page 162.)

By changing the parameters in 'texinfo.tex', you can change the size of the printed document. In addition, you can change the style in which the printed document is formatted; for example, you can change the sizes and fonts used, the amount of indentation for each paragraph, the degree to which words are hyphenated, and the like. By changing the specifications, you can make a book look dignified, old and serious, or light-hearted, young and cheery.

TeX is freely distributable. It is written in a superset of Pascal called WEB and can be compiled either in Pascal or (by using a conversion program that comes with the TeX distribution) in C. (See section "TeX Mode" in *The GNU Emacs Manual*, for information about TeX.)

TeX is very powerful and has a great many features. Because a Texinfo file must be able to present information both on a character-only terminal in Info form and in a typeset book, the formatting commands that Texinfo supports are necessarily limited.

To get a copy of TeX, see Appendix J [How to Obtain TeX], page 228.

1.5 @-commands

In a Texinfo file, the commands that tell TeX how to typeset the printed manual and tell `makeinfo` and `texinfo-format-buffer` how to create an Info file are preceded by '@'; they are called @-*commands*. For example,

---

described here. `texi2roff` is not part of the standard GNU distribution and is not maintained or up-to-date with all the Texinfo features described in this manual.

`@node` is the command to indicate a node and `@chapter` is the command to indicate the start of a chapter.

Please note: All the `@`-commands, with the exception of the `@TeX{}` command, must be written entirely in lower case.

The Texinfo `@`-commands are a strictly limited set of constructs. The strict limits make it possible for Texinfo files to be understood both by TEX and by the code that converts them into Info files. You can display Info files on any terminal that displays alphabetic and numeric characters. Similarly, you can print the output generated by TEX on a wide variety of printers.

Depending on what they do or what arguments[4] they take, you need to write `@`-commands on lines of their own or as part of sentences:

- Write a command such as `@noindent` at the beginning of a line as the only text on the line. (`@noindent` prevents the beginning of the next line from being indented as the beginning of a paragraph.)

- Write a command such as `@chapter` at the beginning of a line followed by the command's arguments, in this case the chapter title, on the rest of the line. (`@chapter` creates chapter titles.)

- Write a command such as `@dots{}` wherever you wish but usually within a sentence. (`@dots{}` creates dots . . .)

- Write a command such as `@code{`*sample-code*`}` wherever you wish (but usually within a sentence) with its argument, *sample-code* in this example, between the braces. (`@code` marks text as being code.)

- Write a command such as `@example` on a line of its own; write the body-text on following lines; and write the matching `@end` command, `@end example` in this case, at the on a line of its own after the body-text. (`@example` . . . `@end example` indents and typesets body-text as an example.) It's usually ok to indent environment commands like this, but in complicated and hard-to-define circumstances the extra spaces cause extra space to appear in the output, so beware.

As a general rule, a command requires braces if it mingles among other text; but it does not need braces if it starts a line of its own. The non-alphabetic commands, such as `@:`, are exceptions to the rule; they do not need braces.

As you gain experience with Texinfo, you will rapidly learn how to write the different commands: the different ways to write commands make it easier to write and read Texinfo files than if all commands followed exactly the same

---

[4] The word *argument* comes from the way it is used in mathematics and does not refer to a dispute between two people; it refers to the information presented to the command. According to the *Oxford English Dictionary*, the word derives from the Latin for *to make clear, prove*; thus it came to mean 'the evidence offered as proof', which is to say, 'the information offered', which led to its mathematical meaning. In its other thread of derivation, the word came to mean 'to assert in a manner against which others may make counter assertions', which led to the meaning of 'argument' as a dispute.

syntax. (For details about @-command syntax, see Appendix I [@-Command Syntax], page 227.)

1.6 General Syntactic Conventions

This section describes the general conventions used in all Texinfo documents.

- All printable ASCII characters except '@', '{' and '}' can appear in a Texinfo file and stand for themselves. '@' is the escape character which introduces commands. '{' and '}' should be used only to surround arguments to certain commands. To put one of these special characters into the document, put an '@' character in front of it, like this: '@@', '@{', and '@}'.

- It is customary in TEX to use doubled single-quote characters to begin and end quotations: ' ' and ' ' . This convention should be followed in Texinfo files. TEX converts doubled single-quote characters to left- and right-hand doubled quotation marks, "like this", and Info converts doubled single-quote characters to ASCII double-quotes: ' ' and ' ' to " .

- Use three hyphens in a row, '---', for a dash—like this. In TEX, a single or double hyphen produces a printed dash that is shorter than the usual typeset dash. Info reduces three hyphens to two for display on the screen.

- To prevent a paragraph from being indented in the printed manual, put the command @noindent on a line by itself before the paragraph.

- If you mark off a region of the Texinfo file with the @iftex and @end iftex commands, that region will appear only in the printed copy; in that region, you can use certain commands borrowed from plain TEX that you cannot use in Info. Likewise, if you mark off a region with the @ifinfo and @end ifinfo commands, that region will appear only in the Info file; in that region, you can use Info commands that you cannot use in TEX. Similarly for @ifhtml ... @end ifhtml, @ifnothtml ... @end ifnothtml, @ifnotinfo ... @end ifnotinfo, @ifnottex ... @end ifnottex. See Chapter 16 [Conditionals], page 139.

  Caution: Do not use tabs in a Texinfo file! TEX uses variable-width fonts, which means that it cannot predefine a tab to work in all circumstances. Consequently, TEX treats tabs like single spaces, and that is not what they look like. Furthermore, makeinfo does nothing special with tabs, and thus a tab character in your input file may appear differently in the output.

  To avoid this problem, Texinfo mode causes GNU Emacs to insert multiple spaces when you press the (TAB) key.

Also, you can run **untabify** in Emacs to convert tabs in a region to multiple spaces.

1.7 Comments

You can write comments in a Texinfo file that will not appear in either the Info file or the printed manual by using the **@comment** command (which may be abbreviated to **@c**). Such comments are for the person who revises the Texinfo file. All the text on a line that follows either **@comment** or **@c** is a comment; the rest of the line does not appear in either the Info file or the printed manual. (Often, you can write the **@comment** or **@c** in the middle of a line, and only the text that follows after the **@comment** or **@c** command does not appear; but some commands, such as **@settitle** and **@setfilename**, work on a whole line. You cannot use **@comment** or **@c** in a line beginning with such a command.)

You can write long stretches of text that will not appear in either the Info file or the printed manual by using the **@ignore** and **@end ignore** commands. Write each of these commands on a line of its own, starting each command at the beginning of the line. Text between these two commands does not appear in the processed output. You can use **@ignore** and **@end ignore** for writing comments. Often, **@ignore** and **@end ignore** is used to enclose a part of the copying permissions that applies to the Texinfo source file of a document, but not to the Info or printed version of the document.

1.8 What a Texinfo File Must Have

By convention, the names of Texinfo files end with one of the extensions '.texinfo', '.texi', '.txi', or '.tex'. The longer extension is preferred since it describes more clearly to a human reader the nature of the file. The shorter extensions are for operating systems that cannot handle long file names.

In order to be made into a printed manual and an Info file, a Texinfo file **must** begin with lines like this:

```
\input texinfo
@setfilename info-file-name
@settitle name-of-manual
```

The contents of the file follow this beginning, and then you **must** end a Texinfo file with a line like this:

```
@bye
```

The '\input texinfo' line tells TeX to use the 'texinfo.tex' file, which tells TeX how to translate the Texinfo @-commands into TeX typesetting commands. (Note the use of the backslash, '\'; this is correct for TeX.) The '@setfilename' line provides a name for the Info file and tells TeX to open auxiliary files. The '@settitle' line specifies a title for the page headers (or footers) of the printed manual.

The @bye line at the end of the file on a line of its own tells the formatters that the file is ended and to stop formatting.

Usually, you will not use quite such a spare format, but will include mode setting and start-of-header and end-of-header lines at the beginning of a Texinfo file, like this:

```
\input texinfo   @c -*-texinfo-*-
@c %**start of header
@setfilename info-file-name
@settitle name-of-manual
@c %**end of header
```

In the first line, '-*-texinfo-*-' causes Emacs to switch into Texinfo mode when you edit the file.

The @c lines which surround the '@setfilename' and '@settitle' lines are optional, but you need them in order to run TEX or Info on just part of the file. (See Section 3.2.2 [Start of Header], page 32, for more information.)

Furthermore, you will usually provide a Texinfo file with a title page, indices, and the like. But the minimum, which can be useful for short documents, is just the three lines at the beginning and the one line at the end.

1.9 Six Parts of a Texinfo File

Generally, a Texinfo file contains more than the minimal beginning and end—it usually contains six parts:

1. Header   The *Header* names the file, tells TEX which definitions' file to use, and performs other "housekeeping" tasks.

2. Summary Description and Copyright
     The *Summary Description and Copyright* segment describes the document and contains the copyright notice and copying permissions for the Info file. The segment must be enclosed between @ifinfo and @end ifinfo commands so that the formatters place it only in the Info file.

3. Title and Copyright
     The *Title and Copyright* segment contains the title and copyright pages and copying permissions for the printed manual. The segment must be enclosed between @titlepage and @end titlepage commands. The title and copyright page appear only in the printed manual.

4. 'Top' Node and Master Menu
     The *Master Menu* contains a complete menu of all the nodes in the whole Info file. It appears only in the Info file, in the 'Top' node.

5. Body   The *Body* of the document may be structured like a traditional
            book or encyclopedia or it may be free form.

6. End   The *End* contains commands for printing indices and generating
            the table of contents, and the @bye command on a line of its own.

1.10 A Short Sample Texinfo File

Here is a complete but very short Texinfo file, in six parts. The first
three parts of the file, from '\input texinfo' through to '@end titlepage',
look more intimidating than they are. Most of the material is standard
boilerplate; when you write a manual, simply insert the names for your own
manual in this segment. (See Chapter 3 [Beginning a File], page 30.)

In the following, the sample text is *indented*; comments on it are not.
The complete file, without any comments, is shown in Appendix C [Sample
Texinfo File], page 204.

Part 1: Header

The header does not appear in either the Info file or the printed output. It
sets various parameters, including the name of the Info file and the title used
in the header.

```
\input texinfo   @c -*-texinfo-*-
@c %**start of header
@setfilename sample.info
@settitle Sample Document
@setchapternewpage odd
@c %**end of header
```

Part 2: Summary Description and Copyright

The summary description and copyright segment does not appear in the
printed document.

```
@ifinfo
This is a short example of a complete Texinfo file.

Copyright @copyright{} 1990 Free Software Foundation, Inc.
@end ifinfo
```

Part 3: Titlepage and Copyright

The titlepage segment does not appear in the Info file.

```
@titlepage
@sp 10
@comment The title is printed in a large font.
@center @titlefont{Sample Title}
```

```
@c The following two commands start the copyright page.
@page
@vskip 0pt plus 1filll
Copyright @copyright{} 1990 Free Software Foundation, Inc.
@end titlepage
```

Part 4: 'Top' Node and Master Menu

The 'Top' node contains the master menu for the Info file. Since a printed manual uses a table of contents rather than a menu, the master menu appears only in the Info file.

```
@node      Top,      First Chapter, ,          (dir)
@comment node-name, next,          previous, up

@menu
* First Chapter::     The first chapter is the
                      only chapter in this sample.
* Concept Index::     This index has two entries.
@end menu
```

Part 5: The Body of the Document

The body segment contains all the text of the document, but not the indices or table of contents. This example illustrates a node and a chapter containing an enumerated list.

```
@node      First Chapter, Concept Index, Top,      Top
@comment node-name,       next,          previous, up
@chapter First Chapter
@cindex Sample index entry

This is the contents of the first chapter.
@cindex Another sample index entry

Here is a numbered list.

@enumerate
@item
This is the first item.

@item
This is the second item.
@end enumerate
```

```
The @code{makeinfo} and @code{texinfo-format-buffer}
commands transform a Texinfo file such as this into
an Info file; and @TeX{} typesets it for a printed
manual.
```

Part 6: The End of the Document

The end segment contains commands for generating an index in a node and
unnumbered chapter of its own, (usually) for generating the table of contents,
and the @bye command that marks the end of the document.

```
@node    Concept Index,    , First Chapter, Top
@unnumbered Concept Index

@printindex cp

@contents
@bye
```

The Results

Here is what the contents of the first chapter of the sample look like:

This is the contents of the first chapter.

Here is a numbered list.

1. This is the first item.

2. This is the second item.

The makeinfo and texinfo-format-buffer commands transform
a Texinfo file such as this into an Info file; and TEX typesets it for
a printed manual.

1.11 Acknowledgements and History

Richard M. Stallman invented the Texinfo format, wrote the initial processors, and created Edition 1.0 of this manual. Robert J. Chassell greatly
revised and extended the manual, starting with Edition 1.1. Brian Fox was
responsible for the standalone Texinfo distribution until version 3.8, and
wrote the standalone makeinfo and info. Karl Berry has made the updates
since Texinfo 3.8 and subsequent releases, starting with Edition 2.22 of the
manual.

Our thanks go out to all who helped improve this work, particularly to
François Pinard and David D. Zuhn, who tirelessly recorded and reported
mistakes and obscurities; our special thanks go to Melissa Weisshaus for
her frequent and often tedious reviews of nearly similar editions. The inde-
fatigable Eli Zaretskii and Andreas Schwab have provided patches beyond

counting. Zack Weinberg did the impossible by implementing the macro syntax in 'texinfo.tex'. Dozens of others have contributed patches and suggestions, they are gratefully acknowledged in the 'ChangeLog' file. Our mistakes are our own.

A bit of history: in the 1970's at CMU, Brian Reid developed a program and format named Scribe to mark up documents for printing. It used the @ character to introduce commands as Texinfo does and strived to describe document contents rather than formatting.

Meanwhile, people at MIT developed another, not too dissimilar format called Bolio. This then was converted to using TeX as its typesetting language: BoTeX.

BoTeX could only be used as a markup language for documents to be printed, not for online documents. Richard Stallman (RMS) worked on both Bolio and BoTeX. He also developed a nifty on-line help format called Info, and then combined BoTeX and Info to create Texinfo, a mark up language for text that is intended to be read both on line and as printed hard copy.

2 Using Texinfo Mode

You may edit a Texinfo file with any text editor you choose. A Texinfo file is no different from any other ASCII file. However, GNU Emacs comes with a special mode, called Texinfo mode, that provides Emacs commands and tools to help ease your work.

This chapter describes features of GNU Emacs' Texinfo mode but not any features of the Texinfo formatting language. If you are reading this manual straight through from the beginning, you may want to skim through this chapter briefly and come back to it after reading succeeding chapters which describe the Texinfo formatting language in detail.

Texinfo mode provides special features for working with Texinfo files. You can:

- Insert frequently used @-commands.
- Automatically create @node lines.
- Show the structure of a Texinfo source file.
- Automatically create or update the 'Next', 'Previous', and 'Up' pointers of a node.
- Automatically create or update menus.
- Automatically create a master menu.
- Format a part or all of a file for Info.
- Typeset and print part or all of a file.

Perhaps the two most helpful features are those for inserting frequently used @-commands and for creating node pointers and menus.

2.1 The Usual GNU Emacs Editing Commands

In most cases, the usual Text mode commands work the same in Texinfo mode as they do in Text mode. Texinfo mode adds new editing commands and tools to GNU Emacs' general purpose editing features. The major difference concerns filling. In Texinfo mode, the paragraph separation variable and syntax table are redefined so that Texinfo commands that should be on lines of their own are not inadvertently included in paragraphs. Thus, the *M-q* (`fill-paragraph`) command will refill a paragraph but not mix an indexing command on a line adjacent to it into the paragraph.

In addition, Texinfo mode sets the `page-delimiter` variable to the value of `texinfo-chapter-level-regexp`; by default, this is a regular expression matching the commands for chapters and their equivalents, such as appendices. With this value for the page delimiter, you can jump from chapter title to chapter title with the *C-x]* (`forward-page`) and *C-x [* (`backward-page`) commands and narrow to a chapter with the *C-x p* (`narrow-to-page`) command. (See section "Pages" in *The GNU Emacs Manual*, for details about the page commands.)

You may name a Texinfo file however you wish, but the convention is to end a Texinfo file name with one of the extensions '`.texinfo`', '`.texi`', '`.txi`', or '`.tex`'. A longer extension is preferred, since it is explicit, but a shorter extension may be necessary for operating systems that limit the length of file names. GNU Emacs automatically enters Texinfo mode when you visit a file with a '`.texinfo`', '`.texi`' or '`.txi`' extension. Also, Emacs switches to Texinfo mode when you visit a file that has '`-*-texinfo-*-`' in its first line. If ever you are in another mode and wish to switch to Texinfo mode, type `M-x texinfo-mode`.

Like all other Emacs features, you can customize or enhance Texinfo mode as you wish. In particular, the keybindings are very easy to change. The keybindings described here are the default or standard ones.

2.2 Inserting Frequently Used Commands

Texinfo mode provides commands to insert various frequently used @-commands into the buffer. You can use these commands to save keystrokes.

The insert commands are invoked by typing *C-c* twice and then the first letter of the @-command:

C-c C-c c
M-x texinfo-insert-@code
> Insert @code{} and put the cursor between the braces.

C-c C-c d
M-x texinfo-insert-@dfn
> Insert @dfn{} and put the cursor between the braces.

C-c C-c e
M-x texinfo-insert-@end
> Insert @end and attempt to insert the correct following word, such as '`example`' or '`table`'. (This command does not handle nested lists correctly, but inserts the word appropriate to the immediately preceding list.)

C-c C-c i
M-x texinfo-insert-@item
> Insert @item and put the cursor at the beginning of the next line.

C-c C-c k
M-x texinfo-insert-@kbd
> Insert @kbd{} and put the cursor between the braces.

C-c C-c n
M-x texinfo-insert-@node
> Insert @node and a comment line listing the sequence for the 'Next', 'Previous', and 'Up' nodes. Leave point after the @node.

`C-c C-c o`
`M-x texinfo-insert-@noindent`
> Insert `@noindent` and put the cursor at the beginning of the next line.

`C-c C-c s`
`M-x texinfo-insert-@samp`
> Insert `@samp{}` and put the cursor between the braces.

`C-c C-c t`
`M-x texinfo-insert-@table`
> Insert `@table` followed by a (SPC) and leave the cursor after the (SPC).

`C-c C-c v`
`M-x texinfo-insert-@var`
> Insert `@var{}` and put the cursor between the braces.

`C-c C-c x`
`M-x texinfo-insert-@example`
> Insert `@example` and put the cursor at the beginning of the next line.

`C-c C-c {`
`M-x texinfo-insert-braces`
> Insert `{}` and put the cursor between the braces.

`C-c C-c }`
`C-c C-c ]`
`M-x up-list`
> Move from between a pair of braces forward past the closing brace. Typing `C-c C-c ]` is easier than typing `C-c C-c }`, which is, however, more mnemonic; hence the two keybindings. (Also, you can move out from between braces by typing `C-f`.)

To put a command such as `@code{...}` around an *existing* word, position the cursor in front of the word and type `C-u 1 C-c C-c c`. This makes it easy to edit existing plain text. The value of the prefix argument tells Emacs how many words following point to include between braces—'1' for one word, '2' for two words, and so on. Use a negative argument to enclose the previous word or words. If you do not specify a prefix argument, Emacs inserts the @-command string and positions the cursor between the braces. This feature works only for those @-commands that operate on a word or words within one line, such as `@kbd` and `@var`.

This set of insert commands was created after analyzing the frequency with which different @-commands are used in the *GNU Emacs Manual* and the *GDB Manual*. If you wish to add your own insert commands, you can bind a keyboard macro to a key, use abbreviations, or extend the code in '`texinfo.el`'.

C-c C-c C-d (`texinfo-start-menu-description`) is an insert command that works differently from the other insert commands. It inserts a node's section or chapter title in the space for the description in a menu entry line. (A menu entry has three parts, the entry name, the node name, and the description. Only the node name is required, but a description helps explain what the node is about. See Section 7.2 [The Parts of a Menu], page 65.)

To use `texinfo-start-menu-description`, position point in a menu entry line and type *C-c C-c C-d*. The command looks for and copies the title that goes with the node name, and inserts the title as a description; it positions point at beginning of the inserted text so you can edit it. The function does not insert the title if the menu entry line already contains a description.

This command is only an aid to writing descriptions; it does not do the whole job. You must edit the inserted text since a title tends to use the same words as a node name but a useful description uses different words.

2.3 Showing the Section Structure of a File

You can show the section structure of a Texinfo file by using the *C-c C-s* command (`texinfo-show-structure`). This command shows the section structure of a Texinfo file by listing the lines that begin with the @-commands for `@chapter`, `@section`, and the like. It constructs what amounts to a table of contents. These lines are displayed in another buffer called the '*Occur*' buffer. In that buffer, you can position the cursor over one of the lines and use the *C-c C-c* command (`occur-mode-goto-occurrence`), to jump to the corresponding spot in the Texinfo file.

C-c C-s
M-x texinfo-show-structure
        Show the `@chapter`, `@section`, and such lines of a Texinfo file.

C-c C-c
M-x occur-mode-goto-occurrence
        Go to the line in the Texinfo file corresponding to the line under the cursor in the '*Occur*' buffer.

If you call `texinfo-show-structure` with a prefix argument by typing *C-u C-c C-s*, it will list not only those lines with the @-commands for `@chapter`, `@section`, and the like, but also the `@node` lines. You can use `texinfo-show-structure` with a prefix argument to check whether the 'Next', 'Previous', and 'Up' pointers of an `@node` line are correct.

Often, when you are working on a manual, you will be interested only in the structure of the current chapter. In this case, you can mark off the region of the buffer that you are interested in by using the *C-x n n* (`narrow-to-region`) command and `texinfo-show-structure` will work on only that region. To see the whole buffer again, use *C-x n w* (`widen`). (See section

"Narrowing" in *The GNU Emacs Manual*, for more information about the
narrowing commands.)

In addition to providing the `texinfo-show-structure` command, Texinfo mode sets the value of the page delimiter variable to match the chapter-
level @-commands. This enables you to use the `C-x ]` (`forward-page`) and
`C-x [` (`backward-page`) commands to move forward and backward by chapter, and to use the `C-x p` (`narrow-to-page`) command to narrow to a chapter. See section "Pages" in *The GNU Emacs Manual*, for more information
about the page commands.

2.4 Updating Nodes and Menus

Texinfo mode provides commands for automatically creating or updating menus and node pointers. The commands are called "update" commands
because their most frequent use is for updating a Texinfo file after you have
worked on it; but you can use them to insert the 'Next', 'Previous', and 'Up'
pointers into an @node line that has none and to create menus in a file that
has none.

If you do not use the updating commands, you need to write menus and
node pointers by hand, which is a tedious task.

You can use the updating commands to:

- insert or update the 'Next', 'Previous', and 'Up' pointers of a node,
- insert or update the menu for a section, and
- create a master menu for a Texinfo source file.

You can also use the commands to update all the nodes and menus in
a region or in a whole Texinfo file.

The updating commands work only with conventional Texinfo files,
which are structured hierarchically like books. In such files, a structuring
command line must follow closely after each @node line, except for the 'Top'
@node line. (A *structuring command line* is a line beginning with @chapter,
@section, or other similar command.)

You can write the structuring command line on the line that follows
immediately after an @node line or else on the line that follows after a single
@comment line or a single @ifinfo line. You cannot interpose more than one
line between the @node line and the structuring command line; and you may
interpose only an @comment line or an @ifinfo line.

Commands which work on a whole buffer require that the 'Top' node
be followed by a node with an @chapter or equivalent-level command. The
menu updating commands will not create a main or master menu for a Texinfo file that has only @chapter-level nodes! The menu updating commands
only create menus *within* nodes for lower level nodes. To create a menu of
chapters, you must provide a 'Top' node.

The menu updating commands remove menu entries that refer to other
Info files since they do not refer to nodes within the current buffer. This

is a deficiency. Rather than use menu entries, you can use cross references to refer to other Info files. None of the updating commands affect cross references.

Texinfo mode has five updating commands that are used most often: two are for updating the node pointers or menu of a single node (or a region); two are for updating every node pointer and menu in a file; and one, the `texinfo-master-menu` command, is for creating a master menu for a complete file, and optionally, for updating every node and menu in the whole Texinfo file.

The `texinfo-master-menu` command is the primary command:

C-c C-u m
M-x texinfo-master-menu

> Create or update a master menu that includes all the other menus (incorporating the descriptions from pre-existing menus, if any).
>
> With an argument (prefix argument, *C-u,* if interactive), first create or update all the nodes and all the regular menus in the buffer before constructing the master menu. (See Section 3.5 [The Top Node and Master Menu], page 43, for more about a master menu.)
>
> For `texinfo-master-menu` to work, the Texinfo file must have a 'Top' node and at least one subsequent node.
>
> After extensively editing a Texinfo file, you can type the following:
>
>   C-u M-x texinfo-master-menu
> or
>   C-u C-c C-u m
>
> This updates all the nodes and menus completely and all at once.

The other major updating commands do smaller jobs and are designed for the person who updates nodes and menus as he or she writes a Texinfo file.

The commands are:

C-c C-u C-n
M-x texinfo-update-node

> Insert the 'Next', 'Previous', and 'Up' pointers for the node that point is within (i.e., for the `@node` line preceding point). If the `@node` line has pre-existing 'Next', 'Previous', or 'Up' pointers in it, the old pointers are removed and new ones inserted. With an argument (prefix argument, *C-u*, if interactive), this command updates all `@node` lines in the region (which is the text between point and mark).

`C-c C-u C-m`
`M-x texinfo-make-menu`

> Create or update the menu in the node that point is within.
> With an argument (`C-u` as prefix argument, if interactive), the
> command makes or updates menus for the nodes which are either
> within or a part of the region.
>
> Whenever **texinfo-make-menu** updates an existing menu, the
> descriptions from that menu are incorporated into the new menu.
> This is done by copying descriptions from the existing menu to
> the entries in the new menu that have the same node names. If
> the node names are different, the descriptions are not copied to
> the new menu.

`C-c C-u C-e`
`M-x texinfo-every-node-update`

> Insert or update the 'Next', 'Previous', and 'Up' pointers for
> every node in the buffer.

`C-c C-u C-a`
`M-x texinfo-all-menus-update`

> Create or update all the menus in the buffer. With an argument
> (`C-u` as prefix argument, if interactive), first insert or update all
> the node pointers before working on the menus.
>
> If a master menu exists, the **texinfo-all-menus-update** com-
> mand updates it; but the command does not create a new mas-
> ter menu if none already exists. (Use the **texinfo-master-menu**
> command for that.)
>
> When working on a document that does not merit a master
> menu, you can type the following:
>
>   C-u C-c C-u C-a
>
> or
>
>   C-u M-x texinfo-all-menus-update
>
> This updates all the nodes and menus.

The **texinfo-column-for-description** variable specifies the column
to which menu descriptions are indented. By default, the value is 32 although
it is often useful to reduce it to as low as 24. You can set the variable with
the `M-x edit-options` command (see section "Editing Variable Values" in
The GNU Emacs Manual) or with the `M-x set-variable` command (see
section "Examining and Setting Variables" in *The GNU Emacs Manual*).

Also, the **texinfo-indent-menu-description** command may be used
to indent existing menu descriptions to a specified column. Finally, if you
wish, you can use the **texinfo-insert-node-lines** command to insert
missing @node lines into a file. (See Section 2.4.2 [Other Updating Com-
mands], page 23, for more information.)

2.4.1 Updating Requirements

To use the updating commands, you must organize the Texinfo file hierarchically with chapters, sections, subsections, and the like. When you construct the hierarchy of the manual, do not 'jump down' more than one level at a time: you can follow the 'Top' node with a chapter, but not with a section; you can follow a chapter with a section, but not with a subsection. However, you may 'jump up' any number of levels at one time—for example, from a subsection to a chapter.

Each @node line, with the exception of the line for the 'Top' node, must be followed by a line with a structuring command such as @chapter, @section, or @unnumberedsubsec.

Each @node line/structuring-command line combination must look either like this:

```
@node       Comments,  Minimum,  Conventions,  Overview
@comment  node-name,  next,      previous,     up
@section Comments
```

or like this (without the @comment line):

```
@node Comments, Minimum, Conventions, Overview
@section Comments
```

In this example, 'Comments' is the name of both the node and the section. The next node is called 'Minimum' and the previous node is called 'Conventions'. The 'Comments' section is within the 'Overview' node, which is specified by the 'Up' pointer. (Instead of an @comment line, you may also write an @ifinfo line.)

If a file has a 'Top' node, it must be called 'top' or 'Top' and be the first node in the file.

The menu updating commands create a menu of sections within a chapter, a menu of subsections within a section, and so on. This means that you must have a 'Top' node if you want a menu of chapters.

Incidentally, the makeinfo command will create an Info file for a hierarchically organized Texinfo file that lacks 'Next', 'Previous' and 'Up' pointers. Thus, if you can be sure that your Texinfo file will be formatted with makeinfo, you have no need for the update node commands. (See Section 20.1 [Creating an Info File], page 165, for more information about makeinfo.) However, both makeinfo and the texinfo-format-... commands require that you insert menus in the file.

2.4.2 Other Updating Commands

In addition to the five major updating commands, Texinfo mode possesses several less frequently used updating commands:

M-x texinfo-insert-node-lines

Insert @node lines before the @chapter, @section, and other
sectioning commands wherever they are missing throughout a
region in a Texinfo file.

With an argument (*C-u* as prefix argument, if interactive), the
texinfo-insert-node-lines command not only inserts @node
lines but also inserts the chapter or section titles as the names of
the corresponding nodes. In addition, it inserts the titles as node
names in pre-existing @node lines that lack names. Since node
names should be more concise than section or chapter titles, you
must manually edit node names so inserted.

For example, the following marks a whole buffer as a region and
inserts @node lines and titles throughout:

C-x h C-u M-x texinfo-insert-node-lines

This command inserts titles as node names in @node lines; the
texinfo-start-menu-description command (see Section 2.2
[Inserting], page 17) inserts titles as descriptions in menu entries,
a different action. However, in both cases, you need to edit the
inserted text.

M-x texinfo-multiple-files-update

Update nodes and menus in a document built from several separate files. With *C-u* as a prefix argument, create and insert a master menu in the outer file. With a numeric prefix
argument, such as *C-u 2*, first update all the menus and all
the 'Next', 'Previous', and 'Up' pointers of all the included
files before creating and inserting a master menu in the outer
file. The texinfo-multiple-files-update command is described in the appendix on @include files. See Section E.2
[texinfo-multiple-files-update], page 209.

M-x texinfo-indent-menu-description

Indent every description in the menu following point to the specified column. You can use this command to give yourself more
space for descriptions. With an argument (*C-u* as prefix argument, if interactive), the texinfo-indent-menu-description
command indents every description in every menu in the region.
However, this command does not indent the second and subsequent lines of a multi-line description.

M-x texinfo-sequential-node-update

Insert the names of the nodes immediately following and preceding the current node as the 'Next' or 'Previous' pointers regardless of those nodes' hierarchical level. This means that the 'Next'
node of a subsection may well be the next chapter. Sequentially
ordered nodes are useful for novels and other documents that you
read through sequentially. (However, in Info, the *g ** command

lets you look through the file sequentially, so sequentially ordered
nodes are not strictly necessary.) With an argument (prefix argument, if interactive), the `texinfo-sequential-node-update`
command sequentially updates all the nodes in the region.

2.5 Formatting for Info

Texinfo mode provides several commands for formatting part or all of
a Texinfo file for Info. Often, when you are writing a document, you want
to format only part of a file—that is, a region.

You can use either the `texinfo-format-region` or the `makeinfo-
region` command to format a region:

`C-c C-e C-r`
`M-x texinfo-format-region`
`C-c C-m C-r`
`M-x makeinfo-region`
Format the current region for Info.

You can use either the `texinfo-format-buffer` or the `makeinfo-
buffer` command to format a whole buffer:

`C-c C-e C-b`
`M-x texinfo-format-buffer`
`C-c C-m C-b`
`M-x makeinfo-buffer`
Format the current buffer for Info.

For example, after writing a Texinfo file, you can type the following:

`C-u C-c C-u m`

or

`C-u M-x texinfo-master-menu`

This updates all the nodes and menus. Then type the following to create an
Info file:

`C-c C-m C-b`

or

`M-x makeinfo-buffer`

For TEX or the Info formatting commands to work, the file *must* include
a line that has `@setfilename` in its header.

See Section 20.1 [Creating an Info File], page 165, for details about Info
formatting.

2.6 Formatting and Printing

Typesetting and printing a Texinfo file is a multi-step process in which
you first create a file for printing (called a DVI file), and then print the

file. Optionally, you may also create indices. To do this, you must run the `texindex` command after first running the `tex` typesetting command; and then you must run the `tex` command again. Or else run the `texi2dvi` command which automatically creates indices as needed (see Section 19.3 [Format with texi2dvi], page 155).

Often, when you are writing a document, you want to typeset and print only part of a file to see what it will look like. You can use the `texinfo-tex-region` and related commands for this purpose. Use the `texinfo-tex-buffer` command to format all of a buffer.

`C-c C-t C-b`
`M-x texinfo-tex-buffer`
> Run `texi2dvi` on the buffer. In addition to running TeX on the buffer, this command automatically creates or updates indices as needed.

`C-c C-t C-r`
`M-x texinfo-tex-region`
> Run TeX on the region.

`C-c C-t C-i`
`M-x texinfo-texindex`
> Run `texindex` to sort the indices of a Texinfo file formatted with `texinfo-tex-region`. The `texinfo-tex-region` command does not run `texindex` automatically; it only runs the `tex` typesetting command. You must run the `texinfo-tex-region` command a second time after sorting the raw index files with the `texindex` command. (Usually, you do not format an index when you format a region, only when you format a buffer. Now that the `texi2dvi` command exists, there is little or no need for this command.)

`C-c C-t C-p`
`M-x texinfo-tex-print`
> Print the file (or the part of the file) previously formatted with `texinfo-tex-buffer` or `texinfo-tex-region`.

For `texinfo-tex-region` or `texinfo-tex-buffer` to work, the file *must* start with a '\input texinfo' line and must include an @settitle line. The file must end with @bye on a line by itself. (When you use `texinfo-tex-region`, you must surround the @settitle line with start-of-header and end-of-header lines.)

See Chapter 19 [Hardcopy], page 153, for a description of the other TeX related commands, such as `tex-show-print-queue`.

2.7 Texinfo Mode Summary

In Texinfo mode, each set of commands has default keybindings that begin with the same keys. All the commands that are custom-created for Texinfo mode begin with *C-c*. The keys are somewhat mnemonic.

Insert Commands

The insert commands are invoked by typing *C-c* twice and then the first letter of the @-command to be inserted. (It might make more sense mnemonically to use *C-c C-i*, for 'custom insert', but *C-c C-c* is quick to type.)

C-c C-c c	Insert '@code'.
C-c C-c d	Insert '@dfn'.
C-c C-c e	Insert '@end'.
C-c C-c i	Insert '@item'.
C-c C-c n	Insert '@node'.
C-c C-c s	Insert '@samp'.
C-c C-c v	Insert '@var'.
C-c C-c {	Insert braces.
C-c C-c]	
C-c C-c }	Move out of enclosing braces.
C-c C-c C-d	Insert a node's section title in the space for the description in a menu entry line.

Show Structure

The `texinfo-show-structure` command is often used within a narrowed region.

C-c C-s	List all the headings.

The Master Update Command

The `texinfo-master-menu` command creates a master menu; and can be used to update every node and menu in a file as well.

C-c C-u m M-x texinfo-master-menu	Create or update a master menu.
C-u C-c C-u m	With *C-u* as a prefix argument, first create or update all nodes and regular menus, and then create a master menu.

Update Pointers

The update pointer commands are invoked by typing *C-c C-u* and then either *C-n* for `texinfo-update-node` or *C-e* for `texinfo-every-node-update`.

C-c C-u C-n   Update a node.
C-c C-u C-e   Update every node in the buffer.

Update Menus

Invoke the update menu commands by typing *C-c C-u* and then either *C-m* for `texinfo-make-menu` or *C-a* for `texinfo-all-menus-update`. To update both nodes and menus at the same time, precede *C-c C-u C-a* with *C-u*.

C-c C-u C-m   Make or update a menu.

C-c C-u C-a   Make or update all
                menus in a buffer.

C-u C-c C-u C-a With *C-u* as a prefix argument,
                first create or update all nodes and
                then create or update all menus.

Format for Info

The Info formatting commands that are written in Emacs Lisp are invoked by typing *C-c C-e* and then either *C-r* for a region or *C-b* for the whole buffer.

The Info formatting commands that are written in C and based on the `makeinfo` program are invoked by typing *C-c C-m* and then either *C-r* for a region or *C-b* for the whole buffer.

Use the `texinfo-format...` commands:

C-c C-e C-r   Format the region.
C-c C-e C-b   Format the buffer.

Use `makeinfo`:

C-c C-m C-r   Format the region.
C-c C-m C-b   Format the buffer.
C-c C-m C-l   Recenter the `makeinfo` output buffer.
C-c C-m C-k   Kill the `makeinfo` formatting job.

Typeset and Print

The TEX typesetting and printing commands are invoked by typing *C-c C-t* and then another control command: *C-r* for `texinfo-tex-region`, *C-b* for `texinfo-tex-buffer`, and so on.

`C-c C-t C-r`	Run T_EX on the region.
`C-c C-t C-b`	Run `texi2dvi` on the buffer.
`C-c C-t C-i`	Run `texindex`.
`C-c C-t C-p`	Print the DVI file.
`C-c C-t C-q`	Show the print queue.
`C-c C-t C-d`	Delete a job from the print queue.
`C-c C-t C-k`	Kill the current T_EX formatting job.
`C-c C-t C-x`	Quit a currently stopped T_EX formatting job.
`C-c C-t C-l`	Recenter the output buffer.

Other Updating Commands

The remaining updating commands do not have standard keybindings because they are rarely used.

`M-x texinfo-insert-node-lines`

> Insert missing @node lines in region.
> With *C-u* as a prefix argument,
> use section titles as node names.

`M-x texinfo-multiple-files-update`

> Update a multi-file document.
> With *C-u 2* as a prefix argument,
> create or update all nodes and menus
> in all included files first.

`M-x texinfo-indent-menu-description`

> Indent descriptions.

`M-x texinfo-sequential-node-update`

> Insert node pointers in strict sequence.

3 Beginning a Texinfo File

Certain pieces of information must be provided at the beginning of a Texinfo file, such as the name of the file and the title of the document.

Generally, the beginning of a Texinfo file has four parts:

1. The header, delimited by special comment lines, that includes the commands for naming the Texinfo file and telling TeX what definitions file to use when processing the Texinfo file.

2. A short statement of what the file is about, with a copyright notice and copying permissions. This is enclosed in `@ifinfo` and `@end ifinfo` commands so that the formatters place it only in the Info file.

3. A title page and copyright page, with a copyright notice and copying permissions. This is enclosed between `@titlepage` and `@end titlepage` commands. The title and copyright page appear only in the printed manual.

4. The 'Top' node that contains a menu for the whole Info file. The contents of this node appear only in the Info file.

Also, optionally, you may include the copying conditions for a program and a warranty disclaimer. The copying section will be followed by an introduction or else by the first chapter of the manual.

Since the copyright notice and copying permissions for the Texinfo document (in contrast to the copying permissions for a program) are in parts that appear only in the Info file or only in the printed manual, this information must be given twice.

3.1 Sample Texinfo File Beginning

The following sample shows what is needed.

```
\input texinfo    @c -*-texinfo-*-
@c %**start of header
@setfilename name-of-info-file
@settitle name-of-manual
@setchapternewpage odd
@c %**end of header

@ifinfo
This file documents ...

Copyright year copyright-owner

Permission is granted to ...
@end ifinfo
```

```
@c  This title page illustrates only one of the
@c  two methods of forming a title page.
@titlepage
@title name-of-manual-when-printed
@subtitle subtitle-if-any
@subtitle second-subtitle
@author author

@c  The following two commands
@c  start the copyright page.
@page
@vskip 0pt plus 1filll
Copyright @copyright{} year copyright-owner

Published by ...

Permission is granted to ...
@end titlepage

@node Top, Overview, , (dir)

@ifinfo
This document describes ...

This document applies to version ...
of the program named ...
@end ifinfo

@menu
* Copying::          Your rights and freedoms.
* First Chapter::    Getting started ...
* Second Chapter::            ...
  ...
  ...
@end menu

@node    First Chapter, Second Chapter, top,    top
@comment node-name,     next,         previous, up
@chapter First Chapter
@cindex Index entry for First Chapter
```

3.2 The Texinfo File Header

Texinfo files start with at least three lines that provide Info and TEX with necessary information. These are the \input texinfo line, the @settitle line, and the @setfilename line. If you want to run TEX on just a part of the Texinfo File, you must write the `@settitle` and `@setfilename` lines between start-of-header and end-of-header lines.

Thus, the beginning of a Texinfo file looks like this:

```
\input texinfo    @c -*-texinfo-*-
@setfilename sample.info
@settitle Sample Document
```

or else like this:

```
\input texinfo    @c -*-texinfo-*-
@c %**start of header
@setfilename sample.info
@settitle Sample Document
@c %**end of header
```

3.2.1 The First Line of a Texinfo File

Every Texinfo file that is to be the top-level input to TeX must begin with a line that looks like this:

```
\input texinfo    @c -*-texinfo-*-
```

This line serves two functions:

1. When the file is processed by TeX, the '`\input texinfo`' command tells TeX to load the macros needed for processing a Texinfo file. These are in a file called '`texinfo.tex`', which is usually located in the '`/usr/lib/tex/macros`' directory. TeX uses the backslash, '`\`', to mark the beginning of a command, just as Texinfo uses '`@`'. The '`texinfo.tex`' file causes the switch from '`\`' to '`@`'; before the switch occurs, TeX requires '`\`', which is why it appears at the beginning of the file.

2. When the file is edited in GNU Emacs, the '`-*-texinfo-*-`' mode specification tells Emacs to use Texinfo mode.

3.2.2 Start of Header

Write a start-of-header line on the second line of a Texinfo file. Follow the start-of-header line with `@setfilename` and `@settitle` lines and, optionally, with other command lines, such as `@smallbook` or `@footnotestyle`; and then by an end-of-header line (see Section 3.2.8 [End of Header], page 36).

With these lines, you can format part of a Texinfo file for Info or typeset part for printing.

A start-of-header line looks like this:

```
@c %**start of header
```

The odd string of characters, '`%**`', is to ensure that no other comment is accidentally taken for a start-of-header line.

3.2.3 @setfilename

In order to serve as the primary input file for either `makeinfo` or TEX, a Texinfo file must contain a line that looks like this:

`@setfilename` *info-file-name*

Write the `@setfilename` command at the beginning of a line and follow it on the same line by the Info file name. Do not write anything else on the line; anything on the line after the command is considered part of the file name, including what would otherwise be a comment.

The `@setfilename` line specifies the name of the output file to be generated. This name should be different from the name of the Texinfo file. There are two conventions for choosing the name: you can either remove the extension (such as '`.texi`') from the input file name, or replace it with the '`.info`' extension. When producing HTML output, `makeinfo` will replace any extension with '`html`', or add '`.html`' if the given name has no extension.

Some operating systems cannot handle long file names. You can run into a problem even when the file name you specify is itself short enough. This occurs because the Info formatters split a long Info file into short indirect subfiles, and name them by appending '`-1`', '`-2`', ..., '`-10`', '`-11`', and so on, to the original file name. (See Section 20.1.8 [Tag Files and Split Files], page 171.) The subfile name '`texinfo.info-10`', for example, is too long for some systems; so the Info file name for this document is '`texinfo`' rather than '`texinfo.info`'. When `makeinfo` is running on operating systems such as MS-DOS which impose grave limits on file names, it will sometimes remove some characters from the original file name to leave enough space for the subfile suffix, thus producing files named '`texin-10`', '`gcc.i12`', etc.

The Info formatting commands ignore everything written before the `@setfilename` line, which is why the very first line of the file (the `\input` line) does not show up in the output.

The `@setfilename` line produces no output when you typeset a manual with TEX, but it is nevertheless essential: it opens the index, cross-reference, and other auxiliary files used by Texinfo, and also reads '`texinfo.cnf`' if that file is present on your system (see Section 19.9 [Preparing for TEX], page 159).

3.2.4 @settitle

In order to be made into a printed manual, a Texinfo file must contain a line that looks like this:

`@settitle` *title*

Write the `@settitle` command at the beginning of a line and follow it on the same line by the title. This tells TEX the title to use in a header or footer. Do not write anything else on the line; anything on the line after the command is considered part of the title, including a comment.

Conventionally, when TEX formats a Texinfo file for double-sided output, the title is printed in the left-hand (even-numbered) page headings and the current chapter title is printed in the right-hand (odd-numbered) page headings. (TEX learns the title of each chapter from each @chapter command.) Page footers are not printed.

Even if you are printing in a single-sided style, TEX looks for an @settitle command line, in case you include the manual title in the heading.

The @settitle command should precede everything that generates actual output in TEX.

Although the title in the @settitle command is usually the same as the title on the title page, it does not affect the title as it appears on the title page. Thus, the two do not need not match exactly; and the title in the @settitle command can be a shortened or expanded version of the title as it appears on the title page. (See Section 3.4.1 [@titlepage], page 37.)

TEX prints page headings only for that text that comes after the @end titlepage command in the Texinfo file, or that comes after an @headings command that turns on headings. (See Section 3.4.6 [The @headings Command], page 42, for more information.)

You may, if you wish, create your own, customized headings and footings. See Appendix F [Page Headings], page 213, for a detailed discussion of this process.

3.2.5 @setchapternewpage

In an officially bound book, text is usually printed on both sides of the paper, chapters start on right-hand pages, and right-hand pages have odd numbers. But in short reports, text often is printed only on one side of the paper. Also in short reports, chapters sometimes do not start on new pages, but are printed on the same page as the end of the preceding chapter, after a small amount of vertical whitespace.

You can use the @setchapternewpage command with various arguments to specify how TEX should start chapters and whether it should format headers for printing on one or both sides of the paper (single-sided or double-sided printing).

Write the @setchapternewpage command at the beginning of a line followed by its argument.

For example, you would write the following to cause each chapter to start on a fresh odd-numbered page:

```
@setchapternewpage odd
```

You can specify one of three alternatives with the @setchapternewpage command:

@setchapternewpage off

> Cause TEX to typeset a new chapter on the same page as the last chapter, after skipping some vertical whitespace. Also, cause TEX to format page headers for single-sided printing. (You can override the headers format with the **@headings double** command; see Section 3.4.6 [The **@headings** Command], page 42.)

@setchapternewpage on

> Cause TEX to start new chapters on new pages and to format page headers for single-sided printing. This is the form most often used for short reports or personal printing.
>
> This alternative is the default.

@setchapternewpage odd

> Cause TEX to start new chapters on new, odd-numbered pages (right-handed pages) and to typeset for double-sided printing. This is the form most often used for books and manuals.

Texinfo does not have an **@setchapternewpage even** command.

You can countermand or modify the effect on headers of an **@setchapternewpage** command with an **@headings** command. See Section 3.4.6 [The **@headings** Command], page 42.

At the beginning of a manual or book, pages are not numbered—for example, the title and copyright pages of a book are not numbered. By convention, table of contents pages are numbered with roman numerals and not in sequence with the rest of the document.

Since an Info file does not have pages, the **@setchapternewpage** command has no effect on it.

We recommend not including any **@setchapternewpage** command in your manual sources at all, since the desired output is not intrinsic to the document. Instead, if you don't want the default option (no blank pages, same headers on all pages) use the '**--texinfo**' option to `texi2dvi` to specify the output you want.

3.2.6 Paragraph Indenting

The Texinfo processors may insert whitespace at the beginning of the first line of each paragraph, thereby indenting that paragraph. You can use the **@paragraphindent** command to specify this indentation. Write an **@paragraphindent** command at the beginning of a line followed by either 'asis' or a number:

@paragraphindent *indent*

The indentation is according to the value of *indent*:

asis
> Do not change the existing indentation (not implemented in TEX).

0
> Omit all indentation.

n   Indent by *n* space characters in Info output, by *n* ems in TeX.

The default value of *indent* is 'asis'. `@paragraphindent` is ignored for HTML output.

Write the `@paragraphindent` command before or shortly after the end-of-header line at the beginning of a Texinfo file. (If you write the command between the start-of-header and end-of-header lines, the region formatting commands indent paragraphs as specified.)

A peculiarity of the `texinfo-format-buffer` and `texinfo-format-region` commands is that they do not indent (nor fill) paragraphs that contain `@w` or `@*` commands. See Appendix H [Refilling Paragraphs], page 226, for further information.

3.2.7 `@exampleindent`: **Environment Indenting**

The Texinfo processors indent each line of `@example` and similar environments. You can use the `@exampleindent` command to specify this indentation. Write an `@exampleindent` command at the beginning of a line followed by either 'asis' or a number:

`@exampleindent` *indent*

The indentation is according to the value of *indent*:

asis   Do not change the existing indentation (not implemented in TeX).

0   Omit all indentation.

n   Indent environments by *n* space characters in Info output, by *n* ems in TeX.

The default value of *indent* is 5. `@exampleindent` is ignored for HTML output.

Write the `@exampleindent` command before or shortly after the end-of-header line at the beginning of a Texinfo file. (If you write the command between the start-of-header and end-of-header lines, the region formatting commands indent examples as specified.)

3.2.8 **End of Header**

Follow the header lines with an end-of-header line. An end-of-header line looks like this:

`@c %**end of header`

If you include the `@setchapternewpage` command between the start-of-header and end-of-header lines, TeX will typeset a region as that command specifies. Similarly, if you include an `@smallbook` command between the start-of-header and end-of-header lines, TeX will typeset a region in the "small" book format.

See Section 3.2.2 [Start of Header], page 32.

3.3 Summary and Copying Permissions for Info

The title page and the copyright page appear only in the printed copy of the manual; therefore, the same information must be inserted in a section that appears only in the Info file. This section usually contains a brief description of the contents of the Info file, a copyright notice, and copying permissions.

The copyright notice should read:

`Copyright` *year copyright-owner*

and be put on a line by itself.

Standard text for the copyright permissions is contained in an appendix to this manual; see Section D.1 ['ifinfo' Copying Permissions], page 206, for the complete text.

The permissions text appears in an Info file *before* the first node. This mean that a reader does *not* see this text when reading the file using Info, except when using the advanced Info command *g* *.

3.4 The Title and Copyright Pages

A manual's name and author are usually printed on a title page. Sometimes copyright information is printed on the title page as well; more often, copyright information is printed on the back of the title page.

The title and copyright pages appear in the printed manual, but not in the Info file. Because of this, it is possible to use several slightly obscure TeX typesetting commands that cannot be used in an Info file. In addition, this part of the beginning of a Texinfo file contains the text of the copying permissions that will appear in the printed manual.

You may wish to include titlepage-like information for plain text output. Simply place any such leading material between `@ifinfo` and `@end ifinfo`; `makeinfo` includes this in its plain text output. It will not show up in the Info readers.

See Section D.2 [Titlepage Copying Permissions], page 207, for the standard text for the copyright permissions.

3.4.1 @titlepage

Start the material for the title page and following copyright page with `@titlepage` on a line by itself and end it with `@end titlepage` on a line by itself.

The `@end titlepage` command starts a new page and turns on page numbering. (See Appendix F [Page Headings], page 213, for details about how to generate page headings.) All the material that you want to appear on unnumbered pages should be put between the `@titlepage` and `@end titlepage` commands. You can force the table of contents to appear there with the `@setcontentsaftertitlepage` command (see Section 4.2 [Contents], page 47).

By using the `@page` command you can force a page break within the region delineated by the `@titlepage` and `@end titlepage` commands and thereby create more than one unnumbered page. This is how the copyright page is produced. (The `@titlepage` command might perhaps have been better named the `@titleandadditionalpages` command, but that would have been rather long!)

When you write a manual about a computer program, you should write the version of the program to which the manual applies on the title page. If the manual changes more frequently than the program or is independent of it, you should also include an edition number[1] for the manual. This helps readers keep track of which manual is for which version of the program. (The 'Top' node should also contain this information; see Section 5.3 [`@top`], page 50.)

Texinfo provides two main methods for creating a title page. One method uses the `@titlefont`, `@sp`, and `@center` commands to generate a title page in which the words on the page are centered.

The second method uses the `@title`, `@subtitle`, and `@author` commands to create a title page with black rules under the title and author lines and the subtitle text set flush to the right hand side of the page. With this method, you do not specify any of the actual formatting of the title page. You specify the text you want, and Texinfo does the formatting.

You may use either method, or you may combine them; see the examples in the sections below.

For extremely simple applications, and for the bastard title page in traditional book front matter, Texinfo also provides a command `@shorttitlepage` which takes a single argument as the title. The argument is typeset on a page by itself and followed by a blank page.

3.4.2 `@titlefont`, `@center`, and `@sp`

You can use the `@titlefont`, `@sp`, and `@center` commands to create a title page for a printed document. (This is the first of the two methods for creating a title page in Texinfo.)

Use the `@titlefont` command to select a large font suitable for the title itself. You can use `@titlefont` more than once if you have an especially long title.

---

[1] We have found that it is helpful to refer to versions of manuals as 'editions' and versions of programs as 'versions'; otherwise, we find we are liable to confuse each other in conversation by referring to both the documentation and the software with the same words.

For example:

```
@titlefont{Texinfo}
```

Use the `@center` command at the beginning of a line to center the remaining text on that line. Thus,

```
@center @titlefont{Texinfo}
```

centers the title, which in this example is "Texinfo" printed in the title font.

Use the `@sp` command to insert vertical space. For example:

```
@sp 2
```

This inserts two blank lines on the printed page. (See Section 14.4 [`@sp`], page 123, for more information about the `@sp` command.)

A template for this method looks like this:

```
@titlepage
@sp 10
@center @titlefont{name-of-manual-when-printed}
@sp 2
@center subtitle-if-any
@sp 2
@center author
...
@end titlepage
```

The spacing of the example fits an 8.5 by 11 inch manual.

3.4.3 `@title`, `@subtitle`, and `@author`

You can use the `@title`, `@subtitle`, and `@author` commands to create a title page in which the vertical and horizontal spacing is done for you automatically. This contrasts with the method described in the previous section, in which the `@sp` command is needed to adjust vertical spacing.

Write the `@title`, `@subtitle`, or `@author` commands at the beginning of a line followed by the title, subtitle, or author.

The `@title` command produces a line in which the title is set flush to the left-hand side of the page in a larger than normal font. The title is underlined with a black rule. Only a single line is allowed; the `@*` command may not be used to break the title into two lines. To handle very long titles, you may find it profitable to use both `@title` and `@titlefont`; see the final example in this section.

The `@subtitle` command sets subtitles in a normal-sized font flush to the right-hand side of the page.

The `@author` command sets the names of the author or authors in a middle-sized font flush to the left-hand side of the page on a line near the bottom of the title page. The names are underlined with a black rule that is thinner than the rule that underlines the title. (The black rule only occurs if the `@author` command line is followed by an `@page` command line.)

There are two ways to use the `@author` command: you can write the name or names on the remaining part of the line that starts with an `@author` command:

```
@author by Jane Smith and John Doe
```

or you can write the names one above each other by using two (or more) `@author` commands:

```
@author Jane Smith
@author John Doe
```

(Only the bottom name is underlined with a black rule.)

A template for this method looks like this:

```
@titlepage
@title name-of-manual-when-printed
@subtitle subtitle-if-any
@subtitle second-subtitle
@author author
@page
...
@end titlepage
```

You may also combine the `@titlefont` method described in the previous section and `@title` method described in this one. This may be useful if you have a very long title. Here is a real-life example:

```
@titlepage
@titlefont{GNU Software}
@sp 1
@title for MS-Windows and MS-DOS
@subtitle Edition @value{edition} for Release @value{cd-edition}
@author by Daniel Hagerty, Melissa Weisshaus
@author and Eli Zaretskii
```

(The use of `@value` here is explained in Section 16.4.3 [`@value` Example], page 143.)

3.4.4 Copyright Page and Permissions

By international treaty, the copyright notice for a book should be either on the title page or on the back of the title page. The copyright notice should include the year followed by the name of the organization or person who owns the copyright.

When the copyright notice is on the back of the title page, that page is customarily not numbered. Therefore, in Texinfo, the information on the copyright page should be within `@titlepage` and `@end titlepage` commands.

Use the `@page` command to cause a page break. To push the copyright notice and the other text on the copyright page towards the bottom of the page, you can write a somewhat mysterious line after the @page command that reads like this:

```
@vskip 0pt plus 1filll
```

This is a TeX command that is not supported by the Info formatting commands. The @vskip command inserts whitespace. The 'Opt plus 1filll' means to put in zero points of mandatory whitespace, and as much optional whitespace as needed to push the following text to the bottom of the page. Note the use of three 'l's in the word 'filll'; this is the correct usage in TeX.

In a printed manual, the @copyright{} command generates a 'c' inside a circle. (In Info, it generates '(C)'.) The copyright notice itself has the following legally defined sequence:

```
Copyright © year copyright-owner
```

It is customary to put information on how to get a manual after the copyright notice, followed by the copying permissions for the manual.

Permissions must be given here as well as in the summary segment within @ifinfo and @end ifinfo that immediately follows the header since this text appears only in the printed manual and the 'ifinfo' text appears only in the Info file.

See Appendix D [Sample Permissions], page 206, for the standard text.

3.4.5 Heading Generation

An @end titlepage command on a line by itself not only marks the end of the title and copyright pages, but also causes TeX to start generating page headings and page numbers.

To repeat what is said elsewhere, Texinfo has two standard page heading formats, one for documents which are printed on one side of each sheet of paper (single-sided printing), and the other for documents which are printed on both sides of each sheet (double-sided printing). (See Section 3.2.5 [@setchapternewpage], page 34.) You can specify these formats in different ways:

- The conventional way is to write an @setchapternewpage command before the title page commands, and then have the @end titlepage command start generating page headings in the manner desired. (See Section 3.2.5 [@setchapternewpage], page 34.)

- Alternatively, you can use the @headings command to prevent page headings from being generated or to start them for either single or double-sided printing. (Write an @headings command immediately after the @end titlepage command. See Section 3.4.6 [The @headings Command], page 42, for more information.)

- Or, you may specify your own page heading and footing format. See Appendix F [Page Headings], page 213, for detailed information about page headings and footings.

Most documents are formatted with the standard single-sided or double-sided format, using `@setchapternewpage odd` for double-sided printing and no `@setchapternewpage` command for single-sided printing.

3.4.6 The `@headings` Command

The `@headings` command is rarely used. It specifies what kind of page headings and footings to print on each page. Usually, this is controlled by the `@setchapternewpage` command. You need the `@headings` command only if the `@setchapternewpage` command does not do what you want, or if you want to turn off pre-defined page headings prior to defining your own. Write an `@headings` command immediately after the `@end titlepage` command.

You can use `@headings` as follows:

`@headings off`
> Turn off printing of page headings.

`@headings single`
> Turn on page headings appropriate for single-sided printing.

`@headings double`
`@headings on`
> Turn on page headings appropriate for double-sided printing. The two commands, `@headings on` and `@headings double`, are synonymous.

`@headings singleafter`
`@headings doubleafter`
> Turn on `single` or `double` headings, respectively, after the current page is output.

`@headings on`
> Turn on page headings: `single` if '`@setchapternewpage on`', `double` otherwise.

For example, suppose you write `@setchapternewpage off` before the `@titlepage` command to tell TEX to start a new chapter on the same page as the end of the last chapter. This command also causes TEX to typeset page headers for single-sided printing. To cause TEX to typeset for double sided printing, write `@headings double` after the `@end titlepage` command.

You can stop TEX from generating any page headings at all by writing `@headings off` on a line of its own immediately after the line containing the `@end titlepage` command, like this:

```
@end titlepage
@headings off
```

The `@headings off` command overrides the `@end titlepage` command, which would otherwise cause TEX to print page headings.

You can also specify your own style of page heading and footing. See Appendix F [Page Headings], page 213, for more information.

3.5 The 'Top' Node and Master Menu

The 'Top' node is the node from which you enter an Info file.

A 'Top' node should contain a brief description of the Info file and an extensive, master menu for the whole Info file. This helps the reader understand what the Info file is about. Also, you should write the version number of the program to which the Info file applies; or, at least, the edition number.

The contents of the 'Top' node should appear only in the Info file; none of it should appear in printed output, so enclose it between @ifinfo and @end ifinfo commands. (TEX does not print either an @node line or a menu; they appear only in Info; strictly speaking, you are not required to enclose these parts between @ifinfo and @end ifinfo, but it is simplest to do so. See Chapter 16 [Conditionally Visible Text], page 139.)

3.5.1 'Top' Node Title

Sometimes, you will want to place an @top sectioning command line containing the title of the document immediately after the @node Top line (see Section 6.3.6 [The @top Sectioning Command], page 61, for more information).

For example, the beginning of the Top node of this manual contains an @top sectioning command, a short description, and edition and version information. It looks like this:

```
...
@end titlepage

@ifnottex
@node Top, Copying, , (dir)
@top Texinfo

Texinfo is a documentation system...
This is edition...
...
@end ifnottex

@menu
* Copying::                     Texinfo is freely
                                redistributable.
* Overview::                    What is Texinfo?
...
@end menu
```

In a 'Top' node, the 'Previous', and 'Up' nodes usually refer to the top level directory of the whole Info system, which is called '(dir)'. The 'Next' node refers to the first node that follows the main or master menu, which is usually the copying permissions, introduction, or first chapter.

3.5.2 Parts of a Master Menu

A *master menu* is a detailed main menu listing all the nodes in a file.

A master menu is enclosed in **@menu** and **@end menu** commands and does not appear in the printed document.

Generally, a master menu is divided into parts.

- The first part contains the major nodes in the Texinfo file: the nodes for the chapters, chapter-like sections, and the appendices.

- The second part contains nodes for the indices.

- The third and subsequent parts contain a listing of the other, lower level nodes, often ordered by chapter. This way, rather than go through an intermediary menu, an inquirer can go directly to a particular node when searching for specific information. These menu items are not required; add them if you think they are a convenience. If you do use them, put **@detailmenu** before the first one, and **@end detailmenu** after the last; otherwise, `makeinfo` will get confused.

Each section in the menu can be introduced by a descriptive line. So long as the line does not begin with an asterisk, it will not be treated as a menu entry. (See Section 7.1 [Writing a Menu], page 64, for more information.)

For example, the master menu for this manual looks like the following (but has many more entries):

```
@menu
* Copying::              Texinfo is freely
                           redistributable.
* Overview::             What is Texinfo?
* Texinfo Mode::         Special features in GNU Emacs.
...
...
* Command and Variable Index::
                         An entry for each @-command.
* Concept Index::        An entry for each concept.
```

```
@detailmenu
 --- The Detailed Node Listing ---

Overview of Texinfo

* Info Files::            What is an Info file?
* Printed Manuals::       Characteristics of
                          a printed manual.
 ...
 ...

Using Texinfo Mode

* Info on a Region::      Formatting part of a file
                          for Info.
 ...
 ...
@end detailmenu
@end menu
```

3.6 Software Copying Permissions

If the Texinfo file has a section containing the "General Public License" and the distribution information and a warranty disclaimer for the software that is documented, this section usually follows the 'Top' node. The General Public License is very important to Project GNU software. It ensures that you and others will continue to have a right to use and share the software.

The copying and distribution information and the disclaimer are followed by an introduction or else by the first chapter of the manual.

Although an introduction is not a required part of a Texinfo file, it is very helpful. Ideally, it should state clearly and concisely what the file is about and who would be interested in reading it. In general, an introduction would follow the licensing and distribution information, although sometimes people put it earlier in the document. Usually, an introduction is put in an @unnumbered section. (See Section 5.5 [The @unnumbered and @appendix Commands], page 51.)

4 Ending a Texinfo File

The end of a Texinfo file should include commands to create indices and (usually) to generate detailed and summary tables of contents. And it must include the @bye command that marks the last line processed by TeX.

For example:

```
@node    Concept Index,     , Variables Index, Top
@c           node-name,    next, previous,        up
@unnumbered Concept Index

@printindex cp

@contents
@bye
```

4.1 Index Menus and Printing an Index

To print an index means to include it as part of a manual or Info file. This does not happen automatically just because you use @cindex or other index-entry generating commands in the Texinfo file; those just cause the raw data for the index to be accumulated. To generate an index, you must include the @printindex command at the place in the document where you want the index to appear. Also, as part of the process of creating a printed manual, you must run a program called texindex (see Chapter 19 [Hardcopy], page 153) to sort the raw data to produce a sorted index file. The sorted index file is what is actually used to print the index.

Texinfo offers six different types of predefined index: the concept index, the function index, the variables index, the keystroke index, the program index, and the data type index (see Section 12.2 [Predefined Indices], page 104). Each index type has a two-letter name: 'cp', 'fn', 'vr', 'ky', 'pg', and 'tp'. You may merge indices, or put them into separate sections (see Section 12.4 [Combining Indices], page 106); or you may define your own indices (see Section 12.5 [Defining New Indices], page 107).

The @printindex command takes a two-letter index name, reads the corresponding sorted index file and formats it appropriately into an index.

The @printindex command does not generate a chapter heading for the index. Consequently, you should precede the @printindex command with a suitable section or chapter command (usually @unnumbered) to supply the chapter heading and put the index into the table of contents. Precede the @unnumbered command with an @node line.

For example:

```
@node Variable Index, Concept Index, Function Index, Top
@comment     node-name,          next,       previous, up
@unnumbered Variable Index


@printindex vr

@node     Concept Index,     , Variable Index, Top
@comment        node-name, next,       previous, up
@unnumbered Concept Index


@printindex cp
```

Readers often prefer that the concept index come last in a book, since that makes it easiest to find. Having just one index helps readers also, since then they have only one place to look (see Section 12.4.2 [synindex], page 107).

4.2 Generating a Table of Contents

The `@chapter`, `@section`, and other structuring commands supply the information to make up a table of contents, but they do not cause an actual table to appear in the manual. To do this, you must use the `@contents` and/or `@summarycontents` command(s).

`@contents`

> Generate a table of contents in a printed manual, including all chapters, sections, subsections, etc., as well as appendices and unnumbered chapters. (Headings generated by the `@heading` series of commands do not appear in the table of contents.)

`@shortcontents`
`@summarycontents`

> (`@summarycontents` is a synonym for `@shortcontents`; the two commands are exactly the same.)

> Generate a short or summary table of contents that lists only the chapters (and appendices and unnumbered chapters). Omit sections, subsections and subsubsections. Only a long manual needs a short table of contents in addition to the full table of contents.

Both contents commands should be written on a line by themselves. The contents commands automatically generate a chapter-like heading at the top of the first table of contents page, so don't include any sectioning command such as `@unnumbered` before them.

Since an Info file uses menus instead of tables of contents, the Info formatting commands ignore the contents commands. But the contents are included in plain text output (generated by `makeinfo --no-headers`).

The contents commands can be placed either at the very end of the file, after any indices (see the previous section) and just before the @bye (see the next section), or near the beginning of the file, after the @end titlepage (see Section 3.4.1 [titlepage], page 37). The advantage to the former is that then the contents output is always up to date, because it reflects the processing just done. The advantage to the latter is that the contents are printed in the proper place, thus you do not need to rearrange the DVI file with dviselect or shuffle paper. However, contents commands at the beginning of the document are ignored when outputting to standard output.

As an author, you can put the contents commands wherever you prefer. But if you are a user simply printing a manual, you may wish to print the contents after the title page even if the author put the contents commands at the end of the document (as is the case in most existing Texinfo documents). You can do this by specifying @setcontentsaftertitlepage and/or @setshortcontentsaftertitlepage. The first prints only the main contents after the @end titlepage; the second prints both the short contents and the main contents. In either case, any subsequent @contents or @shortcontents is ignored (unless no @end titlepage is ever encountered).

You need to include the @set...contentsaftertitlepage commands early in the document (just after @setfilename, for example). Or, if you're using texi2dvi (see Section 19.3 [Format with texi2dvi], page 155), you can use its '--texinfo' option to specify this without altering the source file at all. For example:

```
texi2dvi --texinfo=@setshortcontentsaftertitlepage foo.texi
```

4.3 @bye File Ending

An @bye command terminates TeX or Info formatting. None of the formatting commands see any of the file following @bye. The @bye command should be on a line by itself.

If you wish, you may follow the @bye line with notes. These notes will not be formatted and will not appear in either Info or a printed manual; it is as if text after @bye were within @ignore ... @end ignore. Also, you may follow the @bye line with a local variables list. See Section 19.7 [Using Local Variables and the Compile Command], page 158, for more information.

5 Chapter Structuring

The *chapter structuring* commands divide a document into a hierarchy of chapters, sections, subsections, and subsubsections. These commands generate large headings; they also provide information for the table of contents of a printed manual (see Section 4.2 [Generating a Table of Contents], page 47).

The chapter structuring commands do not create an Info node structure, so normally you should put an @node command immediately before each chapter structuring command (see Chapter 6 [Nodes], page 56). The only time you are likely to use the chapter structuring commands without using the node structuring commands is if you are writing a document that contains no cross references and will never be transformed into Info format.

It is unlikely that you will ever write a Texinfo file that is intended only as an Info file and not as a printable document. If you do, you might still use chapter structuring commands to create a heading at the top of each node—but you don't need to.

5.1 Tree Structure of Sections

A Texinfo file is usually structured like a book with chapters, sections, subsections, and the like. This structure can be visualized as a tree (or rather as an upside-down tree) with the root at the top and the levels corresponding to chapters, sections, subsection, and subsubsections.

Here is a diagram that shows a Texinfo file with three chapters, each of which has two sections.

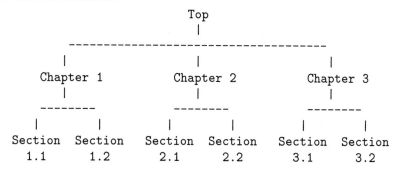

```
                              Top
                               |
          ---------------------------------------------
          |                    |                      |
       Chapter 1            Chapter 2              Chapter 3
          |                    |                      |
       --------             --------               --------
       |      |             |      |               |      |
    Section  Section     Section  Section       Section  Section
      1.1      1.2         2.1      2.2            3.1      3.2
```

In a Texinfo file that has this structure, the beginning of Chapter 2 looks like this:

```
@node      Chapter 2,  Chapter 3, Chapter 1, top
@chapter Chapter 2
```

The chapter structuring commands are described in the sections that follow; the @node and @menu commands are described in following chapters. (See Chapter 6 [Nodes], page 56, and see Chapter 7 [Menus], page 64.)

5.2 Structuring Command Types

The chapter structuring commands fall into four groups or series, each of which contains structuring commands corresponding to the hierarchical levels of chapters, sections, subsections, and subsubsections.

The four groups are the `@chapter` series, the `@unnumbered` series, the `@appendix` series, and the `@heading` series.

Each command produces titles that have a different appearance on the printed page or Info file; only some of the commands produce titles that are listed in the table of contents of a printed book or manual.

- The `@chapter` and `@appendix` series of commands produce numbered or lettered entries both in the body of a printed work and in its table of contents.

- The `@unnumbered` series of commands produce unnumbered entries both in the body of a printed work and in its table of contents. The `@top` command, which has a special use, is a member of this series (see Section 5.3 [`@top`], page 50).

- The `@heading` series of commands produce unnumbered headings that do not appear in a table of contents. The heading commands never start a new page.

- The `@majorheading` command produces results similar to using the `@chapheading` command but generates a larger vertical whitespace before the heading.

- When an `@setchapternewpage` command says to do so, the `@chapter`, `@unnumbered`, and `@appendix` commands start new pages in the printed manual; the `@heading` commands do not.

Here are the four groups of chapter structuring commands:

Numbered	Unnumbered	Lettered and numbered	No new page Unnumbered
In contents	In contents	In contents	Not in contents
	`@top`		`@majorheading`
`@chapter`	`@unnumbered`	`@appendix`	`@chapheading`
`@section`	`@unnumberedsec`	`@appendixsec`	`@heading`
`@subsection`	`@unnumberedsubsec`	`@appendixsubsec`	`@subheading`
`@subsubsection`	`@unnumberedsubsubsec`	`@appendixsubsubsec`	`@subsubheading`

5.3 `@top`

The `@top` command is a special sectioning command that you use only after an '`@node Top`' line at the beginning of a Texinfo file. The `@top` command tells the `makeinfo` formatter which node is the 'Top' node, so it can use it as the root of the node tree if your manual uses implicit pointers. It has the same typesetting effect as `@unnumbered` (see Section 5.5 [`@unnumbered` and `@appendix`], page 51). For detailed information, see Section 6.3.6 [The `@top` Command], page 61.

The `@top` node and its menu (if any) is conventionally wrapped in an `@ifnottex` conditional so that it will appear only in Info and HTML output, not TeX.

5.4 @chapter

`@chapter` identifies a chapter in the document. Write the command at the beginning of a line and follow it on the same line by the title of the chapter.

For example, this chapter in this manual is entitled "Chapter Structuring"; the `@chapter` line looks like this:

```
@chapter Chapter Structuring
```

In TeX, the `@chapter` command creates a chapter in the document, specifying the chapter title. The chapter is numbered automatically.

In Info, the `@chapter` command causes the title to appear on a line by itself, with a line of asterisks inserted underneath. Thus, in Info, the above example produces the following output:

```
Chapter Structuring
*******************
```

Texinfo also provides a command `@centerchap`, which is analogous to `@unnumbered`, but centers its argument in the printed output. This kind of stylistic choice is not usually offered by Texinfo.

5.5 @unnumbered and @appendix

Use the `@unnumbered` command to create a chapter that appears in a printed manual without chapter numbers of any kind. Use the `@appendix` command to create an appendix in a printed manual that is labelled by letter instead of by number.

For Info file output, the `@unnumbered` and `@appendix` commands are equivalent to `@chapter`: the title is printed on a line by itself with a line of asterisks underneath. (See Section 5.4 [`@chapter`], page 51.)

To create an appendix or an unnumbered chapter, write an `@appendix` or `@unnumbered` command at the beginning of a line and follow it on the same line by the title, as you would if you were creating a chapter.

5.6 @majorheading, @chapheading

The `@majorheading` and `@chapheading` commands put chapter-like headings in the body of a document.

However, neither command causes TeX to produce a numbered heading or an entry in the table of contents; and neither command causes TeX to start a new page in a printed manual.

In TEX, an `@majorheading` command generates a larger vertical whitespace before the heading than an `@chapheading` command but is otherwise the same.

In Info, the `@majorheading` and `@chapheading` commands are equivalent to `@chapter`: the title is printed on a line by itself with a line of asterisks underneath. (See Section 5.4 [`@chapter`], page 51.)

5.7 @section

In a printed manual, an `@section` command identifies a numbered section within a chapter. The section title appears in the table of contents. In Info, an `@section` command provides a title for a segment of text, underlined with '='.

This section is headed with an `@section` command and looks like this in the Texinfo file:

```
@section @code{@@section}
```

To create a section, write the `@section` command at the beginning of a line and follow it on the same line by the section title.

Thus,

```
@section This is a section
```

produces

```
This is a section
==================
```

in Info.

5.8 @unnumberedsec, @appendixsec, @heading

The `@unnumberedsec`, `@appendixsec`, and `@heading` commands are, respectively, the unnumbered, appendix-like, and heading-like equivalents of the `@section` command. (See Section 5.7 [`@section`], page 52.)

`@unnumberedsec`

> The `@unnumberedsec` command may be used within an unnumbered chapter or within a regular chapter or appendix to provide an unnumbered section.

`@appendixsec`
`@appendixsection`

> `@appendixsection` is a longer spelling of the `@appendixsec` command; the two are synonymous.

> Conventionally, the `@appendixsec` or `@appendixsection` command is used only within appendices.

`@heading`   You may use the `@heading` command anywhere you wish for a section-style heading that will not appear in the table of contents.

5.9 The @subsection Command

Subsections are to sections as sections are to chapters. (See Section 5.7 [@section], page 52.) In Info, subsection titles are underlined with '-'. For example,

```
@subsection This is a subsection
```
produces

```
This is a subsection
--------------------
```

In a printed manual, subsections are listed in the table of contents and are numbered three levels deep.

5.10 The @subsection-like Commands

The @unnumberedsubsec, @appendixsubsec, and @subheading commands are, respectively, the unnumbered, appendix-like, and heading-like equivalents of the @subsection command. (See Section 5.9 [@subsection], page 53.)

In Info, the @subsection-like commands generate a title underlined with hyphens. In a printed manual, an @subheading command produces a heading like that of a subsection except that it is not numbered and does not appear in the table of contents. Similarly, an @unnumberedsubsec command produces an unnumbered heading like that of a subsection and an @appendixsubsec command produces a subsection-like heading labelled with a letter and numbers; both of these commands produce headings that appear in the table of contents.

5.11 The 'subsub' Commands

The fourth and lowest level sectioning commands in Texinfo are the 'subsub' commands. They are:

@subsubsection
> Subsubsections are to subsections as subsections are to sections. (See Section 5.9 [@subsection], page 53.) In a printed manual, subsubsection titles appear in the table of contents and are numbered four levels deep.

@unnumberedsubsubsec
> Unnumbered subsubsection titles appear in the table of contents of a printed manual, but lack numbers. Otherwise, unnumbered subsubsections are the same as subsubsections. In Info, unnumbered subsubsections look exactly like ordinary subsubsections.

@appendixsubsubsec
> Conventionally, appendix commands are used only for appendices and are lettered and numbered appropriately in a printed manual. They also appear in the table of contents. In Info, appendix subsubsections look exactly like ordinary subsubsections.

`@subsubheading`
>
> The `@subsubheading` command may be used anywhere that you need a small heading that will not appear in the table of contents. In Info, subsubheadings look exactly like ordinary subsubsection headings.

In Info, 'subsub' titles are underlined with periods. For example,

```
@subsubsection This is a subsubsection
```

produces

```
This is a subsubsection
```
. . . .

5.12 `@raisesections` and `@lowersections`

The `@raisesections` and `@lowersections` commands raise and lower the hierarchical level of chapters, sections, subsections and the like. The `@raisesections` command changes sections to chapters, subsections to sections, and so on. The `@lowersections` command changes chapters to sections, sections to subsections, and so on.

An `@lowersections` command is useful if you wish to include text that is written as an outer or standalone Texinfo file in another Texinfo file as an inner, included file. If you write the command at the beginning of the file, all your `@chapter` commands are formatted as if they were `@section` commands, all your `@section` command are formatted as if they were `@subsection` commands, and so on.

`@raisesections` raises a command one level in the chapter structuring hierarchy:

```
    Change          To


    @subsection     @section,
    @section        @chapter,
    @heading        @chapheading,
            etc.
```

`@lowersections` lowers a command one level in the chapter structuring hierarchy:

```
    Change          To


    @chapter        @section,
    @subsection     @subsubsection,
    @heading        @subheading,
            etc.
```

An `@raisesections` or `@lowersections` command changes only those structuring commands that follow the command in the Texinfo file. Write an `@raisesections` or `@lowersections` command on a line of its own.

An `@lowersections` command cancels an `@raisesections` command, and vice versa. Typically, the commands are used like this:

```
@lowersections
@include somefile.texi
@raisesections
```

Without the `@raisesections`, all the subsequent sections in your document will be lowered.

Repeated use of the commands continue to raise or lower the hierarchical level a step at a time.

An attempt to raise above 'chapters' reproduces chapter commands; an attempt to lower below 'subsubsections' reproduces subsubsection commands.

6 Nodes

Nodes are the primary segments of a Texinfo file. They do not themselves impose a hierarchical or any other kind of structure on a file. Nodes contain *node pointers* that name other nodes, and can contain *menus* which are lists of nodes. In Info, the movement commands can carry you to a pointed-to node or to a node listed in a menu. Node pointers and menus provide structure for Info files just as chapters, sections, subsections, and the like, provide structure for printed books.

6.1 Two Paths

The node and menu commands and the chapter structuring commands are technically independent of each other:

- In Info, node and menu commands provide structure. The chapter structuring commands generate headings with different kinds of underlining—asterisks for chapters, hyphens for sections, and so on; they do nothing else.

- In TeX, the chapter structuring commands generate chapter and section numbers and tables of contents. The node and menu commands provide information for cross references; they do nothing else.

You can use node pointers and menus to structure an Info file any way you want; and you can write a Texinfo file so that its Info output has a different structure than its printed output. However, virtually all Texinfo files are written such that the structure for the Info output corresponds to the structure for the printed output. It is neither convenient nor understandable to the reader to do otherwise.

Generally, printed output is structured in a tree-like hierarchy in which the chapters are the major limbs from which the sections branch out. Similarly, node pointers and menus are organized to create a matching structure in the Info output.

6.2 Node and Menu Illustration

Here is a copy of the diagram shown earlier that illustrates a Texinfo file with three chapters, each of which contains two sections.

The "root" is at the top of the diagram and the "leaves" are at the bottom. This is how such a diagram is drawn conventionally; it illustrates an upside-down tree. For this reason, the root node is called the 'Top' node, and 'Up' node pointers carry you closer to the root.

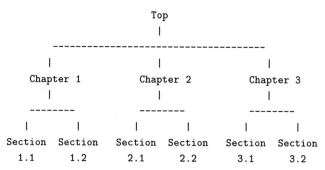

```
                              Top
                               |
        ------------------------------------------
        |                      |                  |
   Chapter 1              Chapter 2           Chapter 3
        |                      |                  |
   --------              --------            --------
   |      |              |      |            |      |
Section Section     Section Section     Section Section
  1.1     1.2         2.1     2.2         3.1     3.2
```

The fully-written command to start Chapter 2 would be this:

```
@node      Chapter 2,  Chapter 3, Chapter 1, Top
@comment   node-name,  next,      previous,  up
```

This `@node` line says that the name of this node is "Chapter 2", the name of the 'Next' node is "Chapter 3", the name of the 'Previous' node is "Chapter 1", and the name of the 'Up' node is "Top". You can omit writing out these node names if your document is hierarchically organized (see Section 6.4 [makeinfo Pointer Creation], page 62), but the pointer relationships still obtain.

> **Please Note:** 'Next' refers to the next node at the same hierarchical level in the manual, not necessarily to the next node within the Texinfo file. In the Texinfo file, the subsequent node may be at a lower level—a section-level node most often follows a chapter-level node, for example. 'Next' and 'Previous' refer to nodes at the *same* hierarchical level. (The 'Top' node contains the exception to this rule. Since the 'Top' node is the only node at that level, 'Next' refers to the first following node, which is almost always a chapter or chapter-level node.)

To go to Sections 2.1 and 2.2 using Info, you need a menu inside Chapter 2. (See Chapter 7 [Menus], page 64.) You would write the menu just before the beginning of Section 2.1, like this:

```
@menu
* Sect. 2.1::    Description of this section.
* Sect. 2.2::
@end menu
```

Write the node for Sect. 2.1 like this:

```
@node      Sect. 2.1, Sect. 2.2, Chapter 2, Chapter 2
@comment   node-name, next,      previous,  up
```

In Info format, the 'Next' and 'Previous' pointers of a node usually lead to other nodes at the same level—from chapter to chapter or from section to section (sometimes, as shown, the 'Previous' pointer points up); an 'Up' pointer usually leads to a node at the level above (closer to the 'Top' node); and a 'Menu' leads to nodes at a level below (closer to 'leaves'). (A cross reference can point to a node at any level; see Chapter 8 [Cross References], page 68.)

Usually, an @node command and a chapter structuring command are used in sequence, along with indexing commands. (You may follow the @node line with a comment line that reminds you which pointer is which.)

Here is the beginning of the chapter in this manual called "Ending a Texinfo File". This shows an @node line followed by a comment line, an @chapter line, and then by indexing lines.

```
@node    Ending a File, Structuring, Beginning a File, Top
@comment node-name,    next,       previous,       up
@chapter Ending a Texinfo File
@cindex Ending a Texinfo file
@cindex Texinfo file ending
@cindex File ending
```

6.3 The @node Command

A *node* is a segment of text that begins at an @node command and continues until the next @node command. The definition of node is different from that for chapter or section. A chapter may contain sections and a section may contain subsections; but a node cannot contain subnodes; the text of a node continues only until the next @node command in the file. A node usually contains only one chapter structuring command, the one that follows the @node line. On the other hand, in printed output nodes are used only for cross references, so a chapter or section may contain any number of nodes. Indeed, a chapter usually contains several nodes, one for each section, subsection, and subsubsection.

To create a node, write an @node command at the beginning of a line, and follow it with up to four arguments, separated by commas, on the rest of the same line. The first argument is required; it is the name of this node. The subsequent arguments are the names of the 'Next', 'Previous', and 'Up' pointers, in that order, and may be omitted if your Texinfo document is hierarchically organized (see Section 6.4 [makeinfo Pointer Creation], page 62).

You may insert spaces before each name if you wish; the spaces are ignored. You must write the name of the node and the names of the 'Next', 'Previous', and 'Up' pointers all on the same line. Otherwise, the formatters fail. (See Info file 'info', node 'Top', for more information about nodes in Info.)

Usually, you write one of the chapter-structuring command lines immediately after an @node line—for example, an @section or @subsection line. (See Section 5.2 [Structuring Command Types], page 50.)

Please note: The GNU Emacs Texinfo mode updating commands work only with Texinfo files in which @node lines are followed by chapter structuring lines. See Section 2.4.1 [Updating Requirements], page 23.

TeX uses @node lines to identify the names to use for cross references. For this reason, you must write @node lines in a Texinfo file that you intend to format for printing, even if you do not intend to format it for Info. (Cross references, such as the one at the end of this sentence, are made with `@xref` and related commands; see Chapter 8 [Cross References], page 68.)

6.3.1 Choosing Node and Pointer Names

The name of a node identifies the node. The pointers enable you to reach other nodes and consist of the names of those nodes.

Normally, a node's 'Up' pointer contains the name of the node whose menu mentions that node. The node's 'Next' pointer contains the name of the node that follows that node in that menu and its 'Previous' pointer contains the name of the node that precedes it in that menu. When a node's 'Previous' node is the same as its 'Up' node, both node pointers name the same node.

Usually, the first node of a Texinfo file is the 'Top' node, and its 'Up' and 'Previous' pointers point to the '`dir`' file, which contains the main menu for all of Info.

The 'Top' node itself contains the main or master menu for the manual. Also, it is helpful to include a brief description of the manual in the 'Top' node. See Section 6.3.5 [First Node], page 61, for information on how to write the first node of a Texinfo file.

Even when you explicitly specify all pointers, that does not mean you can write the nodes in the Texinfo source file in an arbitrary order! Because TEX processes the file sequentially, irrespective of node pointers, you must write the nodes in the order you wish them to appear in the printed output.

6.3.2 How to Write an @node Line

The easiest way to write an `@node` line is to write `@node` at the beginning of a line and then the name of the node, like this:

    @node node-name

If you are using GNU Emacs, you can use the update node commands provided by Texinfo mode to insert the names of the pointers; or you can leave the pointers out of the Texinfo file and let `makeinfo` insert node pointers into the Info file it creates. (See Chapter 2 [Texinfo Mode], page 16, and Section 6.4 [makeinfo Pointer Creation], page 62.)

Alternatively, you can insert the 'Next', 'Previous', and 'Up' pointers yourself. If you do this, you may find it helpful to use the Texinfo mode keyboard command `C-c C-c n`. This command inserts '`@node`' and a comment line listing the names of the pointers in their proper order. The comment line helps you keep track of which arguments are for which pointers. This comment line is especially useful if you are not familiar with Texinfo.

The template for a fully-written-out node line with 'Next', 'Previous', and 'Up' pointers looks like this:

    @node node-name, next, previous, up

If you wish, you can ignore `@node` lines altogether in your first draft and then use the `texinfo-insert-node-lines` command to create `@node` lines for you.

However, we do not recommend this practice. It is better to name the node itself at the same time that you write a segment so you can easily make cross references. A large number of cross references are an especially important feature of a good Info file.

After you have inserted an @node line, you should immediately write an @-command for the chapter or section and insert its name. Next (and this is important!), put in several index entries. Usually, you will find at least two and often as many as four or five ways of referring to the node in the index. Use them all. This will make it much easier for people to find the node.

6.3.3 @node Line Tips

Here are three suggestions:

- Try to pick node names that are informative but short.

  In the Info file, the file name, node name, and pointer names are all inserted on one line, which may run into the right edge of the window. (This does not cause a problem with Info, but is ugly.)

- Try to pick node names that differ from each other near the beginnings of their names. This way, it is easy to use automatic name completion in Info.

- By convention, node names are capitalized just as they would be for section or chapter titles—initial and significant words are capitalized; others are not.

6.3.4 @node Line Requirements

Here are several requirements for @node lines:

- All the node names for a single Info file must be unique.

  Duplicates confuse the Info movement commands. This means, for example, that if you end every chapter with a summary, you must name each summary node differently. You cannot just call each one "Summary". You may, however, duplicate the titles of chapters, sections, and the like. Thus you can end each chapter in a book with a section called "Summary", so long as the node names for those sections are all different.

- A pointer name must be the name of a node.

  The node to which a pointer points may come before or after the node containing the pointer.

- @-commands used in node names generally confuse Info, so you should avoid them. For a few rare cases when this is useful, Texinfo has limited support for using @-commands in node names; see Section 20.1.4 [Pointer Validation], page 168.

Thus, the beginning of the section called @chapter looks like this:

```
@node   chapter, unnumbered & appendix, makeinfo top, Structuring
@comment node-name,  next,  previous,  up
@section @code{@@chapter}
@findex chapter
```

- Unfortunately, you cannot use periods, commas, colons or apostrophes within a node name; these confuse TEX or the Info formatters.

  For example, the following is a section title:

  ```
  @code{@@unnumberedsec}, @code{@@appendixsec}, @code{@@heading}
  ```

  The corresponding node name is:

  ```
  unnumberedsec appendixsec heading
  ```

- Case is significant.

6.3.5 The First Node

The first node of a Texinfo file is the *Top* node, except in an included file (see Appendix E [Include Files], page 209). The Top node contains the main or master menu for the document, and a short summary of the document (see Section 6.3.7 [Top Node Summary], page 62).

The Top node (which must be named 'top' or 'Top') should have as its 'Up' node the name of a node in another file, where there is a menu that leads to this file. Specify the file name in parentheses. If the file is to be installed directly in the Info directory file, use '(dir)' as the parent of the Top node; this is short for '(dir)top', and specifies the Top node in the 'dir' file, which contains the main menu for the Info system as a whole. For example, the @node Top line of this manual looks like this:

```
@node Top, Copying, , (dir)
```

(You can use the Texinfo updating commands or the makeinfo utility to insert these pointers automatically.)

Do not define the 'Previous' node of the Top node to be '(dir)', as it causes confusing behavior for users: if you are in the Top node and hits (DEL) to go backwards, you wind up in the middle of the some other entry in the 'dir' file, which has nothing to do with what you were reading.

See Section 20.2 [Install an Info File], page 173, for more information about installing an Info file in the 'info' directory.

6.3.6 The @top Sectioning Command

A special sectioning command, @top, has been created for use with the @node Top line. The @top sectioning command tells makeinfo that it marks the 'Top' node in the file. It provides the information that makeinfo needs to insert node pointers automatically. Write the @top command at the beginning of the line immediately following the @node Top line. Write the title on the remaining part of the same line as the @top command.

In Info, the @top sectioning command causes the title to appear on a line by itself, with a line of asterisks inserted underneath.

In TEX and `texinfo-format-buffer`, the `@top` sectioning command is merely a synonym for `@unnumbered`. Neither of these formatters require an `@top` command, and do nothing special with it. You can use `@chapter` or `@unnumbered` after the `@node Top` line when you use these formatters. Also, you can use `@chapter` or `@unnumbered` when you use the Texinfo updating commands to create or update pointers and menus.

6.3.7 The 'Top' Node Summary

You can help readers by writing a summary in the 'Top' node, after the `@top` line, before the main or master menu. The summary should briefly describe the document. In Info, this summary will appear just before the master menu. In a printed manual, this summary will appear on a page of its own.

If you do not want the summary to appear on a page of its own in a printed manual, you can enclose the whole of the 'Top' node, including the `@node Top` line and the `@top` sectioning command line or other sectioning command line between `@ifinfo` and `@end ifinfo`. This prevents any of the text from appearing in the printed output. (see Chapter 16 [Conditionally Visible Text], page 139). You can repeat the brief description from the 'Top' node within `@iftex` ... `@end iftex` at the beginning of the first chapter, for those who read the printed manual. This saves paper and may look neater.

You should write the version number of the program to which the manual applies in the summary. This helps the reader keep track of which manual is for which version of the program. If the manual changes more frequently than the program or is independent of it, you should also include an edition number for the manual. (The title page should also contain this information: see Section 3.4.1 [`@titlepage`], page 37.)

6.4 Creating Pointers with `makeinfo`

The `makeinfo` program has a feature for automatically defining node pointers for a hierarchically organized file.

When you take advantage of this feature, you do not need to write the 'Next', 'Previous', and 'Up' pointers after the name of a node. However, you must write a sectioning command, such as `@chapter` or `@section`, on the line immediately following each truncated `@node` line (except that comment lines may intervene).

In addition, you must follow the 'Top' `@node` line with a line beginning with `@top` to mark the 'Top' node in the file. See Section 5.3 [`@top`], page 50.

Finally, you must write the name of each node (except for the 'Top' node) in a menu that is one or more hierarchical levels above the node's hierarchical level.

This node pointer insertion feature in `makeinfo` relieves you from the need to update menus and pointers manually or with Texinfo mode commands. (See Section 2.4 [Updating Nodes and Menus], page 20.)

6.5 @anchor: Defining Arbitrary Cross-reference Targets

An *anchor* is a position in your document, labeled so that cross-references can refer to it, just as they can to nodes. You create an anchor with the `@anchor` command, and give the label as a normal brace-delimited argument. For example:

```
This marks the @anchor{x-spot}spot.
   . . .
@xref{x-spot,,the spot}.
```

produces:

```
This marks the spot.
   . . .
See [the spot], page 1.
```

As you can see, the `@anchor` command itself produces no output. This example defines an anchor 'x-spot' just before the word 'spot'. You can refer to it later with an `@xref` or other cross-reference command, as shown. See Chapter 8 [Cross References], page 68, for details on the cross-reference commands.

It is best to put `@anchor` commands just before the position you wish to refer to; that way, the reader's eye is led on to the correct text when they jump to the anchor. You can put the `@anchor` command on a line by itself if that helps readability of the source. Spaces are always ignored after `@anchor`.

Anchor names and node names may not conflict. Anchors and nodes are given similar treatment in some ways; for example, the `goto-node` command in standalone Info takes either an anchor name or a node name as an argument. (See section "goto-node" in *GNU Info*.)

7 Menus

Menus contain pointers to subordinate nodes.[1] In Info, you use menus to go to such nodes. Menus have no effect in printed manuals and do not appear in them.

By convention, a menu is put at the end of a node since a reader who uses the menu may not see text that follows it. Furthermore, a node that has a menu should not contain much text. If you have a lot of text and a menu, move most of the text into a new subnode—all but a few lines. Otherwise, a reader with a terminal that displays only a few lines may miss the menu and its associated text. As a practical matter, you should locate a menu within 20 lines of the beginning of the node.

The short text before a menu may look awkward in a printed manual. To avoid this, you can write a menu near the beginning of its node and follow the menu by an `@node` line, and then an `@heading` line located within `@ifinfo` and `@end ifinfo`. This way, the menu, `@node` line, and title appear only in the Info file, not the printed document.

For example, the preceding two paragraphs follow an Info-only menu, `@node` line, and heading, and look like this:

```
@menu
* Menu Location::          Put a menu in a short node.
* Writing a Menu::         What is a menu?
* Menu Parts::             A menu entry has three parts.
* Less Cluttered Menu Entry:: Two part menu entry.
* Menu Example::           Two and three part entries.
* Other Info Files::       How to refer to a different
                             Info file.

@end menu


@node Menu Location, Writing a Menu, , Menus
@ifinfo
@heading Menus Need Short Nodes
@end ifinfo
```

The Texinfo file for this document contains more than a dozen examples of this procedure. One is at the beginning of this chapter; another is at the beginning of Chapter 8 [Cross References], page 68.

7.1 Writing a Menu

A menu consists of an `@menu` command on a line by itself followed by menu entry lines or menu comment lines and then by an `@end menu` command on a line by itself.

---

[1] Menus can carry you to any node, regardless of the hierarchical structure; even to nodes in a different Info file. However, the GNU Emacs Texinfo mode updating commands work only to create menus of subordinate nodes. Conventionally, cross references are used to refer to other nodes.

A menu looks like this:

```
@menu
Larger Units of Text

* Files::                        All about handling files.
* Multiples: Buffers.            Multiple buffers; editing
                                    several files at once.
@end menu
```

In a menu, every line that begins with an '*' is a *menu entry*. (Note the space after the asterisk.) A line that does not start with an '*' may also appear in a menu. Such a line is not a menu entry but is a menu comment line that appears in the Info file. In the example above, the line 'Larger Units of Text' is a menu comment line; the two lines starting with '*' are menu entries. Space characters in a menu are preserved as-is; this allows you to format the menu as you wish.

7.2 The Parts of a Menu

A menu entry has three parts, only the second of which is required:

1. The menu entry name (optional).

2. The name of the node (required).

3. A description of the item (optional).

The template for a menu entry looks like this:

```
* menu-entry-name: node-name.    description
```

Follow the menu entry name with a single colon and follow the node name with tab, comma, period, or newline.

In Info, a user selects a node with the m (Info-menu) command. The menu entry name is what the user types after the m command.

The third part of a menu entry is a descriptive phrase or sentence. Menu entry names and node names are often short; the description explains to the reader what the node is about. A useful description complements the node name rather than repeats it. The description, which is optional, can spread over two or more lines; if it does, some authors prefer to indent the second line while others prefer to align it with the first (and all others). It's up to you.

7.3 Less Cluttered Menu Entry

When the menu entry name and node name are the same, you can write the name immediately after the asterisk and space at the beginning of the line and follow the name with two colons.

For example, write

```
* Name::                              description
```

instead of

```
* Name: Name.                         description
```

You should use the node name for the menu entry name whenever possible, since it reduces visual clutter in the menu.

7.4 A Menu Example

A menu looks like this in Texinfo:

```
@menu
* menu entry name: Node name.    A short description.
* Node name::                    This form is preferred.
@end menu
```

This produces:

```
* menu:

* menu entry name: Node name.    A short description.
* Node name::                    This form is preferred.
```

Here is an example as you might see it in a Texinfo file:

```
@menu
Larger Units of Text

* Files::                        All about handling files.
* Multiples: Buffers.            Multiple buffers; editing
                                    several files at once.

@end menu
```

This produces:

```
* menu:
Larger Units of Text

* Files::                        All about handling files.
* Multiples: Buffers.            Multiple buffers; editing
                                    several files at once.
```

In this example, the menu has two entries. 'Files' is both a menu entry name and the name of the node referred to by that name. 'Multiples' is the menu entry name; it refers to the node named 'Buffers'. The line 'Larger Units of Text' is a comment; it appears in the menu, but is not an entry.

Since no file name is specified with either 'Files' or 'Buffers', they must be the names of nodes in the same Info file (see Section 7.5 [Referring to Other Info Files], page 67).

7.5 Referring to Other Info Files

You can create a menu entry that enables a reader in Info to go to a node in another Info file by writing the file name in parentheses just before the node name. In this case, you should use the three-part menu entry format, which saves the reader from having to type the file name.

The format looks like this:

```
@menu
* first-entry-name: (filename) nodename.        description
* second-entry-name: (filename) second-node.  description
@end menu
```

For example, to refer directly to the 'Outlining' and 'Rebinding' nodes in the *Emacs Manual*, you would write a menu like this:

```
@menu
* Outlining: (emacs)Outline Mode. The major mode for
                                  editing outlines.
* Rebinding: (emacs)Rebinding.    How to redefine the
                                  meaning of a key.
@end menu
```

If you do not list the node name, but only name the file, then Info presumes that you are referring to the 'Top' node.

The 'dir' file that contains the main menu for Info has menu entries that list only file names. These take you directly to the 'Top' nodes of each Info document. (See Section 20.2 [Install an Info File], page 173.)

For example:

```
* Info: (info).       Documentation browsing system.
* Emacs: (emacs).     The extensible, self-documenting
                      text editor.
```

(The 'dir' top level directory for the Info system is an Info file, not a Texinfo file, but a menu entry looks the same in both types of file.)

The GNU Emacs Texinfo mode menu updating commands only work with nodes within the current buffer, so you cannot use them to create menus that refer to other files. You must write such menus by hand.

8 Cross References

Cross references are used to refer the reader to other parts of the same or different Texinfo files. In Texinfo, nodes and anchors are the places to which cross references can refer.

Often, but not always, a printed document should be designed so that it can be read sequentially. People tire of flipping back and forth to find information that should be presented to them as they need it.

However, in any document, some information will be too detailed for the current context, or incidental to it; use cross references to provide access to such information. Also, an online help system or a reference manual is not like a novel; few read such documents in sequence from beginning to end. Instead, people look up what they need. For this reason, such creations should contain many cross references to help readers find other information that they may not have read.

In a printed manual, a cross reference results in a page reference, unless it is to another manual altogether, in which case the cross reference names that manual.

In Info, a cross reference results in an entry that you can follow using the Info 'f' command. (See Info file 'info', node 'Help-Adv'.)

The various cross reference commands use nodes (or anchors, see Section 6.5 [@anchor], page 63) to define cross reference locations. This is evident in Info, in which a cross reference takes you to the specified location. TeX also uses nodes to define cross reference locations, but the action is less obvious. When TeX generates a DVI file, it records each node's page number and uses the page numbers in making references. Thus, if you are writing a manual that will only be printed, and will not be used online, you must nonetheless write @node lines to name the places to which you make cross references.

8.1 Different Cross Reference Commands

There are four different cross reference commands:

@xref Used to start a sentence in the printed manual saying 'See ...' or an Info cross-reference saying '*Note *name*: *node*.'.

@ref Used within or, more often, at the end of a sentence; same as @xref for Info; produces just the reference in the printed manual without a preceding 'See'.

@pxref Used within parentheses to make a reference that suits both an Info file and a printed book. Starts with a lower case 'see' within the printed manual. ('p' is for 'parenthesis'.)

@inforef Used to make a reference to an Info file for which there is no printed manual.

(The @cite command is used to make references to books and manuals for which there is no corresponding Info file and, therefore, no node to which to point. See Section 9.1.11 [@cite], page 86.)

8.2 Parts of a Cross Reference

A cross reference command requires only one argument, which is the name of the node to which it refers. But a cross reference command may contain up to four additional arguments. By using these arguments, you can provide a cross reference name for Info, a topic description or section title for the printed output, the name of a different Info file, and the name of a different printed manual.

Here is a simple cross reference example:

```
@xref{Node name}.
```

which produces

```
*Note Node name::.
```

and

See Section *nnn* [Node name], page *ppp*.

Here is an example of a full five-part cross reference:

```
@xref{Node name, Cross Reference Name, Particular Topic,
info-file-name, A Printed Manual}, for details.
```

which produces

```
*Note Cross Reference Name: (info-file-name)Node name,
for details.
```

in Info and

See section "Particular Topic" in *A Printed Manual*, for details.

in a printed book.

The five possible arguments for a cross reference are:

1. The node or anchor name (required). This is the location to which the cross reference takes you. In a printed document, the location of the node provides the page reference only for references within the same document.

2. The cross reference name for the Info reference, if it is to be different from the node name. If you include this argument, it becomes the first part of the cross reference. It is usually omitted.

3. A topic description or section name. Often, this is the title of the section. This is used as the name of the reference in the printed manual. If omitted, the node name is used.

4. The name of the Info file in which the reference is located, if it is different from the current file. You need not include any '.info' suffix on the file name, since Info readers try appending it automatically.

5. The name of a printed manual from a different Texinfo file.

The template for a full five argument cross reference looks like this:

```
@xref{node-name, cross-reference-name, title-or-topic,
info-file-name, printed-manual-title}.
```

Cross references with one, two, three, four, and five arguments are described separately following the description of @xref.

Write a node name in a cross reference in exactly the same way as in the @node line, including the same capitalization; otherwise, the formatters may not find the reference.

You can write cross reference commands within a paragraph, but note how Info and TeX format the output of each of the various commands: write @xref at the beginning of a sentence; write @pxref only within parentheses, and so on.

8.3 @xref

The @xref command generates a cross reference for the beginning of a sentence. The Info formatting commands convert it into an Info cross reference, which the Info 'f' command can use to bring you directly to another node. The TeX typesetting commands convert it into a page reference, or a reference to another book or manual.

Most often, an Info cross reference looks like this:

*Note *node-name*::.

or like this

*Note *cross-reference-name*: *node-name*.

In TeX, a cross reference looks like this:

See Section *section-number* [*node-name*], page *page*.

or like this

See Section *section-number* [*title-or-topic*], page *page*.

The @xref command does not generate a period or comma to end the cross reference in either the Info file or the printed output. You must write that period or comma yourself; otherwise, Info will not recognize the end of the reference. (The @pxref command works differently. See Section 8.6 [@pxref], page 75.)

Please note: A period or comma **must** follow the closing brace of an @xref. It is required to terminate the cross reference. This period or comma will appear in the output, both in the Info file and in the printed manual.

@xref must refer to an Info node by name. Use @node to define the node (see Section 6.3.2 [Writing a Node], page 59).

@xref is followed by several arguments inside braces, separated by commas. Whitespace before and after these commas is ignored.

A cross reference requires only the name of a node; but it may contain up to four additional arguments. Each of these variations produces a cross reference that looks somewhat different.

Please note: Commas separate arguments in a cross reference; avoid including them in the title or other part lest the formatters mistake them for separators.

8.3.1 `@xref` **with One Argument**

The simplest form of `@xref` takes one argument, the name of another node in the same Info file. The Info formatters produce output that the Info readers can use to jump to the reference; TEX produces output that specifies the page and section number for you.

For example,

```
@xref{Tropical Storms}.
```

produces

```
*Note Tropical Storms::.
```

and

See Section 3.1 [Tropical Storms], page 24.

(Note that in the preceding example the closing brace is followed by a period.)

You can write a clause after the cross reference, like this:

```
@xref{Tropical Storms}, for more info.
```

which produces

```
*Note Tropical Storms::, for more info.
```

and

See Section 3.1 [Tropical Storms], page 24, for more info.

(Note that in the preceding example the closing brace is followed by a comma, and then by the clause, which is followed by a period.)

8.3.2 `@xref` **with Two Arguments**

With two arguments, the second is used as the name of the Info cross reference, while the first is still the name of the node to which the cross reference points.

The template is like this:

```
@xref{node-name, cross-reference-name}.
```

For example,

```
@xref{Electrical Effects, Lightning}.
```

produces:

```
*Note Lightning: Electrical Effects.
```

and

See Section 5.2 [Electrical Effects], page 57.

(Note that in the preceding example the closing brace is followed by a period; and that the node name is printed, not the cross reference name.)

You can write a clause after the cross reference, like this:

```
@xref{Electrical Effects, Lightning}, for more info.
```

which produces

```
*Note Lightning: Electrical Effects, for more info.
```

and

See Section 5.2 [Electrical Effects], page 57, for more info.
(Note that in the preceding example the closing brace is followed by a comma, and then by the clause, which is followed by a period.)

8.3.3 @xref with Three Arguments

A third argument replaces the node name in the TEX output. The third argument should be the name of the section in the printed output, or else state the topic discussed by that section. Often, you will want to use initial upper case letters so it will be easier to read when the reference is printed. Use a third argument when the node name is unsuitable because of syntax or meaning.

Remember to avoid placing a comma within the title or topic section of a cross reference, or within any other section. The formatters divide cross references into arguments according to the commas; a comma within a title or other section will divide it into two arguments. In a reference, you need to write a title such as "Clouds, Mist, and Fog" without the commas.

Also, remember to write a comma or period after the closing brace of an @xref to terminate the cross reference. In the following examples, a clause follows a terminating comma.

The template is like this:

```
@xref{node-name, cross-reference-name, title-or-topic}.
```

For example,

```
@xref{Electrical Effects, Lightning, Thunder and Lightning},
for details.
```

produces

```
*Note Lightning: Electrical Effects, for details.
```

and

See Section 5.2 [Thunder and Lightning], page 57, for details.

If a third argument is given and the second one is empty, then the third argument serves both. (Note how two commas, side by side, mark the empty second argument.)

```
@xref{Electrical Effects, , Thunder and Lightning},
for details.
```

produces

```
*Note Thunder and Lightning: Electrical Effects, for details.
```

and

See Section 5.2 [Thunder and Lightning], page 57, for details.

As a practical matter, it is often best to write cross references with just the first argument if the node name and the section title are the same, and with the first and third arguments if the node name and title are different.

Here are several examples from *The GNU Awk User's Guide*:

```
@xref{Sample Program}.
@xref{Glossary}.
```

```
@xref{Case-sensitivity, ,Case-sensitivity in Matching}.
@xref{Close Output, , Closing Output Files and Pipes},
    for more information.
@xref{Regexp, , Regular Expressions as Patterns}.
```

8.3.4 @xref with Four and Five Arguments

In a cross reference, a fourth argument specifies the name of another Info file, different from the file in which the reference appears, and a fifth argument specifies its title as a printed manual.

Remember that a comma or period must follow the closing brace of an @xref command to terminate the cross reference. In the following examples, a clause follows a terminating comma.

The template is:

@xref{*node-name*, *cross-reference-name*, *title-or-topic*,
info-file-name, *printed-manual-title*}.

For example,

```
@xref{Electrical Effects, Lightning, Thunder and Lightning,
weather, An Introduction to Meteorology}, for details.
```

produces

```
*Note Lightning: (weather)Electrical Effects, for details.
```

The name of the Info file is enclosed in parentheses and precedes the name of the node.

In a printed manual, the reference looks like this:

See section "Thunder and Lightning" in *An Introduction to Meteorology*, for details.

The title of the printed manual is typeset in italics; and the reference lacks a page number since TeX cannot know to which page a reference refers when that reference is to another manual.

Often, you will leave out the second argument when you use the long version of @xref. In this case, the third argument, the topic description, will be used as the cross reference name in Info.

The template looks like this:

@xref{*node-name*, , *title-or-topic*, *info-file-name*,
printed-manual-title}, for details.

which produces

```
*Note title-or-topic: (info-file-name)node-name, for details.
```

and

See section *title-or-topic* in *printed-manual-title*, for details.

For example,

```
@xref{Electrical Effects, , Thunder and Lightning,
weather, An Introduction to Meteorology}, for details.
```

produces

```
*Note Thunder and Lightning: (weather)Electrical Effects,
for details.
```
and
See section "Thunder and Lightning" in *An Introduction to Meteorology*, for details.

On rare occasions, you may want to refer to another Info file that is within a single printed manual—when multiple Texinfo files are incorporated into the same TeX run but make separate Info files. In this case, you need to specify only the fourth argument, and not the fifth.

8.4 Naming a 'Top' Node

In a cross reference, you must always name a node. This means that in order to refer to a whole manual, you must identify the 'Top' node by writing it as the first argument to the @xref command. (This is different from the way you write a menu entry; see Section 7.5 [Referring to Other Info Files], page 67.) At the same time, to provide a meaningful section topic or title in the printed cross reference (instead of the word 'Top'), you must write an appropriate entry for the third argument to the @xref command.

Thus, to make a cross reference to *The GNU Make Manual*, write:
```
@xref{Top, , Overview, make, The GNU Make Manual}.
```
which produces
```
*Note Overview: (make)Top.
```
and
See section "Overview" in *The GNU Make Manual*.

In this example, 'Top' is the name of the first node, and 'Overview' is the name of the first section of the manual.

8.5 @ref

@ref is nearly the same as @xref except that it does not generate a 'See' in the printed output, just the reference itself. This makes it useful as the last part of a sentence.

For example,
```
For more information, see @ref{Hurricanes}.
```
produces
```
For more information, see *Note Hurricanes::.
```
and
For more information, see Section 8.2 [Hurricanes], page 123.

The @ref command sometimes leads writers to express themselves in a manner that is suitable for a printed manual but looks awkward in the Info format. Bear in mind that your audience will be using both the printed and the Info format.

For example,

```
Sea surges are described in @ref{Hurricanes}.
```

produces

Sea surges are described in Section 6.7 [Hurricanes], page 72.

in a printed document, and the following in Info:

```
Sea surges are described in *Note Hurricanes::.
```

Caution: You *must* write a period, comma, or right parenthesis immediately after an `@ref` command with two or more arguments. Otherwise, Info will not find the end of the cross reference entry and its attempt to follow the cross reference will fail. As a general rule, you should write a period or comma after every `@ref` command. This looks best in both the printed and the Info output.

8.6 @pxref

The parenthetical reference command, `@pxref`, is nearly the same as `@xref`, but you use it *only* inside parentheses and you do *not* type a comma or period after the command's closing brace. The command differs from `@xref` in two ways:

1. TEX typesets the reference for the printed manual with a lower case 'see' rather than an upper case 'See'.

2. The Info formatting commands automatically end the reference with a closing colon or period.

Because one type of formatting automatically inserts closing punctuation and the other does not, you should use `@pxref` *only* inside parentheses as part of another sentence. Also, you yourself should not insert punctuation after the reference, as you do with `@xref`.

`@pxref` is designed so that the output looks right and works right between parentheses both in printed output and in an Info file. In a printed manual, a closing comma or period should not follow a cross reference within parentheses; such punctuation is wrong. But in an Info file, suitable closing punctuation must follow the cross reference so Info can recognize its end. `@pxref` spares you the need to use complicated methods to put a terminator into one form of the output and not the other.

With one argument, a parenthetical cross reference looks like this:

```
... storms cause flooding (@pxref{Hurricanes}) ...
```

which produces

```
... storms cause flooding (*Note Hurricanes::) ...
```

and

... storms cause flooding (see Section 6.7 [Hurricanes], page 72) ...

With two arguments, a parenthetical cross reference has this template:

... (@pxref{*node-name, cross-reference-name*}) ...

which produces

... (*Note *cross-reference-name*: *node-name*.) ...

and

... (see Section *nnn* [*node-name*], page *ppp*) ...

@pxref can be used with up to five arguments just like @xref (see Section 8.3 [@xref], page 70).

Please note: Use @pxref only as a parenthetical reference. Do not try to use @pxref as a clause in a sentence. It will look bad in either the Info file, the printed output, or both.

Also, parenthetical cross references look best at the ends of sentences. Although you may write them in the middle of a sentence, that location breaks up the flow of text.

8.7 @inforef

@inforef is used for cross references to Info files for which there are no printed manuals. Even in a printed manual, @inforef generates a reference directing the user to look in an Info file.

The command takes either two or three arguments, in the following order:

1. The node name.
2. The cross reference name (optional).
3. The Info file name.

Separate the arguments with commas, as with @xref. Also, you must terminate the reference with a comma or period after the '}', as you do with @xref.

The template is:

@inforef{*node-name, cross-reference-name, info-file-name*},

Thus,

```
@inforef{Expert, Advanced Info commands, info},
for more information.
```

produces

```
*Note Advanced Info commands: (info)Expert,
for more information.
```

and

See Info file 'info', node 'Expert', for more information.

Similarly,

```
@inforef{Expert, , info}, for more information.
```

produces

```
*Note (info)Expert::, for more information.
```
and

See Info file 'info', node 'Expert', for more information.

The converse of @inforef is @cite, which is used to refer to printed works for which no Info form exists. See Section 9.1.11 [@cite], page 86.

8.8 @uref{*url*[, *text*][, *replacement*]}

@uref produces a reference to a uniform resource locator (url). It takes one mandatory argument, the url, and two optional arguments which control the text that is displayed. In HTML output, @uref produces a link you can follow.

The second argument, if specified, is the text to display (the default is the url itself); in Info and DVI output, but not in HTML output, the url is also output.

The third argument, on the other hand, if specified is also the text to display, but the url is *not* output in any format. This is useful when the text is already sufficiently referential, as in a man page. If the third argument is given, the second argument is ignored.

The simple one argument form, where the url is both the target and the text of the link:

```
The official GNU ftp site is @uref{ftp://ftp.gnu.org/gnu}.
```
produces:

The official GNU ftp site is ftp://ftp.gnu.org/gnu.

An example of the two-argument form:

```
The official @uref{ftp://ftp.gnu.org/gnu, GNU ftp site} holds
programs and texts.
```
produces:

The official GNU ftp site (ftp://ftp.gnu.org/gnu) holds
programs and texts.

that is, the Info output is this:

```
The official GNU ftp site (ftp://ftp.gnu.org/gnu) holds
programs and texts.
```
and the HTML output is this:

```
The official <a href="ftp://ftp.gnu.org/gnu">GNU ftp site</a> holds
programs and texts.
```
An example of the three-argument form:

```
The @uref{http://example.org/man.cgi/1/ls,,ls(1)} program ...
```
produces:

The ls(1) program ...

but with HTML:

```
The <a href="http://example.org/man.cgi/1/ls">ls(1)</a> program ...
```

To merely indicate a url without creating a link people can follow, use `@url` (see Section 9.1.13 [url], page 86).

Some people prefer to display url's in the unambiguous format:

<URL:http://*host*/*path*>

You can use this form in the input file if you wish. We feel it's not necessary to clutter up the output with the extra '`<URL:`' and '`>`', since any software that tries to detect url's in text already has to detect them without the '`<URL:`' to be useful.

9 Marking Words and Phrases

In Texinfo, you can mark words and phrases in a variety of ways. The Texinfo formatters use this information to determine how to highlight the text. You can specify, for example, whether a word or phrase is a defining occurrence, a metasyntactic variable, or a symbol used in a program. Also, you can emphasize text, in several different ways.

9.1 Indicating Definitions, Commands, etc.

Texinfo has commands for indicating just what kind of object a piece of text refers to. For example, metasyntactic variables are marked by `@var`, and code by `@code`. Since the pieces of text are labelled by commands that tell what kind of object they are, it is easy to change the way the Texinfo formatters prepare such text. (Texinfo is an *intentional* formatting language rather than a *typesetting* formatting language.)

For example, in a printed manual, code is usually illustrated in a typewriter font; `@code` tells TeX to typeset this text in this font. But it would be easy to change the way TeX highlights code to use another font, and this change would not affect how keystroke examples are highlighted. If straight typesetting commands were used in the body of the file and you wanted to make a change, you would need to check every single occurrence to make sure that you were changing code and not something else that should not be changed.

The highlighting commands can be used to extract useful information from the file, such as lists of functions or file names. It is possible, for example, to write a program in Emacs Lisp (or a keyboard macro) to insert an index entry after every paragraph that contains words or phrases marked by a specified command. You could do this to construct an index of functions if you had not already made the entries.

The commands serve a variety of purposes:

`@code{sample-code}`
　　Indicate text that is a literal example of a piece of a program.

`@kbd{keyboard-characters}`
　　Indicate keyboard input.

`@key{key-name}`
　　Indicate the conventional name for a key on a keyboard.

`@samp{text}`　Indicate text that is a literal example of a sequence of characters.

`@var{metasyntactic-variable}`
　　Indicate a metasyntactic variable.

`@env{environment-variable}`
　　Indicate an environment variable.

`@file{file-name}`
　　Indicate the name of a file.

`@command{`*command-name*`}`
>   Indicate the name of a command.

`@option{`*option*`}`
>   Indicate a command-line option.

`@dfn{`*term*`}`   Indicate the introductory or defining use of a term.

`@cite{`*reference*`}`
>   Indicate the name of a book.

`@acronym{`*acronym*`}`
>   Indicate an acronym.

`@url{`*uniform-resource-locator*`}`
>   Indicate a uniform resource locator for the World Wide Web.

`@email{`*email-address*`[, ` *displayed-text*`]}`
>   Indicate an electronic mail address.

9.1.1 `@code{`*sample-code*`}`

Use the `@code` command to indicate text that is a piece of a program and which consists of entire syntactic tokens. Enclose the text in braces.

Thus, you should use `@code` for an expression in a program, for the name of a variable or function used in a program, or for a keyword in a programming language.

Use `@code` for command names in languages that resemble programming languages, such as Texinfo. For example, `@code` and `@samp` are produced by writing '`@code{@@code}`' and '`@code{@@samp}`' in the Texinfo source, respectively.

It is incorrect to alter the case of a word inside an `@code` command when it appears at the beginning of a sentence. Most computer languages are case sensitive. In C, for example, `Printf` is different from the identifier `printf`, and most likely is a misspelling of it. Even in languages which are not case sensitive, it is confusing to a human reader to see identifiers spelled in different ways. Pick one spelling and always use that. If you do not want to start a sentence with a command name written all in lower case, you should rearrange the sentence.

In the printed manual, `@code` causes TeX to typeset the argument in a typewriter face. In the Info file, it causes the Info formatting commands to use single quotation marks around the text.

For example,

```
The function returns @code{nil}.
```

produces this in the printed manual:

The function returns `nil`.

and this in the Info file:

```
The function returns 'nil'.
```

Here are some cases for which it is preferable not to use `@code`:

- For shell command names such as `ls` (use `@command`).
- For shell options such as '`-c`' when such options stand alone (use `@option`).

- Also, an entire shell command often looks better if written using `@samp` rather than `@code`. In this case, the rule is to choose the more pleasing format.

- For environment variable such as TEXINPUTS (use `@env`).

- For a string of characters shorter than a syntactic token. For example, if you are writing about '`goto-ch`', which is just a part of the name for the `goto-char` Emacs Lisp function, you should use `@samp`.

- In general, when writing about the characters used in a token; for example, do not use `@code` when you are explaining what letters or printable symbols can be used in the names of functions. (Use `@samp`.) Also, you should not use `@code` to mark text that is considered input to programs unless the input is written in a language that is like a programming language. For example, you should not use `@code` for the keystroke commands of GNU Emacs (use `@kbd` instead) although you may use `@code` for the names of the Emacs Lisp functions that the keystroke commands invoke.

Since `@command`, `@option`, and `@env` were introduced relatively recently, it is acceptable to use `@code` or `@samp` for command names, options, and environment variables. The new commands allow you to express the markup more precisely, but there is no real harm in using the older commands, and of course the long-standing manuals do so.

9.1.2 @kbd{*keyboard-characters*}

Use the `@kbd` command for characters of input to be typed by users. For example, to refer to the characters M-a, write

```
@kbd{M-a}
```

and to refer to the characters M-x *shell*, write

```
@kbd{M-x shell}
```

The `@kbd` command has the same effect as `@code` in Info, but by default produces a different font (slanted typewriter instead of normal typewriter) in the printed manual, so users can distinguish the characters they are supposed to type from those the computer outputs.

Since the usage of `@kbd` varies from manual to manual, you can control the font switching with the `@kbdinputstyle` command. This command has no effect on Info output. Write this command at the beginning of a line with a single word as an argument, one of the following:

'`code`'   Always use the same font for `@kbd` as `@code`.

'`example`'   Use the distinguishing font for `@kbd` only in `@example` and similar environments.

'`distinct`'   (the default) Always use the distinguishing font for `@kbd`.

You can embed another `@`-command inside the braces of an `@kbd` command. Here, for example, is the way to describe a command that would be described more verbosely as "press an '`r`' and then press the (RET) key":

```
@kbd{r @key{RET}}
```
This produces: *r* (RET)

You also use the @kbd command if you are spelling out the letters you type; for example:

```
To give the @code{logout} command,

type the characters @kbd{l o g o u t @key{RET}}.
```
This produces:

To give the `logout` command, type the characters *l o g o u t* (RET).

(Also, this example shows that you can add spaces for clarity. If you really want to mention a space character as one of the characters of input, write *@key{SPC}* for it.)

9.1.3 @key{*key-name*}

Use the @key command for the conventional name for a key on a keyboard, as in:

```
@key{RET}
```
You can use the @key command within the argument of an @kbd command when the sequence of characters to be typed includes one or more keys that are described by name.

For example, to produce *C-x* (ESC) you would type:

```
@kbd{C-x @key{ESC}}
```
Here is a list of the recommended names for keys:

SPC	Space
RET	Return
LFD	Linefeed (however, since most keyboards nowadays do not have a Linefeed key, it might be better to call this character *C-j*.
TAB	Tab
BS	Backspace
ESC	Escape
DEL	Delete
SHIFT	Shift
CTRL	Control
META	Meta

There are subtleties to handling words like 'meta' or 'ctrl' that are names of modifier keys. When mentioning a character in which the modifier key is used, such as *Meta-a*, use the @kbd command alone; do not use the @key command; but when you are referring to the modifier key in isolation, use the @key command. For example, write '@kbd{Meta-a}' to produce *Meta-a* and '@key{META}' to produce (META).

9.1.4 @samp{*text*}

Use the `@samp` command to indicate text that is a literal example or 'sample' of a sequence of characters in a file, string, pattern, etc. Enclose the text in braces. The argument appears within single quotation marks in both the Info file and the printed manual; in addition, it is printed in a fixed-width font.

```
To match @samp{foo} at the end of the line,
use the regexp @samp{foo$}.
```

produces

To match 'foo' at the end of the line, use the regexp 'foo$'.

Any time you are referring to single characters, you should use `@samp` unless `@kbd` or `@key` is more appropriate. Also, you may use `@samp` for entire statements in C and for entire shell commands—in this case, `@samp` often looks better than `@code`. Basically, `@samp` is a catchall for whatever is not covered by `@code`, `@kbd`, or `@key`.

Only include punctuation marks within braces if they are part of the string you are specifying. Write punctuation marks outside the braces if those punctuation marks are part of the English text that surrounds the string. In the following sentence, for example, the commas and period are outside of the braces:

```
In English, the vowels are @samp{a}, @samp{e},
@samp{i}, @samp{o}, @samp{u}, and sometimes
@samp{y}.
```

This produces:

In English, the vowels are 'a', 'e', 'i', 'o', 'u', and sometimes 'y'.

9.1.5 @var{*metasyntactic-variable*}

Use the `@var` command to indicate metasyntactic variables. A *metasyntactic variable* is something that stands for another piece of text. For example, you should use a metasyntactic variable in the documentation of a function to describe the arguments that are passed to that function.

Do not use `@var` for the names of particular variables in programming languages. These are specific names from a program, so `@code` is correct for them (see Section 9.1.1 [code], page 80). For example, the Emacs Lisp variable `texinfo-tex-command` is not a metasyntactic variable; it is properly formatted using `@code`.

Do not use `@var` for environment variables either; `@env` is correct for them (see the next section).

The effect of `@var` in the Info file is to change the case of the argument to all upper case. In the printed manual and HTML output, the argument is printed in slanted type.

For example,

```
To delete file @var{filename},

type @samp{rm @var{filename}}.
```

produces

To delete file *filename*, type 'rm *filename*'.

(Note that @var may appear inside @code, @samp, @file, etc.)

Write a metasyntactic variable all in lower case without spaces, and use hyphens to make it more readable. Thus, the Texinfo source for the illustration of how to begin a Texinfo manual looks like this:

```
\input texinfo

@@setfilename @var{info-file-name}

@@settitle @var{name-of-manual}
```

This produces:

```
\input texinfo

@setfilename info-file-name

@settitle name-of-manual
```

In some documentation styles, metasyntactic variables are shown with angle brackets, for example:

```
..., type rm <filename>
```

However, that is not the style that Texinfo uses. (You can, of course, modify the sources to 'texinfo.tex' and the Info formatting commands to output the <...> format if you wish.)

9.1.6 @env{*environment-variable*}

Use the @env command to indicate environment variables, as used by many operating systems, including GNU. Do not use it for metasyntactic variables; use @var instead (see the previous section).

@env is equivalent to @code in its effects. For example:

```
The @env{PATH} environment variable sets the search path for

commands.
```

produces

The PATH environment variable sets the search path for commands.

9.1.7 @file{*file-name*}

Use the @file command to indicate text that is the name of a file, buffer, or directory, or is the name of a node in Info. You can also use the command for file name suffixes. Do not use @file for symbols in a programming language; use @code.

Currently, @file is equivalent to @samp in its effects. For example,

```
The @file{.el} files are in

the @file{/usr/local/emacs/lisp} directory.
```

produces

The '.el' files are in the '/usr/local/emacs/lisp' directory.

9.1.8 @command{*command-name*}

Use the @command command to indicate command names, such as ls or cc.

@command is equivalent to @code in its effects. For example:

```
The command @command{ls} lists directory contents.
```

produces

The command ls lists directory contents.

You should write the name of a program in the ordinary text font, rather than using @command, if you regard it as a new English word, such as 'Emacs' or 'Bison'.

When writing an entire shell command invocation, as in 'ls -l', you should use either @samp or @code at your discretion.

9.1.9 @option{*option-name*}

Use the @option command to indicate a command-line option; for example, '-l' or '--version' or '--output=*filename*'.

@option is equivalent to @samp in its effects. For example:

```
The option @option{-l} produces a long listing.
```

produces

The option '-l' produces a long listing.

In tables, putting options inside @code produces a more pleasing effect.

9.1.10 @dfn{*term*}

Use the @dfn command to identify the introductory or defining use of a technical term. Use the command only in passages whose purpose is to introduce a term which will be used again or which the reader ought to know. Mere passing mention of a term for the first time does not deserve @dfn. The command generates italics in the printed manual, and double quotation marks in the Info file. For example:

```
Getting rid of a file is called @dfn{deleting} it.
```

produces

Getting rid of a file is called *deleting* it.

As a general rule, a sentence containing the defining occurrence of a term should be a definition of the term. The sentence does not need to say explicitly that it is a definition, but it should contain the information of a definition—it should make the meaning clear.

9.1.11 @cite{*reference*}

Use the `@cite` command for the name of a book that lacks a companion Info file. The command produces italics in the printed manual, and quotation marks in the Info file.

If a book is written in Texinfo, it is better to use a cross reference command since a reader can easily follow such a reference in Info. See Section 8.3 [`@xref`], page 70.

9.1.12 @acronym{*acronym*}

Use the `@acronym` command for abbreviations written in all capital letters, such as 'NASA'. The abbreviation is given as the single argument in braces, as in '`@acronym{NASA}`'. As a matter of style, or for particular abbreviations, you may prefer to use periods, as in '`@acronym{F.B.I.}`'.

In TeX and HTML, the argument is printed in a slightly smaller font size. In Info or plain text output, this command changes nothing.

9.1.13 @url{*uniform-resource-locator*}

Use the `@url` command to indicate a uniform resource locator on the World Wide Web. This is analogous to `@file`, `@var`, etc., and is purely for markup purposes. It does not produce a link you can follow in HTML output (use the `@uref` command for that, see Section 8.8 [`@uref`], page 77). It is useful for url's which do not actually exist. For example:

```
For example, the url might be @url{http://example.org/path}.
```
which produces:

For example, the url might be `http://example.org/path`.

9.1.14 @email{*email-address*[, *displayed-text*]}

Use the `@email` command to indicate an electronic mail address. It takes one mandatory argument, the address, and one optional argument, the text to display (the default is the address itself).

In Info and TeX, the address is shown in angle brackets, preceded by the text to display if any. In HTML output, `@email` produces a '`mailto`' link that usually brings up a mail composition window. For example:

```
Send bug reports to @email{bug-texinfo@@gnu.org}.
Send suggestions to the @email{bug-texinfo@@gnu.org, same place}.
```
produces

Send bug reports to `bug-texinfo@gnu.org`.

Send suggestions to the same place (`bug-texinfo@gnu.org`).

9.2 Emphasizing Text

Usually, Texinfo changes the font to mark words in the text according to what category the words belong to; an example is the `@code` command.

Most often, this is the best way to mark words. However, sometimes you will want to emphasize text without indicating a category. Texinfo has two commands to do this. Also, Texinfo has several commands that specify the font in which TeX will typeset text. These commands have no effect on Info and only one of them, the `@r` command, has any regular use.

9.2.1 @emph{*text*} and @strong{*text*}

The `@emph` and `@strong` commands are for emphasis; `@strong` is stronger. In printed output, `@emph` produces *italics* and `@strong` produces **bold**.

For example,

```
@quotation
@strong{Caution:} @samp{rm * .[^.]*} removes @emph{all}
files in the directory.
@end quotation
```

produces the following in printed output:

Caution: 'rm * .[^.]*' removes *all* files in the directory.

and the following in Info:

```
*Caution*: 'rm * .[^.]*' removes _all_
files in the directory.
```

The `@strong` command is seldom used except to mark what is, in effect, a typographical element, such as the word 'Caution' in the preceding example.

In the Info output, `@emph` surrounds the text with underscores ('_'), and `@strong` puts asterisks around the text.

Caution: Do not use `@strong` with the word 'Note'; Info will mistake the combination for a cross reference. Use a phrase such as **Please note** or **Caution** instead.

9.2.2 @sc{*text*}: The Small Caps Font

Use the '`@sc`' command to set text in the printed and the HTML output in A SMALL CAPS FONT and set text in the Info file in upper case letters. Write the text you want to be in small caps (where possible) between braces in lower case, like this:

```
The @sc{acm} and @sc{ieee} are technical societies.
```

This produces:

The ACM and IEEE are technical societies.

TeX typesets the small caps font in a manner that prevents the letters from 'jumping out at you on the page'. This makes small caps text easier to read than text in all upper case—but it's usually better to use regular mixed case anyway. The Info formatting commands set all small caps text in upper case. In HTML, the text is upper-cased and a smaller font is used to render it.

If the text between the braces of an `@sc` command is uppercase, TeX typesets in FULL-SIZE CAPITALS. Use full-size capitals sparingly, if ever, and since it's redundant to mark all-uppercase text with `@sc`, `makeinfo` warns about such usage.

You may also use the small caps font for a jargon word such as ATO (a NASA word meaning 'abort to orbit').

There are subtleties to using the small caps font with a jargon word such as CDR, a word used in Lisp programming. In this case, you should use the small caps font when the word refers to the second and subsequent elements of a list (the CDR of the list), but you should use '`@code`' when the word refers to the Lisp function of the same spelling.

9.2.3 Fonts for Printing, Not Info

Texinfo provides four font commands that specify font changes in the printed manual but have no effect in the Info file. `@i` requests *italic* font (in some versions of TEX, a slanted font is used), `@b` requests **bold** face, `@t` requests the `fixed-width`, typewriter-style font used by `@code`, and `@r` requests a roman font, which is the usual font in which text is printed. All four commands apply to an argument that follows, surrounded by braces.

Only the `@r` command has much use: in example programs, you can use the `@r` command to convert code comments from the fixed-width font to a roman font. This looks better in printed output.

For example,

```
@lisp
(+ 2 2)     ; @r{Add two plus two.}
@end lisp
```

produces

```
(+ 2 2)     ; Add two plus two.
```

If possible, you should avoid using the other three font commands. If you need to use one, it probably indicates a gap in the Texinfo language.

10 Quotations and Examples

Quotations and examples are blocks of text consisting of one or more whole paragraphs that are set off from the bulk of the text and treated differently. They are usually indented.

In Texinfo, you always begin a quotation or example by writing an @-command at the beginning of a line by itself, and end it by writing an @end command that is also at the beginning of a line by itself. For instance, you begin an example by writing @example by itself at the beginning of a line and end the example by writing @end example on a line by itself, at the beginning of that line.

10.1 Block Enclosing Commands

Here are commands for quotations and examples, explained further in the following sections:

@quotation   Indicate text that is quoted. The text is filled, indented, and printed in a roman font by default.

@example   Illustrate code, commands, and the like. The text is printed in a fixed-width font, and indented but not filled.

@smallexample

  Same as @example, except that in TEX this command typesets text in a smaller font for the @smallbook format than for the default 8.5 by 11 inch format.

@lisp   Like @example, but specifically for illustrating Lisp code. The text is printed in a fixed-width font, and indented but not filled.

@smalllisp   Is to @lisp as @smallexample is to @example.

@display   Display illustrative text. The text is indented but not filled, and no font is selected (so, by default, the font is roman).

@smalldisplay

  Is to @display as @smallexample is to @example.

@format   Like @display (the text is not filled and no font is selected), but the text is not indented.

@smallformat

  Is to @format as @smallexample is to @example.

The @exdent command is used within the above constructs to undo the indentation of a line.

The @flushleft and @flushright commands are used to line up the left or right margins of unfilled text.

The @noindent command may be used after one of the above constructs to prevent the following text from being indented as a new paragraph.

You can use the @cartouche command within one of the above constructs to highlight the example or quotation by drawing a box with rounded corners around it. See Section 10.11 [Drawing Cartouches Around Examples], page 95.

10.2 @quotation

The text of a quotation is processed normally except that:

- the margins are closer to the center of the page, so the whole of the quotation is indented;
- the first lines of paragraphs are indented no more than other lines;
- in the printed output, interparagraph spacing is reduced.

This is an example of text written between an `@quotation` command and an `@end quotation` command. An `@quotation` command is most often used to indicate text that is excerpted from another (real or hypothetical) printed work.

Write an `@quotation` command as text on a line by itself. This line will disappear from the output. Mark the end of the quotation with a line beginning with and containing only `@end quotation`. The `@end quotation` line will likewise disappear from the output. Thus, the following,

```
@quotation
This is
a foo.
@end quotation
```

produces

This is a foo.

10.3 @example

The `@example` command is used to indicate an example that is not part of the running text, such as computer input or output.

```
This is an example of text written between an
@example command
and an @end example command.
The text is indented but not filled.

In the printed manual, the text is typeset in a
fixed-width font, and extra spaces and blank lines are
significant.  In the Info file, an analogous result is
obtained by indenting each line with five spaces.
```

Write an `@example` command at the beginning of a line by itself. Mark the end of the example with an `@end example` command, also written at the beginning of a line by itself.

For example,

```
@example
mv foo bar
@end example
```

produces

```
mv foo bar
```

The lines containing `@example` and `@end example` will disappear from the output. To make the output look good, you should put a blank line before the `@example` and another blank line after the `@end example`. Note that blank lines inside the beginning `@example` and the ending `@end example` will appear in the output.

> Caution: Do not use tabs in the lines of an example (or anywhere else in Texinfo, for that matter)! TEX treats tabs as single spaces, and that is not what they look like. This is a problem with TEX. (If necessary, in Emacs, you can use `M-x untabify` to convert tabs in a region to multiple spaces.)

Examples are often, logically speaking, "in the middle" of a paragraph, and the text that continues after an example should not be indented. The `@noindent` command prevents a piece of text from being indented as if it were a new paragraph.

(The `@code` command is used for examples of code that are embedded within sentences, not set off from preceding and following text. See Section 9.1.1 [`@code`], page 80.)

10.4 @noindent

An example or other inclusion can break a paragraph into segments. Ordinarily, the formatters indent text that follows an example as a new paragraph. However, you can prevent this by writing `@noindent` at the beginning of a line by itself preceding the continuation text.

For example:

```
@example
This is an example
@end example


@noindent
This line is not indented.  As you can see, the
beginning of the line is fully flush left with the line
that follows after it.  (This whole example is between
@code{@@display} and @code{@@end display}.)
```

produces

```
        This is an example
```

This line is not indented. As you can see, the beginning of the line is fully flush left with the line that follows after it. (This whole example is between `@display` and `@end display`.)

To adjust the number of blank lines properly in the Info file output, remember that the line containing `@noindent` does not generate a blank line, and neither does the `@end example` line.

In the Texinfo source file for this manual, each line that says 'produces' is preceded by a line containing `@noindent`.

Do not put braces after an `@noindent` command; they are not necessary, since `@noindent` is a command used outside of paragraphs (see Appendix I [Command Syntax], page 227).

10.5 `@lisp`

The `@lisp` command is used for Lisp code. It is synonymous with the `@example` command.

```
This is an example of text written between an

@lisp command and an @end lisp command.
```

Use `@lisp` instead of `@example` to preserve information regarding the nature of the example. This is useful, for example, if you write a function that evaluates only and all the Lisp code in a Texinfo file. Then you can use the Texinfo file as a Lisp library.[1]

Mark the end of `@lisp` with `@end lisp` on a line by itself.

10.6 `@small...` **Block Commands**

In addition to the regular `@example` and `@lisp` commands, Texinfo has "small" example-style commands. These are `@smalldisplay`, `@smallexample`, `@smallformat`, and `@smalllisp`. All of these commands are designed for use with the `@smallbook` command (which causes TeX to format a printed book for a 7 by 9.25 inch trim size rather than the default 8.5 by 11 inch size).

In TeX, the `@small...` commands typeset text in a smaller font for the smaller `@smallbook` format than for the 8.5 by 11 inch format. Consequently, many examples containing long lines fit in a narrower, `@smallbook` page without needing to be shortened. Both commands typeset in the normal font size when you format for the 8.5 by 11 inch size. Indeed, in this situation, the `@small...` commands are equivalent to their non-small versions.

In Info, the `@small...` commands are also equivalent to their non-small companion commands.

Mark the end of an `@small...` block with a corresponding `@end small...`. For example, pair `@smallexample` with `@end smallexample`.

Here is an example written in the small font used by the `@smallexample` and `@smalllisp` commands:

```
... to make sure that you have the freedom to

distribute copies of free software (and charge for

this service if you wish), that you receive source

code or can get it if you want it, that you can

change the software or use pieces of it in new free

programs; and that you know you can do these things.
```

---

[1] It would be straightforward to extend Texinfo to work in a similar fashion for C, Fortran, or other languages.

The @small... commands make it easier to prepare smaller format manuals without forcing you to edit examples by hand to fit them onto narrower pages.

As a general rule, a printed document looks better if you use only one of (for example) @example or in @smallexample consistently within a chapter. Only occasionally should you mix the two formats.

See Section 19.11 [Printing "Small" Books], page 161, for more information about the @smallbook command.

10.7 @display and @smalldisplay

The @display command begins a kind of example. It is like the @example command except that, in a printed manual, @display does not select the fixed-width font. In fact, it does not specify the font at all, so that the text appears in the same font it would have appeared in without the @display command.

This is an example of text written between an @display command
and an @end display command. The @display command
indents the text, but does not fill it.

Texinfo also provides a command @smalldisplay, which is like @display but uses a smaller font in @smallbook format. See Section 10.6 [small], page 92.

10.8 @format and @smallformat

The @format command is similar to @example except that, in the printed manual, @format does not select the fixed-width font and does not narrow the margins.

This is an example of text written between an @format command
and an @end format command. As you can see
from this example,
the @format command does not fill the text.

Texinfo also provides a command @smallformat, which is like @format but uses a smaller font in @smallbook format. See Section 10.6 [small], page 92.

10.9 @exdent: Undoing a Line's Indentation

The @exdent command removes any indentation a line might have. The command is written at the beginning of a line and applies only to the text that follows the command that is on the same line. Do not use braces around the text. In a printed manual, the text on an @exdent line is printed in the roman font.

@exdent is usually used within examples. Thus,

```
@example
This line follows an @@example command.
@exdent This line is exdented.
This line follows the exdented line.
The @@end example comes on the next line.
@end group
```

produces

```
This line follows an @example command.
```
This line is exdented.
```
This line follows the exdented line.

The @end example comes on the next line.
```

In practice, the `@exdent` command is rarely used. Usually, you un-indent text by ending the example and returning the page to its normal width.

10.10 `@flushleft` and `@flushright`

The `@flushleft` and `@flushright` commands line up the ends of lines on the left and right margins of a page, but do not fill the text. The commands are written on lines of their own, without braces. The `@flushleft` and `@flushright` commands are ended by `@end flushleft` and `@end flushright` commands on lines of their own.

For example,

```
@flushleft
This text is
written flushleft.
@end flushleft
```

produces

This text is
written flushleft.

`@flushright` produces the type of indentation often used in the return address of letters. For example,

```
@flushright
Here is an example of text written
flushright.  The @code{@flushright} command
right justifies every line but leaves the
left end ragged.
@end flushright
```

produces

Here is an example of text written
flushright. The `@flushright` command
right justifies every line but leaves the
left end ragged.

10.11 Drawing Cartouches Around Examples

In a printed manual, the `@cartouche` command draws a box with rounded corners around its contents. You can use this command to further highlight an example or quotation. For instance, you could write a manual in which one type of example is surrounded by a cartouche for emphasis.

`@cartouche` affects only the printed manual; it has no effect in other output files.

For example,

```
@example
@cartouche
% pwd
/usr/local/share/emacs
@end cartouche
@end example
```

surrounds the two-line example with a box with rounded corners, in the printed manual.

In a printed manual, the example looks like this:

```
% pwd
/usr/local/lib/emacs/info
```

11 Lists and Tables

Texinfo has several ways of making lists and tables. Lists can be bulleted or numbered; two-column tables can highlight the items in the first column; multi-column tables are also supported.

Texinfo automatically indents the text in lists or tables, and numbers an enumerated list. This last feature is useful if you modify the list, since you do not need to renumber it yourself.

Numbered lists and tables begin with the appropriate @-command at the beginning of a line, and end with the corresponding @end command on a line by itself. The table and itemized-list commands also require that you write formatting information on the same line as the beginning @-command.

Begin an enumerated list, for example, with an @enumerate command and end the list with an @end enumerate command. Begin an itemized list with an @itemize command, followed on the same line by a formatting command such as @bullet, and end the list with an @end itemize command.

Precede each element of a list with an @item or @itemx command.

Here is an itemized list of the different kinds of table and lists:

- Itemized lists with and without bullets.
- Enumerated lists, using numbers or letters.
- Two-column tables with highlighting.

Here is an enumerated list with the same items:

1. Itemized lists with and without bullets.
2. Enumerated lists, using numbers or letters.
3. Two-column tables with highlighting.

And here is a two-column table with the same items and their @-commands:

@itemize   Itemized lists with and without bullets.

@enumerate Enumerated lists, using numbers or letters.

@table
@ftable
@vtable   Two-column tables, optionally with indexing.

11.1 @itemize: Making an Itemized List

The @itemize command produces sequences of indented paragraphs, with a bullet or other mark inside the left margin at the beginning of each paragraph for which such a mark is desired.

Begin an itemized list by writing @itemize at the beginning of a line. Follow the command, on the same line, with a character or a Texinfo command that generates a mark. Usually, you will write @bullet after @itemize, but you can use @minus, or any command or character that results in a single character in the Info file. If you don't want any mark at all, use `@w`. (When you write the mark command such as `@bullet` after an `@itemize` command, you may omit the '`{}`'.) If you don't specify a mark command, the default is `@bullet`.

Write the text of the indented paragraphs themselves after the `@itemize`, up to another line that says `@end itemize`.

Before each paragraph for which a mark in the margin is desired, write a line that says just `@item`. It is ok to have text following the `@item`.

Usually, you should put a blank line before an `@item`. This puts a blank line in the Info file. (TEX inserts the proper interline whitespace in either case.) Except when the entries are very brief, these blank lines make the list look better.

Here is an example of the use of `@itemize`, followed by the output it produces. `@bullet` produces an '`*`' in Info and a round dot in TEX.

```
@itemize @bullet
@item
Some text for foo.

@item
Some text
for bar.
@end itemize
```

This produces:

- Some text for foo.
- Some text for bar.

Itemized lists may be embedded within other itemized lists. Here is a list marked with dashes embedded in a list marked with bullets:

```
@itemize @bullet
@item
First item.

@itemize @minus
@item
Inner item.

@item
Second inner item.
@end itemize

@item
Second outer item.
@end itemize
```

This produces:

- First item.

      – Inner item.

      – Second inner item.

    • Second outer item.

11.2 @enumerate: Making a Numbered or Lettered List

@enumerate is like @itemize (see Section 11.1 [@itemize], page 96), except that the labels on the items are successive integers or letters instead of bullets.

Write the @enumerate command at the beginning of a line. The command does not require an argument, but accepts either a number or a letter as an option. Without an argument, @enumerate starts the list with the number '1'. With a numeric argument, such as '3', the command starts the list with that number. With an upper or lower case letter, such as 'a' or 'A', the command starts the list with that letter.

Write the text of the enumerated list in the same way you write an itemized list: put @item on a line of its own before the start of each paragraph that you want enumerated. Do not write any other text on the line beginning with @item.

You should put a blank line between entries in the list. This generally makes it easier to read the Info file.

Here is an example of @enumerate without an argument:

```
@enumerate
@item
Underlying causes.

@item
Proximate causes.
@end enumerate
```

This produces:

1. Underlying causes.

2. Proximate causes.

Here is an example with an argument of *3*:

```
@enumerate 3
@item
Predisposing causes.

@item
Precipitating causes.

@item
Perpetuating causes.
@end enumerate
```

This produces:

3. Predisposing causes.

4. Precipitating causes.

5. Perpetuating causes.

Here is a brief summary of the alternatives. The summary is constructed using `@enumerate` with an argument of `a`.

a. `@enumerate`

    Without an argument, produce a numbered list, starting with the number 1.

b. `@enumerate` *positive-integer*

    With a (positive) numeric argument, start a numbered list with that number. You can use this to continue a list that you interrupted with other text.

c. `@enumerate` *upper-case-letter*

    With an upper case letter as argument, start a list in which each item is marked by a letter, beginning with that upper case letter.

d. `@enumerate` *lower-case-letter*

    With a lower case letter as argument, start a list in which each item is marked by a letter, beginning with that lower case letter.

    You can also nest enumerated lists, as in an outline.

11.3 Making a Two-column Table

`@table` is similar to `@itemize` (see Section 11.1 [`@itemize`], page 96), but allows you to specify a name or heading line for each item. The `@table` command is used to produce two-column tables, and is especially useful for glossaries, explanatory exhibits, and command-line option summaries.

Write the `@table` command at the beginning of a line and follow it on the same line with an argument that is a Texinfo "indicating" command such as `@code`, `@samp`, `@var`, or `@kbd` (see Section 9.1 [Indicating], page 79). Although these commands are usually followed by arguments in braces, in this case you use the command name without an argument because `@item` will supply the argument. This command will be applied to the text that goes into the first column of each item and determines how it will be highlighted. For example, @code will cause the text in the first column to be highlighted with an @code command. (We recommend @code for @table's of command-line options.)

You may also choose to use the @asis command as an argument to @table. @asis is a command that does nothing; if you use this command after @table, TeX and the Info formatting commands output the first column entries without added highlighting ("as is").

(The @table command may work with other commands besides those listed here. However, you can only use commands that normally take arguments in braces.)

Begin each table entry with an @item command at the beginning of a line. Write the first column text on the same line as the @item command. Write the second column text on the line following the @item line and on subsequent lines. (You do not need to type anything for an empty second column entry.) You may write as many lines of supporting text as you wish, even several paragraphs. But only text on the same line the @item will be placed in the first column, including any footnote.

Normally, you should put a blank line before an @item line. This puts a blank like in the Info file. Except when the entries are very brief, a blank line looks better.

The following table, for example, highlights the text in the first column with an @samp command:

```
@table @samp
@item foo
This is the text for
@samp{foo}.

@item bar
Text for @samp{bar}.
@end table
```

This produces:

'foo'   This is the text for 'foo'.

'bar'   Text for 'bar'.

If you want to list two or more named items with a single block of text, use the @itemx command. (See Section 11.3.2 [@itemx], page 101.)

11.3.1 @ftable and @vtable

The @ftable and @vtable commands are the same as the @table command except that @ftable automatically enters each of the items in the first column of the table into the index of functions and @vtable automatically enters each of the items in the first column of the table into the index of variables. This simplifies the task of creating indices. Only the items on the same line as the @item commands are indexed, and they are indexed in exactly the form that they appear on that line. See Chapter 12 [Indices], page 104, for more information about indices.

Begin a two-column table using `@ftable` or `@vtable` by writing the `@`-command at the beginning of a line, followed on the same line by an argument that is a Texinfo command such as `@code`, exactly as you would for an `@table` command; and end the table with an `@end ftable` or `@end vtable` command on a line by itself.

See the example for `@table` in the previous section.

11.3.2 `@itemx`

Use the `@itemx` command inside a table when you have two or more first column entries for the same item, each of which should appear on a line of its own. Use `@itemx` for all but the first entry; `@itemx` should always follow an `@item` command. The `@itemx` command works exactly like `@item` except that it does not generate extra vertical space above the first column text.

For example,

```
@table @code
@item upcase
@itemx downcase
These two functions accept a character or a string as
argument, and return the corresponding upper case (lower
case) character or string.
@end table
```

This produces:

```
upcase
downcase        These two functions accept a character or a string as argument,
                and return the corresponding upper case (lower case) character
                or string.
```

(Note also that this example illustrates multi-line supporting text in a two-column table.)

11.4 Multi-column Tables

`@multitable` allows you to construct tables with any number of columns, with each column having any width you like.

You define the column widths on the `@multitable` line itself, and write each row of the actual table following an `@item` command, with columns separated by an `@tab` command. Finally, `@end multitable` completes the table. Details in the sections below.

11.4.1 Multitable Column Widths

You can define the column widths for a multitable in two ways: as fractions of the line length; or with a prototype row. Mixing the two methods is not supported. In either case, the widths are defined entirely on the same line as the `@multitable` command.

1. To specify column widths as fractions of the line length, write `@columnfractions` and the decimal numbers (presumably less than 1) after the `@multitable` command, as in:

    ```
    @multitable @columnfractions .33 .33 .33
    ```

    The fractions need not add up exactly to 1.0, as these do not. This allows you to produce tables that do not need the full line length. You can use a leading zero if you wish.

2. To specify a prototype row, write the longest entry for each column enclosed in braces after the `@multitable` command. For example:

    ```
    @multitable {some text for column one} {for column two}
    ```

    The first column will then have the width of the typeset 'some text for column one', and the second column the width of 'for column two'.

    The prototype entries need not appear in the table itself.

    Although we used simple text in this example, the prototype entries can contain Texinfo commands; markup commands such as `@code` are particularly likely to be useful.

11.4.2 Multitable Rows

After the `@multitable` command defining the column widths (see the previous section), you begin each row in the body of a multitable with `@item`, and separate the column entries with `@tab`. Line breaks are not special within the table body, and you may break input lines in your source file as necessary.

Here is a complete example of a multi-column table (the text is from *The GNU Emacs Manual*, see section "Splitting Windows" in *The GNU Emacs Manual*):

```
@multitable @columnfractions .15 .45 .4
@item Key @tab Command @tab Description
@item C-x 2
@tab @code{split-window-vertically}
@tab Split the selected window into two windows,
with one above the other.
@item C-x 3
@tab @code{split-window-horizontally}
@tab Split the selected window into two windows
positioned side by side.
@item C-Mouse-2
@tab
@tab In the mode line or scroll bar of a window,
split that window.
@end multitable
```

produces:

| Key | Command | Description |

C-x 2	`split-window-vertically`	Split the selected window into two windows, with one above the other.
C-x 3	`split-window-horizontally`	Split the selected window into two windows positioned side by side.
C-Mouse-2		In the mode line or scroll bar of a window, split that window.

12 Indices

Using Texinfo, you can generate indices without having to sort and collate entries manually. In an index, the entries are listed in alphabetical order, together with information on how to find the discussion of each entry. In a printed manual, this information consists of page numbers. In an Info file, this information is a menu entry leading to the first node referenced.

Texinfo provides several predefined kinds of index: an index for functions, an index for variables, an index for concepts, and so on. You can combine indices or use them for other than their canonical purpose. If you wish, you can define your own indices.

12.1 Making Index Entries

When you are making index entries, it is good practice to think of the different ways people may look for something. Different people *do not* think of the same words when they look something up. A helpful index will have items indexed under all the different words that people may use. For example, one reader may think it obvious that the two-letter names for indices should be listed under "Indices, two-letter names", since the word "Index" is the general concept. But another reader may remember the specific concept of two-letter names and search for the entry listed as "Two letter names for indices". A good index will have both entries and will help both readers.

Like typesetting, the construction of an index is a highly skilled, professional art, the subtleties of which are not appreciated until you need to do it yourself.

See Section 4.1 [Printing Indices & Menus], page 46, for information about printing an index at the end of a book or creating an index menu in an Info file.

12.2 Predefined Indices

Texinfo provides six predefined indices:

- A *concept index* listing concepts that are discussed.
- A *function index* listing functions (such as entry points of libraries).
- A *variables index* listing variables (such as global variables of libraries).
- A *keystroke index* listing keyboard commands.
- A *program index* listing names of programs.
- A *data type index* listing data types (such as structures defined in header files).

Not every manual needs all of these, and most manuals use two or three of them. This manual has two indices: a concept index and an @-command index (that is actually the function index but is called a command index in the chapter heading). Two or more indices can be combined into one using the @synindex or @syncodeindex commands. See Section 12.4 [Combining Indices], page 106.

12.3 Defining the Entries of an Index

The data to make an index come from many individual indexing commands scattered throughout the Texinfo source file. Each command says to add one entry to a particular index; after formatting, the index will give the current page number or node name as the reference.

An index entry consists of an indexing command at the beginning of a line followed, on the rest of the line, by the entry.

For example, this section begins with the following five entries for the concept index:

```
@cindex Defining indexing entries
@cindex Index entries
@cindex Entries for an index
@cindex Specifying index entries
@cindex Creating index entries
```

Each predefined index has its own indexing command—`@cindex` for the concept index, `@findex` for the function index, and so on.

Concept index entries consist of text. The best way to write an index is to choose entries that are terse yet clear. If you can do this, the index often looks better if the entries are not capitalized, but written just as they would appear in the middle of a sentence. (Capitalize proper names and acronyms that always call for upper case letters.) This is the case convention we use in most GNU manuals' indices.

If you don't see how to make an entry terse yet clear, make it longer and clear—not terse and confusing. If many of the entries are several words long, the index may look better if you use a different convention: to capitalize the first word of each entry. But do not capitalize a case-sensitive name such as a C or Lisp function name or a shell command; that would be a spelling error.

Whichever case convention you use, please use it consistently!

Entries in indices other than the concept index are symbol names in programming languages, or program names; these names are usually case-sensitive, so use upper and lower case as required for them.

By default, entries for a concept index are printed in a small roman font and entries for the other indices are printed in a small `@code` font. You may change the way part of an entry is printed with the usual Texinfo commands, such as `@file` for file names and `@emph` for emphasis (see Chapter 9 [Marking Text], page 79).

The six indexing commands for predefined indices are:

`@cindex` *concept*
>   Make an entry in the concept index for *concept*.

`@findex` *function*
>   Make an entry in the function index for *function*.

`@vindex` *variable*
>   Make an entry in the variable index for *variable*.

`@kindex` *keystroke*

> Make an entry in the key index for *keystroke*.

`@pindex` *program*

> Make an entry in the program index for *program*.

`@tindex` *data type*

> Make an entry in the data type index for *data type*.

> **Caution:** Do not use a colon in an index entry. In Info, a colon separates the menu entry name from the node name, so a colon in the entry itself confuses Info. See Section 7.2 [The Parts of a Menu], page 65, for more information about the structure of a menu entry.

You are not actually required to use the predefined indices for their canonical purposes. For example, suppose you wish to index some C preprocessor macros. You could put them in the function index along with actual functions, just by writing `@findex` commands for them; then, when you print the "Function Index" as an unnumbered chapter, you could give it the title 'Function and Macro Index' and all will be consistent for the reader. Or you could put the macros in with the data types by writing `@tindex` commands for them, and give that index a suitable title so the reader will understand. (See Section 4.1 [Printing Indices & Menus], page 46.)

12.4 Combining Indices

Sometimes you will want to combine two disparate indices such as functions and concepts, perhaps because you have few enough of one of them that a separate index for them would look silly.

You could put functions into the concept index by writing `@cindex` commands for them instead of `@findex` commands, and produce a consistent manual by printing the concept index with the title 'Function and Concept Index' and not printing the 'Function Index' at all; but this is not a robust procedure. It works only if your document is never included as part of another document that is designed to have a separate function index; if your document were to be included with such a document, the functions from your document and those from the other would not end up together. Also, to make your function names appear in the right font in the concept index, you would need to enclose every one of them between the braces of `@code`.

12.4.1 `@syncodeindex`

When you want to combine functions and concepts into one index, you should index the functions with `@findex` and index the concepts with `@cindex`, and use the `@syncodeindex` command to redirect the function index entries into the concept index.

The `@syncodeindex` command takes two arguments; they are the name of the index to redirect, and the name of the index to redirect it to. The template looks like this:

`@syncodeindex` *from to*

For this purpose, the indices are given two-letter names:

'cp'   concept index

'fn'   function index

'vr'   variable index

'ky'   key index

'pg'   program index

'tp'   data type index

Write an @syncodeindex command before or shortly after the end-of-header line at the beginning of a Texinfo file. For example, to merge a function index with a concept index, write the following:

    @syncodeindex fn cp

This will cause all entries designated for the function index to merge in with the concept index instead.

To merge both a variables index and a function index into a concept index, write the following:

    @syncodeindex vr cp

    @syncodeindex fn cp

The @syncodeindex command puts all the entries from the 'from' index (the redirected index) into the @code font, overriding whatever default font is used by the index to which the entries are now directed. This way, if you direct function names from a function index into a concept index, all the function names are printed in the @code font as you would expect.

12.4.2 @synindex

The @synindex command is nearly the same as the @syncodeindex command, except that it does not put the 'from' index entries into the @code font; rather it puts them in the roman font. Thus, you use @synindex when you merge a concept index into a function index.

See Section 4.1 [Printing Indices & Menus], page 46, for information about printing an index at the end of a book or creating an index menu in an Info file.

12.5 Defining New Indices

In addition to the predefined indices, you may use the @defindex and @defcodeindex commands to define new indices. These commands create new indexing @-commands with which you mark index entries. The @defindex command is used like this:

    @defindex name

The name of an index should be a two letter word, such as 'au'. For example:

```
@defindex au
```

This defines a new index, called the 'au' index. At the same time, it creates a new indexing command, `@auindex`, that you can use to make index entries. Use the new indexing command just as you would use a predefined indexing command.

For example, here is a section heading followed by a concept index entry and two 'au' index entries.

```
@section Cognitive Semantics

@cindex kinesthetic image schemas

@auindex Johnson, Mark

@auindex Lakoff, George
```

(Evidently, 'au' serves here as an abbreviation for "author".) Texinfo constructs the new indexing command by concatenating the name of the index with 'index'; thus, defining an 'au' index leads to the automatic creation of an `@auindex` command.

Use the `@printindex` command to print the index, as you do with the predefined indices. For example:

```
@node Author Index, Subject Index, , Top

@unnumbered Author Index
```

```
@printindex au
```

The `@defcodeindex` is like the `@defindex` command, except that, in the printed output, it prints entries in an `@code` font instead of a roman font. Thus, it parallels the `@findex` command rather than the `@cindex` command.

You should define new indices within or right after the end-of-header line of a Texinfo file, before any `@synindex` or `@syncodeindex` commands (see Section 3.2 [Header], page 31).

13 Special Insertions

Texinfo provides several commands for inserting characters that have special meaning in Texinfo, such as braces, and for other graphic elements that do not correspond to simple characters you can type.

These are:

- Braces and '@'.
- Whitespace within and around a sentence.
- Accents.
- Dots and bullets.
- The TEX logo and the copyright symbol.
- The pounds currency symbol.
- The minus sign.
- Mathematical expressions.
- Glyphs for evaluation, macros, errors, etc.
- Footnotes.
- Images.

13.1 Inserting @ and Braces

'@' and curly braces are special characters in Texinfo. To insert these characters so they appear in text, you must put an '@' in front of these characters to prevent Texinfo from misinterpreting them.

Do not put braces after any of these commands; they are not necessary.

13.1.1 Inserting '@' with @@

@@ stands for a single '@' in either printed or Info output.

Do not put braces after an @@ command.

13.1.2 Inserting '{' and '}'with @{ and @}

@{ stands for a single '{' in either printed or Info output.

@} stands for a single '}' in either printed or Info output.

Do not put braces after either an @{ or an @} command.

13.2 Inserting Space

The following sections describe commands that control spacing of various kinds within and after sentences.

13.2.1 Not Ending a Sentence

Depending on whether a period or exclamation point or question mark
is inside or at the end of a sentence, less or more space is inserted after
a period in a typeset manual. Since it is not always possible to determine
when a period ends a sentence and when it is used in an abbreviation, special
commands are needed in some circumstances. Usually, Texinfo can guess
how to handle periods, so you do not need to use the special commands;
you just enter a period as you would if you were using a typewriter, which
means you put two spaces after the period, question mark, or exclamation
mark that ends a sentence.

Use the @: command after a period, question mark, exclamation mark,
or colon that should not be followed by extra space. For example, use @:
after periods that end abbreviations which are not at the ends of sentences.

For example,

```
The s.o.p.@: has three parts ...
The s.o.p. has three parts ...
```

produces the following. If you look carefully at this printed output, you will
see a little more whitespace after 's.o.p.' in the second line.

The s.o.p. has three parts ...
The s.o.p. has three parts ...

(Incidentally, 's.o.p.' is an abbreviation for "Standard Operating Procedure".)

@: has no effect on the Info output. Do not put braces after @:.

13.2.2 Ending a Sentence

Use @. instead of a period, @! instead of an exclamation point, and @?
instead of a question mark at the end of a sentence that ends with a single
capital letter. Otherwise, TeX will think the letter is an abbreviation and
will not insert the correct end-of-sentence spacing. Here is an example:

```
Give it to M.I.B. and to M.E.W@.  Also, give it to R.J.C@.
Give it to M.I.B. and to M.E.W.  Also, give it to R.J.C.
```

produces the following. If you look carefully at this printed output, you will
see a little more whitespace after the 'W' in the first line.

Give it to M.I.B. and to M.E.W. Also, give it to R.J.C.
Give it to M.I.B. and to M.E.W. Also, give it to R.J.C.

In the Info file output, @. is equivalent to a simple '.'; likewise for @!
and @?.

The meanings of @: and @. in Texinfo are designed to work well with
the Emacs sentence motion commands (see section "Sentences" in *The GNU
Emacs Manual*).

Do not put braces after any of these commands.

13.2.3 Multiple Spaces

Ordinarily, TEX collapses multiple whitespace characters (space, tab, and newline) into a single space. Info output, on the other hand, preserves whitespace as you type it, except for changing a newline into a space; this is why it is important to put two spaces at the end of sentences in Texinfo documents.

Occasionally, you may want to actually insert several consecutive spaces, either for purposes of example (what your program does with multiple spaces as input), or merely for purposes of appearance in headings or lists. Texinfo supports three commands: `@SPACE`, `@TAB`, and `@NL`, all of which insert a single space into the output. (Here, `@SPACE` represents an '`@`' character followed by a space, i.e., '`@ `', and `TAB` and `NL` represent the tab character and end-of-line, i.e., when '`@`' is the last character on a line.)

For example,

```
Spacey@ @ @ @
example.
```

produces

```
Spacey    example.
```

Other possible uses of `@SPACE` have been subsumed by `@multitable` (see Section 11.4 [Multi-column Tables], page 101).

Do not follow any of these commands with braces.

13.2.4 `@dmn{`*dimension*`}`: Format a Dimension

At times, you may want to write '`12 pt`' or '`8.5 in`' with little or no space between the number and the abbreviation for the dimension. You can use the `@dmn` command to do this. On seeing the command, TEX inserts just enough space for proper typesetting; the Info formatting commands insert no space at all, since the Info file does not require it.

To use the `@dmn` command, write the number and then follow it immediately, with no intervening space, by `@dmn`, and then by the dimension within braces. For example,

```
A4 paper is 8.27@dmn{in} wide.
```

produces

A4 paper is 8.27 in wide.

Not everyone uses this style. Some people prefer '`8.27 in.@:`' or '`8.27 inches`' to '`8.27@dmn{in}`' in the Texinfo file. In these cases, however, the formatters may insert a line break between the number and the dimension, so use `@w` (see Section 14.3 [w], page 122). Also, if you write a period after an abbreviation within a sentence, you should write '`@:`' after the period to prevent TEX from inserting extra whitespace, as shown here. See Section 13.2.1 [Not Ending a Sentence], page 110.

13.3 Inserting Accents

Here is a table with the commands Texinfo provides for inserting float-ing accents. The commands with non-alphabetic names do not take braces around their argument (which is taken to be the next character). (Excep-tion: @, *does* take braces around its argument.) This is so as to make the source as convenient to type and read as possible, since accented characters are very common in some languages.

Command	Output	What
@"o	ö	umlaut accent
@'o	ó	acute accent
@,{c}	ç	cedilla accent
@=o	ō	macron/overbar accent
@^o	ô	circumflex accent
@`o	ò	grave accent
@~o	õ	tilde accent
@dotaccent{o}	ȯ	overdot accent
@H{o}	ő	long Hungarian umlaut
@ringaccent{o}	o̊	ring accent
@tieaccent{oo}	o͡o	tie-after accent
@u{o}	ŏ	breve accent
@ubaraccent{o}	o̲	underbar accent
@udotaccent{o}	ọ	underdot accent
@v{o}	ǒ	hacek or check accent

This table lists the Texinfo commands for inserting other characters commonly used in languages other than English.

@exclamdown{}	¡	upside-down !
@questiondown{}	¿	upside-down ?
@aa{},@AA{}	å,Å	a,A with circle
@ae{},@AE{}	æ,Æ	ae,AE ligatures
@dotless{i}	ı	dotless i
@dotless{j}	ȷ	dotless j
@l{},@L{}	ł,Ł	suppressed-L,l
@o{},@O{}	ø,Ø	O,o with slash
@oe{},@OE{}	œ,Œ	oe,OE ligatures
@ss{}	ß	es-zet or sharp S

13.4 Inserting Ellipsis and Bullets

An *ellipsis* (a line of dots) is not typeset as a string of periods, so a special command is used for ellipsis in Texinfo. The @bullet command is special, too. Each of these commands is followed by a pair of braces, '{}', without any whitespace between the name of the command and the braces. (You need to use braces with these commands because you can use them next to other text; without the braces, the formatters would be confused. See Appendix I [@-Command Syntax], page 227, for further information.)

13.4.1 @dots{} (...) and @enddots{} (....)

Use the `@dots{}` command to generate an ellipsis, which is three dots in a row, appropriately spaced, like this: '...'. Do not simply write three periods in the input file; that would work for the Info file output, but would produce the wrong amount of space between the periods in the printed manual.

Similarly, the `@enddots{}` command generates an end-of-sentence ellipsis (four dots) ....

Here is an ellipsis: ... Here are three periods in a row: ...

In printed output, the three periods in a row are closer together than the dots in the ellipsis.

13.4.2 @bullet{} (•)

Use the `@bullet{}` command to generate a large round dot, or the closest possible thing to one. In Info, an asterisk is used.

Here is a bullet: •

When you use `@bullet` in `@itemize`, you do not need to type the braces, because `@itemize` supplies them. (See Section 11.1 [`@itemize`], page 96.)

13.5 Inserting TEX and the Copyright Symbol

The logo 'TEX' is typeset in a special fashion and it needs an `@`-command. The copyright symbol, '©', is also special. Each of these commands is followed by a pair of braces, '{}', without any whitespace between the name of the command and the braces.

13.5.1 @TeX{} (TEX)

Use the `@TeX{}` command to generate 'TEX'. In a printed manual, this is a special logo that is different from three ordinary letters. In Info, it just looks like 'TeX'. The `@TeX{}` command is unique among Texinfo commands in that the 'T' and the 'X' are in upper case.

13.5.2 @copyright{} (©)

Use the `@copyright{}` command to generate '©'. In a printed manual, this is a 'c' inside a circle, and in Info, this is '(c)'.

13.6 @pounds{} (£): Pounds Sterling

Use the `@pounds{}` command to generate '£'. In a printed manual, this is the symbol for the currency pounds sterling. In Info, it is a '#'. Other currency symbols are unfortunately not available.

13.7 @minus{} (−): Inserting a Minus Sign

Use the `@minus{}` command to generate a minus sign. In a fixed-width font, this is a single hyphen, but in a proportional font, the symbol is the customary length for a minus sign—a little longer than a hyphen, shorter than an em-dash:

'−' is a minus sign generated with '`@minus{}`',

'-' is a hyphen generated with the character '-',

'—' is an em-dash for text.

In the fixed-width font used by Info, `@minus{}` is the same as a hyphen.

You should not use `@minus{}` inside `@code` or `@example` because the width distinction is not made in the fixed-width font they use.

When you use `@minus` to specify the mark beginning each entry in an itemized list, you do not need to type the braces (see Section 11.1 [`@itemize`], page 96.)

13.8 @math: Inserting Mathematical Expressions

You can write a short mathematical expression with the `@math` command. Write the mathematical expression between braces, like this:

```
@math{(a + b)(a + b) = a^2 + 2ab + b^2}
```

This produces the following in TEX:

$(a + b)(a + b) \;=\; a\char`\^2 + 2ab + b\char`\^2$

and the following in Info:

```
(a + b)(a + b) = a^2 + 2ab + b^2
```

Thus, the `@math` command has no effect on the Info output.

For complex mathematical expressions, you can also use TEX directly (see Section 16.3 [Raw Formatter Commands], page 140). When you use TEX directly, remember to write the mathematical expression between one or two '`$`' (dollar-signs) as appropriate.

13.9 Glyphs for Examples

In Texinfo, code is often illustrated in examples that are delimited by `@example` and `@end example`, or by `@lisp` and `@end lisp`. In such examples, you can indicate the results of evaluation or an expansion using '⇒' or '↦'. Likewise, there are commands to insert glyphs to indicate printed output, error messages, equivalence of expressions, and the location of point.

The glyph-insertion commands do not need to be used within an example, but most often they are. Every glyph-insertion command is followed by a pair of left- and right-hand braces.

⇒   `@result{}` points to the result of an expression.

↦   @expansion{} shows the results of a macro expansion.

⊣   @print{} indicates printed output.

[error]   @error{} indicates that the following text is an error message.

≡   @equiv{} indicates the exact equivalence of two forms.

⋆   @point{} shows the location of point.

13.9.1 @result{} (⇒): Indicating Evaluation

Use the @result{} command to indicate the result of evaluating an expression.

The @result{} command is displayed as '=>' in Info and as '⇒' in the printed output.

Thus, the following,

```
(cdr '(1 2 3))
    ⇒ (2 3)
```

may be read as "(cdr '(1 2 3)) evaluates to (2 3)".

13.9.2 @expansion{} (↦): Indicating an Expansion

When an expression is a macro call, it expands into a new expression. You can indicate the result of the expansion with the @expansion{} command.

The @expansion{} command is displayed as '==>' in Info and as '↦' in the printed output.

For example, the following

```
@lisp
(third '(a b c))
    @expansion{} (car (cdr (cdr '(a b c))))
    @result{} c
@end lisp
```

produces

```
(third '(a b c))
    ↦ (car (cdr (cdr '(a b c))))
    ⇒ c
```

which may be read as:

(third '(a b c)) expands to (car (cdr (cdr '(a b c)))); the result of evaluating the expression is c.

Often, as in this case, an example looks better if the @expansion{} and @result{} commands are indented five spaces.

13.9.3 @print{} (⊣): Indicating Printed Output

Sometimes an expression will print output during its execution. You can indicate the printed output with the @print{} command.

The @print{} command is displayed as '-|' in Info and as '⊣' in the printed output.

In the following example, the printed text is indicated with '⊣', and the value of the expression follows on the last line.

```
(progn (print 'foo) (print 'bar))
     ⊣ foo
     ⊣ bar
    ⇒ bar
```

In a Texinfo source file, this example is written as follows:

```
@lisp
(progn (print 'foo) (print 'bar))
     @print{} foo
     @print{} bar
     @result{} bar
@end lisp
```

13.9.4 @error{} (error): Indicating an Error Message

A piece of code may cause an error when you evaluate it. You can designate the error message with the @error{} command.

The @error{} command is displayed as 'error-->' in Info and as ' error ' in the printed output.

Thus,

```
@lisp
(+ 23 'x)
@error{} Wrong type argument: integer-or-marker-p, x
@end lisp
```

produces

```
(+ 23 'x)
```
    error   Wrong type argument: integer-or-marker-p, x

This indicates that the following error message is printed when you evaluate the expression:

```
Wrong type argument: integer-or-marker-p, x
```
' error ' itself is not part of the error message.

13.9.5 @equiv{} (≡): Indicating Equivalence

Sometimes two expressions produce identical results. You can indicate the exact equivalence of two forms with the @equiv{} command.

The @equiv{} command is displayed as '==' in Info and as '≡' in the printed output.

Thus,

```
@lisp
(make-sparse-keymap) @equiv{} (list 'keymap)
```

```
@end lisp
```

produces

```
(make-sparse-keymap) ≡ (list 'keymap)
```

This indicates that evaluating `(make-sparse-keymap)` produces identical results to evaluating `(list 'keymap)`.

13.9.6 @point{} (⋆): Indicating Point in a Buffer

Sometimes you need to show an example of text in an Emacs buffer. In such examples, the convention is to include the entire contents of the buffer in question between two lines of dashes containing the buffer name.

You can use the '`@point{}`' command to show the location of point in the text in the buffer. (The symbol for point, of course, is not part of the text in the buffer; it indicates the place *between* two characters where point is located.)

The `@point{}` command is displayed as '`-!-`' in Info and as '⋆' in the printed output.

The following example shows the contents of buffer '`foo`' before and after evaluating a Lisp command to insert the word `changed`.

```
---------- Buffer: foo ----------
This is the ⋆contents of foo.
---------- Buffer: foo ----------


(insert "changed ")
     ⇒ nil
---------- Buffer: foo ----------
This is the changed ⋆contents of foo.
---------- Buffer: foo ----------
```

In a Texinfo source file, the example is written like this:

```
@example
---------- Buffer: foo ----------
This is the @point{}contents of foo.
---------- Buffer: foo ----------


(insert "changed ")
     @result{} nil
---------- Buffer: foo ----------
This is the changed @point{}contents of foo.
---------- Buffer: foo ----------
@end example
```

13.10 Footnotes

A *footnote* is for a reference that documents or elucidates the primary text.[1]

13.10.1 Footnote Commands

In Texinfo, footnotes are created with the `@footnote` command. This command is followed immediately by a left brace, then by the text of the footnote, and then by a terminating right brace. Footnotes may be of any length (they will be broken across pages if necessary), but are usually short. The template is:

```
ordinary text@footnote{text of footnote}
```

As shown here, the `@footnote` command should come right after the text being footnoted, with no intervening space; otherwise, the footnote marker might end up starting a line.

For example, this clause is followed by a sample footnote[2]; in the Texinfo source, it looks like this:

```
...a sample footnote@footnote{Here is the sample

footnote.}; in the Texinfo source...
```

In a printed manual or book, the reference mark for a footnote is a small, superscripted number; the text of the footnote appears at the bottom of the page, below a horizontal line.

In Info, the reference mark for a footnote is a pair of parentheses with the footnote number between them, like this: '(1)'. The reference mark is followed by a cross-reference link to the footnote's text.

In the HTML output, footnote references are marked with a small, superscripted number which is rendered as a hypertext link to the footnote text.

By the way, footnotes in the argument of an `@item` command for a `@table` must be on the same line as the `@item` (as usual). See Section 11.3 [Two-column Tables], page 99.

13.10.2 Footnote Styles

Info has two footnote styles, which determine where the text of the footnote is located:

- In the 'End' node style, all the footnotes for a single node are placed at the end of that node. The footnotes are separated from the rest of the node by a line of dashes with the word 'Footnotes' within it. Each footnote begins with an '(n)' reference mark.

---

[1] A footnote should complement or expand upon the primary text, but a reader should not need to read a footnote to understand the primary text. For a thorough discussion of footnotes, see *The Chicago Manual of Style*, which is published by the University of Chicago Press.

[2] Here is the sample footnote.

Here is an example of a single footnote in the end of node style:

```
--------- Footnotes ---------
```

```
(1)  Here is a sample footnote.
```

- In the 'Separate' node style, all the footnotes for a single node are placed in an automatically constructed node of their own. In this style, a "footnote reference" follows each '(*n*)' reference mark in the body of the node. The footnote reference is actually a cross reference which you use to reach the footnote node.

The name of the node with the footnotes is constructed by appending '-Footnotes' to the name of the node that contains the footnotes. (Consequently, the footnotes' node for the 'Footnotes' node is 'Footnotes-Footnotes'!) The footnotes' node has an 'Up' node pointer that leads back to its parent node.

Here is how the first footnote in this manual looks after being formatted for Info in the separate node style:

```
File: texinfo.info  Node: Overview-Footnotes, Up: Overview
```

```
(1) The first syllable of "Texinfo" is pronounced like "speck", not
"hex". ...
```

A Texinfo file may be formatted into an Info file with either footnote style.

Use the @footnotestyle command to specify an Info file's footnote style. Write this command at the beginning of a line followed by an argument, either 'end' for the end node style or 'separate' for the separate node style.

For example,

```
@footnotestyle end
```

or

```
@footnotestyle separate
```

Write an @footnotestyle command before or shortly after the end-of-header line at the beginning of a Texinfo file. (If you include the @footnotestyle command between the start-of-header and end-of-header lines, the region formatting commands will format footnotes as specified.)

If you do not specify a footnote style, the formatting commands use their default style. Currently, texinfo-format-buffer and texinfo-format-region use the 'separate' style and makeinfo uses the 'end' style.

13.11 Inserting Images

You can insert an image given in an external file with the @image command:

```
@image{filename, [width], [height]}
```

The *filename* argument is mandatory, and must not have an extension, because the different processors support different formats:

- TeX reads the file 'filename.eps' (Encapsulated PostScript format).
- PDFTeX reads 'filename.pdf' (Adobe's Portable Document Format).
- makeinfo uses 'filename.txt' verbatim for Info output (more or less as if it was an @example).
- makeinfo producing HTML output tries 'filename.png'; if that does not exist, it tries 'filename.jpg'. If that does not exist either, it complains. (We cannot support GIF format due to patents.)

The optional *width* and *height* arguments specify the size to scale the image to (they are ignored for Info output). If neither is specified, the image is presented in its natural size (given in the file); if only one is specified, the other is scaled proportionately; and if both are specified, both are respected, thus possibly distorting the original image by changing its aspect ratio.

The *width* and *height* may be specified using any valid TeX dimension, namely:

pt	point (72.27pt = 1in)
pc	pica (1pc = 12pt)
bp	big point (72bp = 1in)
in	inch
cm	centimeter (2.54cm = 1in)
mm	millimeter (10mm = 1cm)
dd	didôt point (1157dd = 1238pt)
cc	cicero (1cc = 12dd)
sp	scaled point (65536sp = 1pt)

For example, the following will scale a file 'ridt.eps' to one inch vertically, with the width scaled proportionately:

```
@image{ridt,,1in}
```

For @image to work with TeX, the file 'epsf.tex' must be installed somewhere that TeX can find it. (The standard location is '*texmf*/tex/generic/dvips/epsf.tex', where *texmf* is a root of your TeX directory tree.) This file is included in the Texinfo distribution and is available from ftp://tug.org/tex/epsf.tex.

@image can be used within a line as well as for displayed figures. Therefore, if you intend it to be displayed, be sure to leave a blank line before the command, or the output will run into the preceding text.

14 Making and Preventing Breaks

Usually, a Texinfo file is processed both by TEX and by one of the Info formatting commands. Line, paragraph, or page breaks sometimes occur in the 'wrong' place in one or other form of output. You must ensure that text looks right both in the printed manual and in the Info file.

For example, in a printed manual, page breaks may occur awkwardly in the middle of an example; to prevent this, you can hold text together using a grouping command that keeps the text from being split across two pages. Conversely, you may want to force a page break where none would occur normally. Fortunately, problems like these do not often arise. When they do, use the break, break prevention, or pagination commands.

The break commands create or allow line and paragraph breaks:

@*   Force a line break.

@sp *n*   Skip *n* blank lines.

@-   Insert a discretionary hyphen.

@hyphenation{*hy-phen-a-ted words*}
                Define hyphen points in *hy-phen-a-ted words*.

The line-break-prevention command holds text together all on one line:

@w{*text*}   Prevent *text* from being split and hyphenated across two lines.

The pagination commands apply only to printed output, since Info files do not have pages.

@page   Start a new page in the printed manual.

@group   Hold text together that must appear on one printed page.

@need *mils*   Start a new printed page if not enough space on this one.

14.1 @*: Generate Line Breaks

The @* command forces a line break in both the printed manual and in Info.

For example,

```
This line @* is broken @*in two places.
```
produces

```
This line
 is broken
in two places.
```

(Note that the space after the first @* command is faithfully carried down to the next line.)

The @* command is often used in a file's copyright page:

```
This is edition 2.0 of the Texinfo documentation,@*
and is for ...
```

In this case, the `@*` command keeps TEX from stretching the line across the whole page in an ugly manner.

> **Please note:** Do not write braces after an `@*` command; they are not needed.

Do not write an `@refill` command at the end of a paragraph containing an `@*` command; it will cause the paragraph to be refilled after the line break occurs, negating the effect of the line break.

14.2 `@-` and `@hyphenation`: Helping TEX hyphenate

Although TEX's hyphenation algorithm is generally pretty good, it does miss useful hyphenation points from time to time. (Or, far more rarely, insert an incorrect hyphenation.) So, for documents with an unusual vocabulary or when fine-tuning for a printed edition, you may wish to help TEX out. Texinfo supports two commands for this:

`@-` Insert a discretionary hyphen, i.e., a place where TEX can (but does not have to) hyphenate. This is especially useful when you notice an overfull hbox is due to TEX missing a hyphenation (see Section 19.10 [Overfull hboxes], page 160). TEX will not insert any hyphenation points in a word containing `@-`.

`@hyphenation{`*hy-phen-a-ted words*`}`
  Tell TEX how to hyphenate *hy-phen-a-ted words*. As shown, you put a '-' at each hyphenation point. For example:

```
@hyphenation{man-u-script man-u-scripts}
```

TEX only uses the specified hyphenation points when the words match exactly, so give all necessary variants.

Info output is not hyphenated, so these commands have no effect there.

14.3 `@w{`*text*`}`: Prevent Line Breaks

`@w{`*text*`}` outputs *text* and prohibits line breaks within *text*.

You can use the `@w` command to prevent TEX from automatically hyphenating a long name or phrase that happens to fall near the end of a line. For example:

```
You can copy GNU software from @w{@samp{ftp.gnu.org}}.
```

produces

You can copy GNU software from 'ftp.gnu.org'.

You can also use `@w` to produce a non-breakable space:

```
None of the formatters will break at this@w{ }space.
```

14.4 @sp *n*: Insert Blank Lines

A line beginning with and containing only @sp *n* generates *n* blank lines of space in both the printed manual and the Info file. @sp also forces a paragraph break. For example,

```
@sp 2
```

generates two blank lines.

The @sp command is most often used in the title page.

14.5 @page: Start a New Page

A line containing only @page starts a new page in a printed manual. The command has no effect on Info files since they are not paginated. An @page command is often used in the @titlepage section of a Texinfo file to start the copyright page.

14.6 @group: Prevent Page Breaks

The @group command (on a line by itself) is used inside an @example or similar construct to begin an unsplittable vertical group, which will appear entirely on one page in the printed output. The group is terminated by a line containing only @end group. These two lines produce no output of their own, and in the Info file output they have no effect at all.

Although @group would make sense conceptually in a wide variety of contexts, its current implementation works reliably only within @example and variants, and within @display, @format, @flushleft and @flushright. See Chapter 10 [Quotations and Examples], page 89. (What all these commands have in common is that each line of input produces a line of output.) In other contexts, @group can cause anomalous vertical spacing.

This formatting requirement means that you should write:

```
@example
@group
...
@end group
@end example
```

with the @group and @end group commands inside the @example and @end example commands.

The @group command is most often used to hold an example together on one page. In this Texinfo manual, more than 100 examples contain text that is enclosed between @group and @end group.

If you forget to end a group, you may get strange and unfathomable error messages when you run TeX. This is because TeX keeps trying to put the rest of the Texinfo file onto the one page and does not start to generate error messages until it has processed considerable text. It is a good rule of thumb to look for a missing @end group if you get incomprehensible error messages in TeX.

14.7 @need *mils*: Prevent Page Breaks

A line containing only @need *n* starts a new page in a printed manual if fewer than *n* mils (thousandths of an inch) remain on the current page. Do not use braces around the argument *n*. The @need command has no effect on Info files since they are not paginated.

This paragraph is preceded by an @need command that tells T_EX to start a new page if fewer than 800 mils (eight-tenths inch) remain on the page. It looks like this:

```
@need 800

This paragraph is preceded by ...
```

The @need command is useful for preventing orphans (single lines at the bottoms of printed pages).

15 Definition Commands

The `@deffn` command and the other *definition commands* enable you to describe functions, variables, macros, commands, user options, special forms and other such artifacts in a uniform format.

In the Info file, a definition causes the entity category—'Function', 'Variable', or whatever—to appear at the beginning of the first line of the definition, followed by the entity's name and arguments. In the printed manual, the command causes TEX to print the entity's name and its arguments on the left margin and print the category next to the right margin. In both output formats, the body of the definition is indented. Also, the name of the entity is entered into the appropriate index: `@deffn` enters the name into the index of functions, `@defvr` enters it into the index of variables, and so on.

A manual need not and should not contain more than one definition for a given name. An appendix containing a summary should use `@table` rather than the definition commands.

15.1 The Template for a Definition

The `@deffn` command is used for definitions of entities that resemble functions. To write a definition using the `@deffn` command, write the `@deffn` command at the beginning of a line and follow it on the same line by the category of the entity, the name of the entity itself, and its arguments (if any). Then write the body of the definition on succeeding lines. (You may embed examples in the body.) Finally, end the definition with an `@end deffn` command written on a line of its own. (The other definition commands follow the same format.)

The template for a definition looks like this:

```
@deffn category name arguments...
body-of-definition
@end deffn
```

For example,

```
@deffn Command forward-word count
This command moves point forward @var{count} words
(or backward if @var{count} is negative). ...
@end deffn
```

produces

> **forward-word** *count*   Command
>
>   This function moves point forward *count* words (or backward if *count* is negative). ...

Capitalize the category name like a title. If the name of the category contains spaces, as in the phrase 'Interactive Command', write braces around it. For example:

```
@deffn {Interactive Command} isearch-forward

...

@end deffn
```

Otherwise, the second word will be mistaken for the name of the entity.

Some of the definition commands are more general than others. The `@deffn` command, for example, is the general definition command for functions and the like—for entities that may take arguments. When you use this command, you specify the category to which the entity belongs. The `@deffn` command possesses three predefined, specialized variations, `@defun`, `@defmac`, and `@defspec`, that specify the category for you: "Function", "Macro", and "Special Form" respectively. (In Lisp, a special form is an entity much like a function.) The `@defvr` command also is accompanied by several predefined, specialized variations for describing particular kinds of variables.

The template for a specialized definition, such as `@defun`, is similar to the template for a generalized definition, except that you do not need to specify the category:

```
@defun name arguments...
body-of-definition
@end defun
```

Thus,

```
@defun buffer-end flag
This function returns @code{(point-min)} if @var{flag}
is less than 1, @code{(point-max)} otherwise.

...

@end defun
```

produces

buffer-end *flag*   Function

   This function returns (`point-min`) if *flag* is less than 1, (`point-max`)
   otherwise. ...

See Section 15.6 [A Sample Function Definition], page 136, for a more detailed example of a function definition, including the use of `@example` inside the definition.

The other specialized commands work like `@defun`.

15.2 Optional and Repeated Arguments

Some entities take optional or repeated arguments, which may be specified by a distinctive glyph that uses square brackets and ellipses. For example, a special form often breaks its argument list into separate arguments in more complicated ways than a straightforward function.

An argument enclosed within square brackets is optional. Thus, the phrase '[*optional-arg*]' means that *optional-arg* is optional. An argument followed by an ellipsis is optional and may be repeated more than once. Thus, '*repeated-args*...' stands for zero or more arguments. Parentheses are used when several arguments are grouped into additional levels of list structure in Lisp.

Here is the `@defspec` line of an example of an imaginary special form:

foobar (*var* [*from* *to* [*inc*]]) *body*...   Special Form

In this example, the arguments *from* and *to* are optional, but must both be present or both absent. If they are present, *inc* may optionally be specified as well. These arguments are grouped with the argument *var* into a list, to distinguish them from *body*, which includes all remaining elements of the form.

In a Texinfo source file, this `@defspec` line is written like this (except it would not be split over two lines, as it is in this example).

```
@defspec foobar (@var{var} [@var{from} @var{to}
      [@var{inc}]]) @var{body}@dots{}
```
The function is listed in the Command and Variable Index under 'foobar'.

15.3 Two or More 'First' Lines

To create two or more 'first' or header lines for a definition, follow the first `@deffn` line by a line beginning with `@deffnx`. The `@deffnx` command works exactly like `@deffn` except that it does not generate extra vertical white space between it and the preceding line.

For example,

```
@deffn {Interactive Command} isearch-forward
@deffnx {Interactive Command} isearch-backward
These two search commands are similar except ...
@end deffn
```
produces

isearch-forward   Interactive Command
isearch-backward   Interactive Command
These two search commands are similar except ...

Each definition command has an 'x' form: `@defunx`, `@defvrx`, `@deftypefunx`, etc.

The 'x' forms work just like `@itemx`; see Section 11.3.2 [@itemx], page 101.

15.4 The Definition Commands

Texinfo provides more than a dozen definition commands, all of which are described in this section.

The definition commands automatically enter the name of the entity in the appropriate index: for example, `@deffn`, `@defun`, and `@defmac` enter function names in the index of functions; `@defvr` and `@defvar` enter variable names in the index of variables.

Although the examples that follow mostly illustrate Lisp, the commands can be used for other programming languages.

15.4.1 Functions and Similar Entities

This section describes the commands for describing functions and similar entities:

@deffn *category name arguments*...

> The `@deffn` command is the general definition command for functions, interactive commands, and similar entities that may take arguments. You must choose a term to describe the category of entity being defined; for example, "Function" could be used if the entity is a function. The `@deffn` command is written at the beginning of a line and is followed on the same line by the category of entity being described, the name of this particular entity, and its arguments, if any. Terminate the definition with `@end deffn` on a line of its own.
>
> For example, here is a definition:
>
> ```
> @deffn Command forward-char nchars
> Move point forward @var{nchars} characters.
> @end deffn
> ```
>
> This shows a rather terse definition for a "command" named `forward-char` with one argument, *nchars*.
>
> `@deffn` prints argument names such as *nchars* in italics or upper case, as if `@var` had been used, because we think of these names as metasyntactic variables—they stand for the actual argument values. Within the text of the description, write an argument name explicitly with `@var` to refer to the value of the argument. In the example above, we used '`@var{nchars}`' in this way.
>
> The template for `@deffn` is:
>
> ```
> @deffn category name arguments...
> body-of-definition
> @end deffn
> ```

@defun *name arguments*...

> The `@defun` command is the definition command for functions. `@defun` is equivalent to '`@deffn Function ...`'.
>
> For example,
>
> ```
> @defun set symbol new-value
> Change the value of the symbol @var{symbol}
> to @var{new-value}.
> @end defun
> ```
>
> shows a rather terse definition for a function `set` whose arguments are *symbol* and *new-value*. The argument names on the `@defun` line automatically appear in italics or upper case as if

they were enclosed in `@var`. Terminate the definition with `@end defun` on a line of its own.

The template is:

```
@defun function-name arguments...
body-of-definition
@end defun
```

`@defun` creates an entry in the index of functions.

`@defmac` *name arguments...*

The `@defmac` command is the definition command for macros. `@defmac` is equivalent to '`@deffn Macro ...`' and works like `@defun`.

`@defspec` *name arguments...*

The `@defspec` command is the definition command for special forms. (In Lisp, a special form is an entity much like a function, see section "Special Forms" in *GNU Emacs Lisp Reference Manual*.) `@defspec` is equivalent to '`@deffn {Special Form} ...`' and works like `@defun`.

15.4.2 Variables and Similar Entities

Here are the commands for defining variables and similar entities:

`@defvr` *category name*

The `@defvr` command is a general definition command for something like a variable—an entity that records a value. You must choose a term to describe the category of entity being defined; for example, "Variable" could be used if the entity is a variable. Write the `@defvr` command at the beginning of a line and follow it on the same line by the category of the entity and the name of the entity.

Capitalize the category name like a title. If the name of the category contains spaces, as in the name "User Option", enclose it in braces. Otherwise, the second word will be mistaken for the name of the entity. For example,

```
@defvr {User Option} fill-column
This buffer-local variable specifies
the maximum width of filled lines.
...
@end defvr
```

Terminate the definition with `@end defvr` on a line of its own.

The template is:

```
@defvr category name
body-of-definition
@end defvr
```

`@defvr` creates an entry in the index of variables for *name*.

@defvar *name*

> The @defvar command is the definition command for variables. @defvar is equivalent to '@defvr Variable ...'.
>
> For example:
>
> ```
> @defvar kill-ring
>
> ...
>
> @end defvar
> ```
>
> The template is:
>
> ```
> @defvar name
> body-of-definition
> @end defvar
> ```
>
> @defvar creates an entry in the index of variables for *name*.

@defopt *name*

> The @defopt command is the definition command for *user options*, i.e., variables intended for users to change according to taste; Emacs has many such (see section "Variables" in *The GNU Emacs Manual*). @defopt is equivalent to '@defvr {User Option} ...' and works like @defvar.

15.4.3 Functions in Typed Languages

The @deftypefn command and its variations are for describing functions in languages in which you must declare types of variables and functions, such as C and C++.

@deftypefn *category data-type name arguments*...

> The @deftypefn command is the general definition command for functions and similar entities that may take arguments and that are typed. The @deftypefn command is written at the beginning of a line and is followed on the same line by the category of entity being described, the type of the returned value, the name of this particular entity, and its arguments, if any.
>
> For example,
>
> ```
> @deftypefn {Library Function} int foobar
>     (int @var{foo}, float @var{bar})
>
>   ...
>
> @end deftypefn
> ```
>
> (where the text before the "...", shown above as two lines, would actually be a single line in a real Texinfo file) produces the following in Info:
>
> ```
> -- Library Function: int foobar (int FOO, float BAR)
>
>   ...
> ```
>
> In a printed manual, it produces:

int foobar (int *foo*, float *bar*)   *Library Function*
    . . .

This means that `foobar` is a "library function" that returns an
`int`, and its arguments are *foo* (an `int`) and *bar* (a `float`).

The argument names that you write in `@deftypefn` are not subject
to an implicit `@var`—since the actual names of the arguments in
`@deftypefn` are typically scattered among data type names and
keywords, Texinfo cannot find them without help. Instead, you
must write `@var` explicitly around the argument names. In the
example above, the argument names are 'foo' and 'bar'.

The template for `@deftypefn` is:

```
@deftypefn category data-type name arguments ...
    body-of-description
@end deftypefn
```

Note that if the *category* or *data type* is more than one word then
it must be enclosed in braces to make it a single argument.

If you are describing a procedure in a language that has packages, such as Ada, you might consider using `@deftypefn` in a manner somewhat contrary to the convention described in the preceding paragraphs.

For example:

```
@deftypefn stacks private push
        (@var{s}:in out stack;
        @var{n}:in integer)

    . . .

@end deftypefn
```

(The `@deftypefn` arguments are shown split into three lines, but
would be a single line in a real Texinfo file.)

In this instance, the procedure is classified as belonging to the
package `stacks` rather than classified as a 'procedure' and its
data type is described as `private`. (The name of the procedure
is `push`, and its arguments are *s* and *n*.)

`@deftypefn` creates an entry in the index of functions for *name*.

`@deftypefun` *data-type name arguments*...
    The `@deftypefun` command is the specialized definition command
    for functions in typed languages. The command is equivalent to
    '`@deftypefn Function ...`'.

Thus,

```
@deftypefun int foobar (int @var{foo}, float @var{bar})

    . . .

@end deftypefun
```

produces the following in Info:

```
-- Function: int foobar (int FOO, float BAR)
...
```

and the following in a printed manual:

> int **foobar** (int *foo*, float *bar*)   Function
>   ...

The template is:

```
@deftypefun type name arguments...
body-of-description
@end deftypefun
```

`@deftypefun` creates an entry in the index of functions for *name*.

15.4.4 Variables in Typed Languages

Variables in typed languages are handled in a manner similar to functions in typed languages. See Section 15.4.3 [Typed Functions], page 130. The general definition command `@deftypevr` corresponds to `@deftypefn` and the specialized definition command `@deftypevar` corresponds to `@deftypefun`.

`@deftypevr` *category data-type name*
> The `@deftypevr` command is the general definition command for something like a variable in a typed language—an entity that records a value. You must choose a term to describe the category of the entity being defined; for example, "Variable" could be used if the entity is a variable.
>
> The `@deftypevr` command is written at the beginning of a line and is followed on the same line by the category of the entity being described, the data type, and the name of this particular entity.
>
> For example:
>
> ```
> @deftypevr {Global Flag} int enable
> ...
> @end deftypevr
> ```
>
> produces the following in Info:
>
> ```
> -- Global Flag: int enable
> ...
> ```

and the following in a printed manual:

> int **enable**   Global Flag
>   ...

The template is:

```
@deftypevr category data-type name
body-of-description
@end deftypevr
```

`@deftypevr` creates an entry in the index of variables for *name*.

`@deftypevar` *data-type name*

The `@deftypevar` command is the specialized definition command for variables in typed languages. `@deftypevar` is equivalent to '`@deftypevr Variable ...`'.

For example:

```
@deftypevar int fubar
...
@end deftypevar
```

produces the following in Info:

```
-- Variable: int fubar
...
```

and the following in a printed manual:

int fubar   Variable

   ...

The template is:

```
@deftypevar data-type name
body-of-description
@end deftypevar
```

`@deftypevar` creates an entry in the index of variables for *name*.

15.4.5 Object-Oriented Programming

Here are the commands for formatting descriptions about abstract objects, such as are used in object-oriented programming. A class is a defined type of abstract object. An instance of a class is a particular object that has the type of the class. An instance variable is a variable that belongs to the class but for which each instance has its own value.

In a definition, if the name of a class is truly a name defined in the programming system for a class, then you should write an `@code` around it. Otherwise, it is printed in the usual text font.

`@defcv` *category class name*

The `@defcv` command is the general definition command for variables associated with classes in object-oriented programming. The `@defcv` command is followed by three arguments: the category of thing being defined, the class to which it belongs, and its name. Thus,

```
@defcv {Class Option} Window border-pattern
...
@end defcv
```

illustrates how you would write the first line of a definition of the `border-pattern` class option of the class `Window`.

The template is:

```
@defcv category class name
...
@end defcv
```

`@defcv` creates an entry in the index of variables.

`@defivar` *class name*

The `@defivar` command is the definition command for instance variables in object-oriented programming. `@defivar` is equivalent to '`@defcv {Instance Variable} ...`'

The template is:

```
@defivar class instance-variable-name
body-of-definition
@end defivar
```

`@defivar` creates an entry in the index of variables.

`@deftypeivar` *class data-type name*

The `@deftypeivar` command is the definition command for typed instance variables in object-oriented programming. It is similar to `@defivar` with the addition of the *data-type* parameter to specify the type of the instance variable. `@deftypeivar` creates an entry in the index of variables.

`@defop` *category class name arguments...*

The `@defop` command is the general definition command for entities that may resemble methods in object-oriented programming. These entities take arguments, as functions do, but are associated with particular classes of objects.

For example, some systems have constructs called *wrappers* that are associated with classes as methods are, but that act more like macros than like functions. You could use `@defop Wrapper` to describe one of these.

Sometimes it is useful to distinguish methods and *operations*. You can think of an operation as the specification for a method. Thus, a window system might specify that all window classes have a method named `expose`; we would say that this window system defines an `expose` operation on windows in general. Typically, the operation has a name and also specifies the pattern of arguments; all methods that implement the operation must accept the same arguments, since applications that use the operation do so without knowing which method will implement it.

Often it makes more sense to document operations than methods. For example, window application developers need to know about the `expose` operation, but need not be concerned with whether a given class of windows has its own method to implement this operation. To describe this operation, you would write:

```
@defop Operation windows expose
```

The `@defop` command is written at the beginning of a line and is followed on the same line by the overall name of the category of operation, the name of the class of the operation, the name of the operation, and its arguments, if any.

The template is:

```
@defop category class name arguments...
body-of-definition
@end defop
```

`@defop` creates an entry, such as 'expose on windows', in the index of functions.

`@deftypeop` *category class data-type name arguments...*

The `@deftypeop` command is the definition command for typed operations in object-oriented programming. It is similar to `@defop` with the addition of the *data-type* parameter to specify the return type of the method. `@deftypeop` creates an entry in the index of functions.

`@defmethod` *class name arguments...*

The `@defmethod` command is the definition command for methods in object-oriented programming. A method is a kind of function that implements an operation for a particular class of objects and its subclasses.

`@defmethod` is equivalent to '`@defop Method ...`'. The command is written at the beginning of a line and is followed by the name of the class of the method, the name of the method, and its arguments, if any.

For example:

```
@defmethod bar-class bar-method argument
...
@end defmethod
```

illustrates the definition for a method called `bar-method` of the class `bar-class`. The method takes an argument.

The template is:

```
@defmethod class method-name arguments...
body-of-definition
@end defmethod
```

`@defmethod` creates an entry, such as 'bar-method on bar-class', in the index of functions.

@deftypemethod *class data-type name arguments*...

> The `@deftypemethod` command is the definition command for
> methods in object-oriented typed languages, such as C++ and
> Java. It is similar to the `@defmethod` command with the addi-
> tion of the *data-type* parameter to specify the return type of the
> method.

15.4.6 Data Types

Here is the command for data types:

@deftp *category name attributes*...

> The `@deftp` command is the generic definition command for data
> types. The command is written at the beginning of a line and
> is followed on the same line by the category, by the name of
> the type (which is a word like `int` or `float`), and then by names
> of attributes of objects of that type. Thus, you could use this
> command for describing `int` or `float`, in which case you could
> use `data type` as the category. (A data type is a category of
> certain objects for purposes of deciding which operations can be
> performed on them.)
>
> In Lisp, for example, *pair* names a particular data type, and an
> object of that type has two slots called the CAR and the CDR.
> Here is how you would write the first line of a definition of `pair`.

```
@deftp {Data type} pair car cdr
...
@end deftp
```

> The template is:

```
@deftp category name-of-type attributes...
body-of-definition
@end deftp
```

> `@deftp` creates an entry in the index of data types.

15.5 Conventions for Writing Definitions

When you write a definition using `@deffn`, `@defun`, or one of the other
definition commands, please take care to use arguments that indicate the
meaning, as with the *count* argument to the `forward-word` function. Also, if
the name of an argument contains the name of a type, such as *integer*, take
care that the argument actually is of that type.

15.6 A Sample Function Definition

A function definition uses the `@defun` and `@end defun` commands. The
name of the function follows immediately after the `@defun` command and it
is followed, on the same line, by the parameter list.

Here is a definition from section "Calling Functions" in *The GNU Emacs Lisp Reference Manual.*

apply *function* &rest *arguments*   Function

    `apply` calls *function* with *arguments*, just like `funcall` but with one difference: the last of *arguments* is a list of arguments to give to *function*, rather than a single argument. We also say that this list is *appended* to the other arguments.

    `apply` returns the result of calling *function*. As with `funcall`, *function* must either be a Lisp function or a primitive function; special forms and macros do not make sense in `apply`.

```
(setq f 'list)
    ⇒ list
(apply f 'x 'y 'z)
error   Wrong type argument: listp, z
(apply '+ 1 2 '(3 4))
    ⇒ 10
(apply '+ '(1 2 3 4))
    ⇒ 10

(apply 'append '((a b c) nil (x y z) nil))
    ⇒ (a b c x y z)
```

An interesting example of using `apply` is found in the description of `mapcar`.

In the Texinfo source file, this example looks like this:

```
@defun apply function &rest arguments
@code{apply} calls @var{function} with
@var{arguments}, just like @code{funcall} but with one
difference: the last of @var{arguments} is a list of
arguments to give to @var{function}, rather than a single
argument.  We also say that this list is @dfn{appended}
to the other arguments.

@code{apply} returns the result of calling
@var{function}.  As with @code{funcall},
@var{function} must either be a Lisp function or a
primitive function; special forms and macros do not make
sense in @code{apply}.
```

```
@example
(setq f 'list)
     @result{} list
(apply f 'x 'y 'z)
@error{} Wrong type argument: listp, z
(apply '+ 1 2 '(3 4))
     @result{} 10
(apply '+ '(1 2 3 4))
     @result{} 10

(apply 'append '((a b c) nil (x y z) nil))
     @result{} (a b c x y z)
@end example

An interesting example of using @code{apply} is found
in the description of @code{mapcar}.
@end defun
```

In this manual, this function is listed in the Command and Variable Index under apply.

Ordinary variables and user options are described using a format like that for functions except that variables do not take arguments.

16 Conditionally Visible Text

Sometimes it is good to use different text for different output formats. For example, you can use the *conditional commands* to specify different text for the printed manual and the Info output.

Conditional commands may not be nested.

The conditional commands comprise the following categories.

- Commands for HTML, Info, or TEX.
- Commands for not HTML, Info, or TEX.
- Raw TEX or HTML commands.
- Substituting text for all formats, and testing if a flag is set or clear.

16.1 Conditional Commands

`@ifinfo` begins segments of text that should be ignored by TEX when it typesets the printed manual. The segment of text appears only in the Info file. The `@ifinfo` command should appear on a line by itself; end the Info-only text with a line containing `@end ifinfo` by itself. At the beginning of a Texinfo file, the Info permissions are contained within a region marked by `@ifinfo` and `@end ifinfo`. (See Section 3.3 [Info Summary and Permissions], page 37.)

The `@iftex` and `@end iftex` commands are similar to the `@ifinfo` and `@end ifinfo` commands, except that they specify text that will appear in the printed manual but not in the Info file. Likewise for `@ifhtml` and `@end ifhtml`, which specify text to appear only in HTML output.

For example,

```
@iftex
This text will appear only in the printed manual.
@end iftex
@ifinfo
However, this text will appear only in Info.
@end ifinfo
@ifhtml
And this text will only appear in HTML.
@end ifhtml
```

The preceding example produces the following line: This text will appear only in the printed manual.

Notice that you only see one of the input lines, depending on which version of the manual you are reading.

16.2 Conditional Not Commands

You can specify text to be included in any output format *other* than some given one with the `@ifnot...` commands:

```
@ifnothtml ... @end ifnothtml

@ifnotinfo ... @end ifnotinfo

@ifnottex ... @end ifnottex
```

(The @ifnot... command and the @end command must actually appear on lines by themselves.)

If the output file is not being made for the given format, the region is included. Otherwise, it is ignored.

The regions delimited by these commands are ordinary Texinfo source as with @iftex, not raw formatter source as with @tex (see Section 16.3 [Raw Formatter Commands], page 140).

16.3 Raw Formatter Commands

Inside a region delineated by @iftex and @end iftex, you can embed some raw TeX commands. Info will ignore these commands since they are only in that part of the file which is seen by TeX. You can write the TeX commands as you would write them in a normal TeX file, except that you must replace the '\' used by TeX with an '@'. For example, in the @titlepage section of a Texinfo file, you can use the TeX command @vskip to format the copyright page. (The @titlepage command causes Info to ignore the region automatically, as it does with the @iftex command.)

However, many features of plain TeX will not work, as they are overridden by Texinfo features.

You can enter plain TeX completely, and use '\' in the TeX commands, by delineating a region with the @tex and @end tex commands. (The @tex command also causes Info to ignore the region, like the @iftex command.) The sole exception is that the @ character still introduces a command, so that @end tex can be recognized properly.

For example, here is a mathematical expression written in plain TeX:

```
@tex
$$ \chi^2 = \sum_{i=1}^N
          \left (y_i - (a + b x_i)
          \over \sigma_i\right)^2 $$
@end tex
```

The output of this example will appear only in a printed manual. If you are reading this in Info, you will not see the equation that appears in the printed manual. In a printed manual, the above expression looks like this:

$$\chi^2 = \sum_{i=1}^N \left(\frac{y_i - (a + bx_i)}{\sigma_i} \right)^2$$

Analogously, you can use @ifhtml ... @end ifhtml to delimit a region to be included in HTML output only, and @html ... @end html for a region of raw HTML (again, except that @ is still the escape character, so the @end command can be recognized.)

16.4 @set, @clear, and @value

You can direct the Texinfo formatting commands to format or ignore parts of a Texinfo file with the @set, @clear, @ifset, and @ifclear commands.

In addition, you can use the @set *flag* command to set the value of *flag* to a string of characters; and use @value{*flag*} to insert that string. You can use @set, for example, to set a date and use @value to insert the date in several places in the Texinfo file.

16.4.1 @ifset and @ifclear

When a *flag* is set, the Texinfo formatting commands format text between subsequent pairs of @ifset *flag* and @end ifset commands. When the *flag* is cleared, the Texinfo formatting commands do *not* format the text.

Use the @set *flag* command to turn on, or *set*, a *flag*; a *flag* name can be any single word, containing letters, numerals, hyphens, or underscores.

The format for the command looks like this:

> @set *flag*

Write the conditionally formatted text between @ifset *flag* and @end ifset commands, like this:

> @ifset *flag*
> *conditional-text*
> @end ifset

For example, you can create one document that has two variants, such as a manual for a 'large' and 'small' model:

```
You can use this machine to dig up shrubs
without hurting them.

@set large

@ifset large
It can also dig up fully grown trees.
@end ifset

Remember to replant promptly ...
```

In the example, the formatting commands will format the text between @ifset large and @end ifset because the large flag is set.

Use the @clear *flag* command to turn off, or *clear*, a *flag*. Clearing a flag is the opposite of setting a flag. The command looks like this:

> @clear *flag*

Write the command on a line of its own.

When *flag* is cleared, the Texinfo formatting commands do *not* format the text between @ifset *flag* and @end ifset; that text is ignored and does not appear in either printed or Info output.

For example, if you clear the flag of the preceding example by writing an `@clear large` command after the `@set large` command (but before the conditional text), then the Texinfo formatting commands ignore the text between the `@ifset large` and `@end ifset` commands. In the formatted output, that text does not appear; in both printed and Info output, you see only the lines that say, "You can use this machine to dig up shrubs without hurting them. Remember to replant promptly . . .".

If a flag is cleared with an `@clear` *flag* command, then the formatting commands format text between subsequent pairs of `@ifclear` and `@end ifclear` commands. But if the flag is set with `@set` *flag*, then the formatting commands do *not* format text between an `@ifclear` and an `@end ifclear` command; rather, they ignore that text. An `@ifclear` command looks like this:

    @ifclear flag

In brief, the commands are:

`@set` *flag*   Tell the Texinfo formatting commands that *flag* is set.

`@clear` *flag*   Tell the Texinfo formatting commands that *flag* is cleared.

`@ifset` *flag*   If *flag* is set, tell the Texinfo formatting commands to format the text up to the following `@end ifset` command.

If *flag* is cleared, tell the Texinfo formatting commands to ignore text up to the following `@end ifset` command.

`@ifclear` *flag*

If *flag* is set, tell the Texinfo formatting commands to ignore the text up to the following `@end ifclear` command.

If *flag* is cleared, tell the Texinfo formatting commands to format the text up to the following `@end ifclear` command.

16.4.2 `@set` and `@value`

You can use the `@set` command to specify a value for a flag, which is expanded by the `@value` command. A flag is an identifier; for best results, use only letters and numerals in a flag name, not '-' or '_'—they will work in some contexts, but not all, due to limitations in TeX. The value is just a string of characters, the remainder of the input line.

Write the `@set` command like this:

    @set foo This is a string.

This sets the value of the flag `foo` to "This is a string.".

The Texinfo formatters then replace an `@value{`*flag*`}` command with the string to which *flag* is set. Thus, when `foo` is set as shown above, the Texinfo formatters convert

    @value{foo}

to

    This is a string.

You can write an `@value` command within a paragraph; but you must write an `@set` command on a line of its own.

If you write the `@set` command like this:

```
@set foo
```
without specifying a string, the value of `foo` is an empty string.

If you clear a previously set flag with `@clear` *flag*, a subsequent `@value{flag}` command is invalid and the string is replaced with an error message that says '`{No value for "flag"}`'.

For example, if you set `foo` as follows:

```
@set how-much very, very, very
```
then the formatters transform

```
It is a @value{how-much} wet day.
```
into
```
It is a very, very, very wet day.
```

If you write

```
@clear how-much
```
then the formatters transform

```
It is a @value{how-much} wet day.
```
into
```
It is a {No value for "how-much"} wet day.
```

16.4.3 `@value` Example

You can use the `@value` command to limit the number of places you need to change when you record an update to a manual. Here is how it is done in *The GNU Make Manual*:

1. Set the flags:

   ```
   @set EDITION 0.35 Beta
   @set VERSION 3.63 Beta
   @set UPDATED 14 August 1992
   @set UPDATE-MONTH August 1992
   ```

2. Write text for the first `@ifinfo` section, for people reading the Texinfo file:

   ```
   This is Edition @value{EDITION},
   last updated @value{UPDATED},
   of @cite{The GNU Make Manual},
   for @code{make}, version @value{VERSION}.
   ```

3. Write text for the title page, for people reading the printed manual:

   ```
   @title GNU Make
   @subtitle A Program for Directing Recompilation
   @subtitle Edition @value{EDITION}, ...
   @subtitle @value{UPDATE-MONTH}
   ```

   (On a printed cover, a date listing the month and the year looks less fussy than a date listing the day as well as the month and year.)

4. Write text for the Top node, for people reading the Info file:

```
This is Edition @value{EDITION}
of the @cite{GNU Make Manual},
last updated @value{UPDATED}
for @code{make} Version @value{VERSION}.
```

After you format the manual, the text in the first @ifinfo section looks like this:

```
This is Edition 0.35 Beta, last updated 14 August 1992,
of 'The GNU Make Manual', for 'make', Version 3.63 Beta.
```

When you update the manual, change only the values of the flags; you do not need to edit the three sections.

17 Internationalization

Texinfo has some support for writing in languages other than English, although this area still needs considerable work.

For a list of the various accented and special characters Texinfo supports, see Section 13.3 [Inserting Accents], page 112.

17.1 @documentlanguage *cc*: Set the Document Language

The @documentlanguage command declares the current document language. Write it on a line by itself, with a two-letter ISO-639 language code following (list is included below). If you have a multilingual document, the intent is to be able to use this command multiple times, to declare each language change. If the command is not used at all, the default is en for English.

At present, this command is ignored in Info and HTML output. For TEX, it causes the file 'txi-*cc*.tex' to be read (if it exists). Such a file appropriately redefines the various English words used in TEX output, such as 'Chapter', 'See', and so on.

It would be good if this command also changed TEX's ideas of the current hyphenation patterns (via the TEX primitive \language), but this is unfortunately not currently implemented.

Here is the list of valid language codes. This list comes from the free translation project (http://www.iro.umontreal.ca/contrib/po/iso-639). In the future we may wish to allow the 3-letter POV codes described at http://www.sil.org/ethnologue/#contents. This will be necessary to support African languages.

aa	Afar	ab	Abkhazian
af	Afrikaans	am	Amharic
ar	Arabic	as	Assamese
ay	Aymara	az	Azerbaijani
ba	Bashkir	be	Byelorussian
bg	Bulgarian	bh	Bihari
bi	Bislama	bn	Bengali; Bangla
bo	Tibetan	br	Breton
ca	Catalan	co	Corsican
cs	Czech	cy	Welsh
da	Danish	de	German
dz	Bhutani	el	Greek
en	English	eo	Esperanto
es	Spanish	et	Estonian
eu	Basque	fa	Persian
fi	Finnish	fj	Fiji
fo	Faroese	fr	French
fy	Frisian	ga	Irish
gd	Scots Gaelic	gl	Galician
gn	Guarani	gu	Gujarati

ha	Hausa	he	Hebrew
hi	Hindi	hr	Croatian
hu	Hungarian	hy	Armenian
ia	Interlingua	id	Indonesian
ie	Interlingue	ik	Inupiak
is	Icelandic	it	Italian
iu	Inuktitut	ja	Japanese
jw	Javanese	ka	Georgian
kk	Kazakh	kl	Greenlandic
km	Cambodian	kn	Kannada
ks	Kashmiri	ko	Korean
ku	Kurdish	ky	Kirghiz
la	Latin	ln	Lingala
lt	Lithuanian	lo	Laothian
lv	Latvian, Lettish	mg	Malagasy
mi	Maori	mk	Macedonian
ml	Malayalam	mn	Mongolian
mo	Moldavian	mr	Marathi
ms	Malay	mt	Maltese
my	Burmese	na	Nauru
ne	Nepali	nl	Dutch
no	Norwegian	oc	Occitan
om	(Afan) Oromo	or	Oriya
pa	Punjabi	pl	Polish
ps	Pashto, Pushto	pt	Portuguese
qu	Quechua	rm	Rhaeto-Romance
rn	Kirundi	ro	Romanian
ru	Russian	rw	Kinyarwanda
sa	Sanskrit	sd	Sindhi
sg	Sangro	sh	Serbo-Croatian
si	Sinhalese	sk	Slovak
sl	Slovenian	sm	Samoan
sn	Shona	so	Somali
sq	Albanian	sr	Serbian
ss	Siswati	st	Sesotho
su	Sundanese	sv	Swedish
sw	Swahili	ta	Tamil
te	Telugu	tg	Tajik
th	Thai	ti	Tigrinya
tk	Turkmen	tl	Tagalog
tn	Setswana	to	Tonga
tr	Turkish	ts	Tsonga
tt	Tatar	tw	Twi
ug	Uighur	uk	Ukrainian
ur	Urdu	uz	Uzbek
vi	Vietnamese	vo	Volapuk
wo	Wolof	xh	Xhosa
yi	Yiddish	yo	Yoruba
za	Zhuang	zh	Chinese
zu	Zulu		

17.2 @documentencoding *enc*: Set Input Encoding

The @documentencoding command declares the input document encoding. Write it on a line by itself, with a valid encoding specification following, such as 'ISO-8859-1'.

At present, this is used only in HTML output from makeinfo. If a document encoding *enc* is specified, it is used in the '<meta>' tag is included in the '<head>' of the output:

```
<meta http-equiv="Content-Type" content="text/html; charset=enc">
```

18 Defining New Texinfo Commands

Texinfo provides several ways to define new commands:

- A Texinfo *macro* allows you to define a new Texinfo command as any sequence of text and/or existing commands (including other macros). The macro can have any number of *parameters*—text you supply each time you use the macro.

  Incidentally, these macros have nothing to do with the `@defmac` command, which is for documenting macros in the subject of the manual (see Section 15.1 [Def Cmd Template], page 125).

- '`@alias`' is a convenient way to define a new name for an existing command.

- '`@definfoenclose`' allows you to define new commands with customized output in the Info file.

18.1 Defining Macros

You use the Texinfo `@macro` command to define a macro, like this:

```
@macro macroname{param1, param2, ...}
text ... \param1\ ...

@end macro
```

The *parameters param1, param2, ...* correspond to arguments supplied when the macro is subsequently used in the document (described in the next section).

For a macro to work with TeX, *macroname* must consist entirely of letters: no digits, hyphens, underscores, or other special characters.

If a macro needs no parameters, you can define it either with an empty list ('`@macro foo {}`') or with no braces at all ('`@macro foo`').

The definition or *body* of the macro can contain most Texinfo commands, including previously-defined macros. Not-yet-defined macro invocations are not allowed; thus, it is not possible to have mutually recursive Texinfo macros. Also, a macro definition that defines another macro does not work in TeX due to limitations in the design of `@macro`.

In the macro body, instances of a parameter name surrounded by backslashes, as in '`\param1\`' in the example above, are replaced by the corresponding argument from the macro invocation. You can use parameter names any number of times in the body, including zero.

To get a single '`\`' in the macro expansion, use '`\\`'. Any other use of '`\`' in the body yields a warning.

The newlines after the `@macro` line and before the `@end macro` line are ignored, that is, not included in the macro body. All other whitespace is treated according to the usual Texinfo rules.

To allow a macro to be used recursively, that is, in an argument to a call to itself, you must define it with '`@rmacro`', like this:

```
@rmacro rmac
a\arg\b
```

```
@end rmacro
```

```
...
```

```
@rmac{1@rmac{text}2}
```

This produces the output 'a1atextb2b'. With '@macro' instead of '@rmacro', an error message is given.

You can undefine a macro *foo* with **@unmacro** *foo*. It is not an error to undefine a macro that is already undefined. For example:

```
@unmacro foo
```

18.2 Invoking Macros

After a macro is defined (see the previous section), you can use (*invoke*) it in your document like this:

```
@macroname {arg1, arg2, ...}
```

and the result will be just as if you typed the body of *macroname* at that spot. For example:

```
@macro foo {p, q}
Together: \p\ & \q\.
@end macro
@foo{a, b}
```

produces:

Together: a & b.

Thus, the arguments and parameters are separated by commas and delimited by braces; any whitespace after (but not before) a comma is ignored. The braces are required in the invocation (but not the definition), even when the macro takes no arguments, consistent with all other Texinfo commands. For example:

```
@macro argless {}
No arguments here.
@end macro
@argless{}
```

produces:

No arguments here.

To insert a comma, brace, or backslash in an argument, prepend a backslash, as in

```
@macname {\\\{\}\,}
```

which will pass the (almost certainly error-producing) argument '\{},' to *macname*.

If the macro is defined to take a single argument, and is invoked without any braces, the entire rest of the line after the macro name is supplied as the argument. For example:

```
@macro bar {p}
Twice: \p\ & \p\.
@end macro
```

```
@bar aah
```
produces:

> Twice: aah & aah.

If the macro is defined to take a single argument, and is invoked with braces, the braced text is passed as the argument, regardless of commas. For example:

```
@macro bar {p}
Twice: \p\ & \p\.
@end macro
@bar{a,b}
```
produces:

> Twice: a,b & a,b.

18.3 Macro Details

Due to unavoidable disparities in the TEX and `makeinfo` implementations, Texinfo macros have the following limitations.

- All macros are expanded inside at least one TEX group. This means that
- Macros containing a command which must be on a line by itself, such as a conditional, cannot be invoked in the middle of a line.
- The TEX implementation cannot construct macros that define macros in the natural way. To do this, you must use conditionals and raw TEX. For example:

```
@ifinfo
@macro ctor {name, arg}
@macro \name\
something involving \arg\ somehow
@end macro
@end macro
@end ifinfo
@tex
\gdef\ctor#1{\ctorx#1,}
\gdef\ctorx#1,#2,{\def#1{something involving #2 somehow}}
@end tex
```
- It is best to avoid comments inside macro definitions.

18.4 '@alias *new=existing*'

The '`@alias`' command defines a new command to be just like an existing one. This is useful for defining additional markup names, thus preserving semantic information in the input even though the output result may be the same.

Write the '@alias' command on a line by itself, followed by the new command name, an equals sign, and the existing command name. Whitespace around the equals sign is ignored. Thus:

```
@alias new = existing
```

For example, if your document contains citations for both books and some other media (movies, for example), you might like to define a macro @moviecite{} that does the same thing as an ordinary @cite{} but conveys the extra semantic information as well. You'd do this as follows:

```
@alias moviecite = cite
```

Macros do not always have the same effect due to vagaries of argument parsing. Also, aliases are much simpler to define than macros. So the command is not redundant. (It was also heavily used in the Jargon File!)

Aliases must not be recursive, directly or indirectly.

18.5 'definfoenclose': Customized Highlighting

A @definfoenclose command may be used to define a highlighting command for Info, but not for TeX. A command defined using @definfoenclose marks text by enclosing it in strings that precede and follow the text. You can use this to get closer control of your Info output.

Presumably, if you define a command with @definfoenclose for Info, you will create a corresponding command for TeX, either in 'texinfo.tex', 'texinfo.cnf', or within an '@iftex' in your document.

Write a @definfoenclose command on a line and follow it with three arguments separated by commas. The first argument to @definfoenclose is the @-command name (without the @); the second argument is the Info start delimiter string; and the third argument is the Info end delimiter string. The latter two arguments enclose the highlighted text in the Info file. A delimiter string may contain spaces. Neither the start nor end delimiter is required. If you do not want a start delimiter but do want an end delimiter, you must follow the command name with two commas in a row; otherwise, the Info formatting commands will naturally misinterpret the end delimiter string you intended as the start delimiter string.

If you do a @definfoenclose on the name of a pre-defined macro (such as @emph, @strong, @t, or @i), the enclosure definition will override the built-in definition.

An enclosure command defined this way takes one argument in braces; this is intended for new markup commands (see Chapter 9 [Marking Text], page 79).

For example, you can write:

```
@definfoenclose phoo,//,\\
```

near the beginning of a Texinfo file to define @phoo as an Info formatting command that inserts '//' before and '\\' after the argument to @phoo. You can then write @phoo{bar} wherever you want '//bar\\' highlighted in Info.

Also, for TeX formatting, you could write

```
@iftex
```

```
@global@let@phoo=@i
@end iftex
```

to define `@phoo` as a command that causes TeX to typeset the argument to `@phoo` in italics.

Note that each definition applies to its own formatter: one for TeX, the other for `texinfo-format-buffer` or `texinfo-format-region`. The `@definfoenclose` command need not be within '`@ifinfo`', but the raw TeX commands do need to be in '`@iftex`'.

Here is another example: write

```
@definfoenclose headword, , :
```

near the beginning of the file, to define `@headword` as an Info formatting command that inserts nothing before and a colon after the argument to `@headword`.

'`@definfoenclose`' definitions must not be recursive, directly or indirectly.

19 Formatting and Printing Hardcopy

There are three major shell commands for making a printed manual from a Texinfo file: one for converting the Texinfo file into a file that will be printed, a second for sorting indices, and a third for printing the formatted document. When you use the shell commands, you can either work directly in the operating system shell or work within a shell inside GNU Emacs.

If you are using GNU Emacs, you can use commands provided by Texinfo mode instead of shell commands. In addition to the three commands to format a file, sort the indices, and print the result, Texinfo mode offers key bindings for commands to recenter the output buffer, show the print queue, and delete a job from the print queue.

19.1 Use TeX

The typesetting program called TeX is used for formatting a Texinfo file. TeX is a very powerful typesetting program and, if used correctly, does an exceptionally good job. (See Appendix J [How to Obtain TeX], page 228, for information on how to obtain TeX.)

The `makeinfo`, `texinfo-format-region`, and `texinfo-format-buffer` commands read the very same @-commands in the Texinfo file as does TeX, but process them differently to make an Info file (see Section 20.1 [Creating an Info File], page 165).

19.2 Format with `tex` and `texindex`

Format the Texinfo file with the shell command `tex` followed by the name of the Texinfo file. For example:

```
tex foo.texi
```

TeX will produce a *DVI file* as well as several auxiliary files containing information for indices, cross references, etc. The DVI file (for *DeVice Independent* file) can be printed on virtually any device (see the following sections).

The `tex` formatting command itself does not sort the indices; it writes an output file of unsorted index data. (The `texi2dvi` command automatically generates indices; see Section 19.3 [Format with `texi2dvi`], page 155.) To generate a printed index after running the `tex` command, you first need a sorted index to work from. The `texindex` command sorts indices. (The source file 'texindex.c' comes as part of the standard Texinfo distribution, among other places.)

The `tex` formatting command outputs unsorted index files under names that obey a standard convention: the name of your main input file with any '.tex' (or similar, see section "tex invocation" in *Web2c*) extension removed, followed by the two letter names of indices. For example, the raw index output files for the input file 'foo.texinfo' would be 'foo.cp', 'foo.vr', 'foo.fn', 'foo.tp', 'foo.pg' and 'foo.ky'. Those are exactly the arguments to give to `texindex`.

Instead of specifying all the unsorted index file names explicitly, you can use '??' as shell wildcards and give the command in this form:

```
texindex foo.??
```

This command will run `texindex` on all the unsorted index files, including any that you have defined yourself using `@defindex` or `@defcodeindex`. (You may execute 'texindex foo.??' even if there are similarly named files with two letter extensions that are not index files, such as 'foo.el'. The `texindex` command reports but otherwise ignores such files.)

For each file specified, `texindex` generates a sorted index file whose name is made by appending 's' to the input file name. The `@printindex` command looks for a file with that name (see Section 4.1 [Printing Indices & Menus], page 46). `texindex` does not alter the raw index output file.

After you have sorted the indices, you need to rerun the `tex` formatting command on the Texinfo file. This regenerates the DVI file, this time with up-to-date index entries.

Finally, you may need to run `tex` one more time, to get the page numbers in the cross-references correct.

To summarize, this is a five step process:

1. Run `tex` on your Texinfo file. This generates a DVI file (with undefined cross-references and no indices), and the raw index files (with two letter extensions).

2. Run `texindex` on the raw index files. This creates the corresponding sorted index files (with three letter extensions).

3. Run `tex` again on your Texinfo file. This regenerates the DVI file, this time with indices and defined cross-references, but with page numbers for the cross-references from last time, generally incorrect.

4. Sort the indices again, with `texindex`.

5. Run `tex` one last time. This time the correct page numbers are written for the cross-references.

Alternatively, it's a one-step process: run `texi2dvi` (see Section 19.3 [Format with texi2dvi], page 155).

You need not run `texindex` each time after you run `tex`. If you do not, on the next run, the `tex` formatting command will use whatever sorted index files happen to exist from the previous use of `texindex`. This is usually ok while you are debugging.

Sometimes you may wish to print a document while you know it is incomplete, or to print just one chapter of a document. In that case, the usual auxiliary files that TeX creates and warnings TeX gives when cross-references are not satisfied are just nuisances. You can avoid them with the `@novalidate` command, which you must give *before* the `@setfilename` command (see Section 3.2.3 [@setfilename], page 33). Thus, the beginning of your file would look approximately like this:

```
\input texinfo
@novalidate
@setfilename myfile.info
```

· · ·

`@novalidate` also turns off validation in `makeinfo`, just like its `--no-validate` option (see Section 20.1.4 [Pointer Validation], page 168).

19.3 Format with `texi2dvi`

The `texi2dvi` command automatically runs both `tex` and `texindex` as many times as necessary to produce a DVI file with sorted indices and all cross-references resolved. It simplifies the `tex`—`texindex`—`tex`—`tex` sequence described in the previous section.

To run `texi2dvi` on an input file 'foo.texi', do this (where 'prompt$ ' is your shell prompt):

```
prompt$ texi2dvi foo.texi
```

As shown in this example, the input filenames to `texi2dvi` must include any extension ('.texi', '.texinfo', etc.). Under MS-DOS and perhaps in other circumstances, you may need to run 'sh texi2dvi foo.texi' instead of relying on the operating system to invoke the shell on the 'texi2dvi' script.

Perhaps the most useful option to `texi2dvi` is '--texinfo=cmd'. This inserts cmd on a line by itself after the `@setfilename` in a temporary copy of the input file before running TeX. With this, you can specify different printing formats, such as `@smallbook` (see Section 19.11 [smallbook], page 161), `@afourpaper` (see Section 19.12 [A4 Paper], page 162), or `@pageparams` (see Section 19.13 [pagesizes], page 162), without actually changing the document source. (You can also do this on a site-wide basis with 'texinfo.cnf'; see Section 19.9 [Preparing for TeX], page 159).

For a list of other options, run 'texi2dvi --help'.

19.4 Shell Print Using `lpr -d`

The precise command to print a DVI file depends on your system installation, but 'lpr -d' is common. The command may require the DVI file name without any extension or with a '.dvi' extension. (If it is 'lpr', you must include the '.dvi'.)

For example, the following commands, will (perhaps) suffice to sort the indices, format, and print the *Bison Manual*:

```
tex bison.texinfo
texindex bison.??
tex bison.texinfo
lpr -d bison.dvi
```

(Remember that the shell commands may be different at your site; but these are commonly used versions.)

Using the `texi2dvi` shell script, you simply need type:

```
texi2dvi bison.texinfo
lpr -d bison.dvi
```

`lpr` is a standard program on Unix systems, but it is usually absent on MS-DOS/MS-Windows. Some network packages come with a program named `lpr`, but these are usually limited to sending files to a print server over the network, and generally don't support the '`-d`' option. If you are unfortunate enough to work on one of these systems, you have several alternative ways of printing DVI files:

- Find and install a Unix-like `lpr` program, or its clone. If you can do that, you will be able to print DVI files just like described above.

- Send the DVI files to a network printer queue for DVI files. Some network printers have special queues for printing DVI files. You should be able to set up your network software to send files to that queue. In some cases, the version of `lpr` which comes with your network software will have a special option to send a file to specific queues, like this:

  ```
  lpr -Qdvi -hprint.server.domain bison.dvi
  ```

- Convert the DVI file to a Postscript or PCL file and send it to your local printer. See section "dvips invocation" in *Dvips*, and the man pages for `dvilj`, for detailed description of these tools. Once the DVI file is converted to the format your local printer understands directly, just send it to the appropriate port, usually '`PRN`'.

19.5 From an Emacs Shell

You can give formatting and printing commands from a shell within GNU Emacs. To create a shell within Emacs, type `M-x shell`. In this shell, you can format and print the document. See Chapter 19 [Format and Print Hardcopy], page 153, for details.

You can switch to and from the shell buffer while `tex` is running and do other editing. If you are formatting a long document on a slow machine, this can be very convenient.

You can also use `texi2dvi` from an Emacs shell. For example, here is how to use `texi2dvi` to format and print *Using and Porting GNU CC* from a shell within Emacs:

```
texi2dvi gcc.texinfo
lpr -d gcc.dvi
```

19.6 Formatting and Printing in Texinfo Mode

Texinfo mode provides several predefined key commands for TEX formatting and printing. These include commands for sorting indices, looking at the printer queue, killing the formatting job, and recentering the display of the buffer in which the operations occur.

```
C-c C-t C-b
M-x texinfo-tex-buffer
```
> Run `texi2dvi` on the current buffer.

```
C-c C-t C-r
M-x texinfo-tex-region
```
> Run TEX on the current region.

```
C-c C-t C-i
M-x texinfo-texindex
```
> Sort the indices of a Texinfo file formatted with `texinfo-tex-region`.

```
C-c C-t C-p
M-x texinfo-tex-print
```
> Print a DVI file that was made with `texinfo-tex-region` or `texinfo-tex-buffer`.

```
C-c C-t C-q
M-x tex-show-print-queue
```
> Show the print queue.

```
C-c C-t C-d
M-x texinfo-delete-from-print-queue
```
> Delete a job from the print queue; you will be prompted for the job number shown by a preceding `C-c C-t C-q` command (`texinfo-show-tex-print-queue`).

```
C-c C-t C-k
M-x tex-kill-job
```
> Kill the currently running TEX job started by either `texinfo-tex-region` or `texinfo-tex-buffer`, or any other process running in the Texinfo shell buffer.

```
C-c C-t C-x
M-x texinfo-quit-job
```
> Quit a TEX formatting job that has stopped because of an error by sending an ⓧ to it. When you do this, TEX preserves a record of what it did in a '.log' file.

```
C-c C-t C-l
M-x tex-recenter-output-buffer
```
> Redisplay the shell buffer in which the TEX printing and formatting commands are run to show its most recent output.

Thus, the usual sequence of commands for formatting a buffer is as follows (with comments to the right):

`C-c C-t C-b`	Run `texi2dvi` on the buffer.
`C-c C-t C-p`	Print the DVI file.
`C-c C-t C-q`	Display the printer queue.

The Texinfo mode TEX formatting commands start a subshell in Emacs called the '`*tex-shell*`'. The `texinfo-tex-command`, `texinfo-texindex-command`, and `tex-dvi-print-command` commands are all run in this shell.

You can watch the commands operate in the '`*tex-shell*`' buffer, and you can switch to and from and use the '`*tex-shell*`' buffer as you would any other shell buffer.

The formatting and print commands depend on the values of several variables. The default values are:

Variable	Default value
`texinfo-texi2dvi-command`	`"texi2dvi"`
`texinfo-tex-command`	`"tex"`
`texinfo-texindex-command`	`"texindex"`
`texinfo-delete-from-print-queue-command`	`"lprm"`
`texinfo-tex-trailer`	`"@bye"`
`tex-start-of-header`	`"%**start"`
`tex-end-of-header`	`"%**end"`
`tex-dvi-print-command`	`"lpr -d"`
`tex-show-queue-command`	`"lpq"`

You can change the values of these variables with the `M-x edit-options` command (see section "Editing Variable Values" in *The GNU Emacs Manual*), with the `M-x set-variable` command (see section "Examining and Setting Variables" in *The GNU Emacs Manual*), or with your '`.emacs`' initialization file (see section "Init File" in *The GNU Emacs Manual*).

Beginning with version 20, GNU Emacs offers a user-friendly interface, called *Customize*, for changing values of user-definable variables. See section "Easy Customization Interface" in *The GNU Emacs Manual*, for more details about this. The Texinfo variables can be found in the '`Development/Docs/Texinfo`' group, once you invoke the `M-x customize` command.

19.7 Using the Local Variables List

Yet another way to apply the TeX formatting command to a Texinfo file is to put that command in a *local variables list* at the end of the Texinfo file. You can then specify the `tex` or `texi2dvi` commands as a `compile-command` and have Emacs run it by typing `M-x compile`. This creates a special shell called the '`*compilation*`' buffer in which Emacs runs the compile command. For example, at the end of the '`gdb.texinfo`' file, after the `@bye`, you could put the following:

```
Local Variables:
compile-command: "texi2dvi gdb.texinfo"
End:
```

This technique is most often used by programmers who also compile programs this way; see section "Compilation" in *The GNU Emacs Manual*.

19.8 TeX Formatting Requirements Summary

Every Texinfo file that is to be input to TeX must begin with a `\input` command and must contain an `@setfilename` command:

```
\input texinfo
```
@setfilename *arg-not-used-by-TEX*

The first command instructs TEX to load the macros it needs to process a Texinfo file and the second command opens auxiliary files.

Every Texinfo file must end with a line that terminates TEX's processing and forces out unfinished pages:

```
@bye
```

Strictly speaking, these lines are all a Texinfo file needs to be processed successfully by TEX.

Usually, however, the beginning includes an @settitle command to define the title of the printed manual, an @setchapternewpage command, a title page, a copyright page, and permissions. Besides an @bye, the end of a file usually includes indices and a table of contents. (And of course most manuals contain a body of text as well.)

For more information, see:

- Section 3.2.4 [@settitle], page 33
- Section 3.2.5 [@setchapternewpage], page 34
- Appendix F [Page Headings], page 213
- Section 3.4 [Titlepage & Copyright Page], page 37
- Section 4.1 [Printing Indices & Menus], page 46
- Section 4.2 [Contents], page 47

19.9 Preparing for TEX

TEX needs to know where to find the 'texinfo.tex' file that you have told it to input with the '\input texinfo' command at the beginning of the first line. The 'texinfo.tex' file tells TEX how to handle @-commands; it is included in all standard GNU distributions.

Usually, the 'texinfo.tex' file is put under the default directory that contains TEX macros ('/usr/local/share/texmf/tex/texinfo/' by default) when GNU Emacs or other GNU software is installed. In this case, TEX will find the file and you do not need to do anything special. Alternatively, you can put 'texinfo.tex' in the current directory when you run TEX, and TEX will find it there.

Also, you should install 'epsf.tex' in the same place as 'texinfo.tex', if it is not already installed from another distribution. This file is needed to support the @image command (see Section 13.11 [Images], page 119).

Optionally, you may create an additional 'texinfo.cnf', and install it as well. This file is read by TEX when the @setfilename command is executed (see Section 3.2.3 [@setfilename], page 33). You can put any commands you like there, according to local site-wide conventions. They will be read by TEX when processing any Texinfo document. For example, if 'texinfo.cnf' contains the line '@afourpaper' (see Section 19.12 [A4 Paper], page 162), then all Texinfo documents will be processed with that page size in effect. If you have nothing to put in 'texinfo.cnf', you do not need to create it.

If neither of the above locations for these system files suffice for you, you can specify the directories explicitly. For 'texinfo.tex', you can do this by writing the complete path for the file after the \input command. Another way, that works for both 'texinfo.tex' and 'texinfo.cnf' (and any other file TeX might read), is to set the TEXINPUTS environment variable in your '.cshrc' or '.profile' file.

Which you use of '.cshrc' or '.profile' depends on whether you use a Bourne shell-compatible (sh, bash, ksh, ...) or C shell-compatible (csh, tcsh) command interpreter. The latter read the '.cshrc' file for initialization information, and the former read '.profile'.

In a '.cshrc' file, you could use the following csh command sequence:

```
setenv TEXINPUTS .:/home/me/mylib:/usr/lib/tex/macros
```

In a '.profile' file, you could use the following sh command sequence:

```
TEXINPUTS=.:/home/me/mylib:/usr/lib/tex/macros
export TEXINPUTS
```

On MS-DOS/MS-Windows, you would say it like this[1]:

```
set TEXINPUTS=.;d:/home/me/mylib;c:/usr/lib/tex/macros
```

It is customary for DOS/Windows users to put such commands in the 'autoexec.bat' file, or in the Windows Registry.

These settings would cause TeX to look for '\input' file first in the current directory, indicated by the '.', then in a hypothetical user's 'me/mylib' directory, and finally in a system directory '/usr/lib/tex/macros'.

Finally, you may wish to dump a '.fmt' file (see section "Memory dumps" in *Web2c*) so that TeX can load Texinfo faster. (The disadvantage is that then updating 'texinfo.tex' requires redumping.) You can do this by running this command, assuming 'epsf.tex' is findable by TeX:

```
initex texinfo @dump
```

(@dump is a TeX primitive.) You'll then need to move 'texinfo.fmt' to wherever your .fmt files are found; typically this will be in the subdirectory 'web2c' of your TeX installation, for example, '/usr/local/share/tex/web2c'.

19.10 Overfull "hboxes"

TeX is sometimes unable to typeset a line without extending it into the right margin. This can occur when TeX comes upon what it interprets as a long word that it cannot hyphenate, such as an electronic mail network address or a very long title. When this happens, TeX prints an error message like this:

```
Overfull @hbox (20.76302pt too wide)
```

(In TeX, lines are in "horizontal boxes", hence the term, "hbox". '@hbox' is a TeX primitive not needed in the Texinfo language.)

---

[1] Note the use of the ';' character, instead of ':', as directory separator on these systems.

TEX also provides the line number in the Texinfo source file and the text of the offending line, which is marked at all the places that TEX considered hyphenation. See Section G.2 [Catching Errors with TEX Formatting], page 219, for more information about typesetting errors.

If the Texinfo file has an overfull hbox, you can rewrite the sentence so the overfull hbox does not occur, or you can decide to leave it. A small excursion into the right margin often does not matter and may not even be noticeable.

If you have many overfull boxes and/or an antipathy to rewriting, you can coerce TEX into greatly increasing the allowable interword spacing, thus (if you're lucky) avoiding many of the bad line breaks, like this:

```
@tex

\global\emergencystretch = .9\hsize

@end tex
```

(You can adjust the fraction as needed.) This huge value for \emergencystretch cannot be the default, since then the typeset output would generally be of noticeably lower quality. The default value is '.15\hsize'. \hsize is the TEX dimension containing the current line width.

For what overfull boxes you have, however, TEX will print a large, ugly, black rectangle beside the line that contains the overfull hbox unless told otherwise. This is so you will notice the location of the problem if you are correcting a draft.

To prevent such a monstrosity from marring your final printout, write the following in the beginning of the Texinfo file on a line of its own, before the @titlepage command:

```
@finalout
```

19.11 Printing "Small" Books

By default, TEX typesets pages for printing in an 8.5 by 11 inch format. However, you can direct TEX to typeset a document in a 7 by 9.25 inch format that is suitable for bound books by inserting the following command on a line by itself at the beginning of the Texinfo file, before the title page:

```
@smallbook
```

(Since many books are about 7 by 9.25 inches, this command might better have been called the @regularbooksize command, but it came to be called the @smallbook command by comparison to the 8.5 by 11 inch format.)

If you write the @smallbook command between the start-of-header and end-of-header lines, the Texinfo mode TEX region formatting command, texinfo-tex-region, will format the region in "small" book size (see Section 3.2.2 [Start of Header], page 32).

See Section 10.6 [small], page 92, for information about commands that make it easier to produce examples for a smaller manual.

See Section 19.3 [Format with texi2dvi], page 155, and Section 19.9 [Preparing for TEX], page 159, for other ways to format with @smallbook that do not require changing the source file.

19.12 Printing on A4 Paper

You can tell T_EX to format a document for printing on European size A4 paper with the `@afourpaper` command. Write the command on a line by itself near the beginning of the Texinfo file, before the title page. For example, this is how you would write the header for this manual:

```
\input texinfo    @c -*-texinfo-*-

@c %**start of header

@setfilename texinfo

@settitle Texinfo

@afourpaper

@c %**end of header
```

See Section 19.3 [Format with texi2dvi], page 155, and Section 19.9 [Preparing for T_EX], page 159, for other ways to format with `@afourpaper` that do not require changing the source file.

You may or may not prefer the formatting that results from the command `@afourlatex`. There's also `@afourwide` for A4 paper in wide format.

19.13 @pagesizes [*width*][, *height*]: Custom page sizes

You can explicitly specify the height and (optionally) width of the main text area on the page with the `@pagesizes` command. Write this on a line by itself near the beginning of the Texinfo file, before the title page. The height comes first, then the width if desired, separated by a comma. Examples:

```
@pagesizes 200mm,150mm
```

and

```
@pagesizes 11.5in
```

This would be reasonable for printing on B5-size paper. To emphasize, this command specifies the size of the *text area*, not the size of the paper (which is 250 mm by 177 mm for B5, 14 in by 8.5 in for legal).

To make more elaborate changes, such as changing any of the page margins, you must define a new command in 'texinfo.tex' (or 'texinfo.cnf', see Section 19.9 [Preparing for T_EX], page 159).

See Section 19.3 [Format with texi2dvi], page 155, and Section 19.9 [Preparing for T_EX], page 159, for other ways to specify `@pagesizes` that do not require changing the source file.

`@pagesizes` is ignored by `makeinfo`.

19.14 Cropmarks and Magnification

You can (attempt to) direct T_EX to print cropmarks at the corners of pages with the `@cropmarks` command. Write the `@cropmarks` command on a line by itself between `@iftex` and `@end iftex` lines near the beginning of the Texinfo file, before the title page, like this:

```
@iftex

@cropmarks

@end iftex
```

This command is mainly for printers that typeset several pages on one sheet of film; but you can attempt to use it to mark the corners of a book set to 7 by 9.25 inches with the `@smallbook` command. (Printers will not produce cropmarks for regular sized output that is printed on regular sized paper.) Since different printing machines work in different ways, you should explore the use of this command with a spirit of adventure. You may have to redefine the command in '`texinfo.tex`'.

You can attempt to direct TEX to typeset pages larger or smaller than usual with the `\mag` TEX command. Everything that is typeset is scaled proportionally larger or smaller. (`\mag` stands for "magnification".) This is *not* a Texinfo @-command, but is a plain TEX command that is prefixed with a backslash. You have to write this command between `@tex` and `@end tex` (see Section 16.3 [Raw Formatter Commands], page 140).

Follow the `\mag` command with an '`=`' and then a number that is 1000 times the magnification you desire. For example, to print pages at 1.2 normal size, write the following near the beginning of the Texinfo file, before the title page:

```
@tex

\mag=1200

@end tex
```

With some printing technologies, you can print normal-sized copies that look better than usual by giving a larger-than-normal master to your print shop. They do the reduction, thus effectively increasing the resolution.

Depending on your system, DVI files prepared with a nonstandard-`\mag` may not print or may print only with certain magnifications. Be prepared to experiment.

19.15 PDF Output

You can generate a PDF output file from Texinfo source by using the `pdftex` program to process your file instead of plain `tex`. Just run '`pdftex foo.texi`' instead of '`tex foo.texi`', or give the '`--pdf`' option to `texi2dvi`.

PDF stands for Portable Document Format, and was invented by Adobe Systems. The file format definition (`http://www.adobe.com/prodindex/acrobat/adobepdf.html`) is freely available, as is a free viewer (`http://www.foolabs.com/xpdf/`) for the X window system. Since PDF is a binary format, there is no '`@ifpdf`' or '`@pdf`' command by analogy with the other output formats.

Despite the 'portable' in the name, PDF files are nowhere near as portable in practice as the plain ASCII formats (Info, HTML) Texinfo also supports (portability relative to DVI is arguable). They also tend to be much larger and do not support the bitmap fonts used by TEX (by default) very well. Nevertheless, a PDF file does preserve an actual printed document on a screen as faithfully as possible, unlike HTML, say, so have their place.

PDF support in Texinfo is fairly rudimentary.

20 Creating and Installing Info Files

This chapter describes how to create and install info files. See Section 1.3 [Info Files], page 5, for general information about the file format itself.

20.1 Creating an Info File

`makeinfo` is a program that converts a Texinfo file into an Info file, HTML file, or plain text. `texinfo-format-region` and `texinfo-format-buffer` are GNU Emacs functions that convert Texinfo to Info.

For information on installing the Info file in the Info system, see Section 20.2 [Install an Info File], page 173.

20.1.1 `makeinfo` Preferred

The `makeinfo` utility creates an Info file from a Texinfo source file more quickly than either of the Emacs formatting commands and provides better error messages. We recommend it. `makeinfo` is a C program that is independent of Emacs. You do not need to run Emacs to use `makeinfo`, which means you can use `makeinfo` on machines that are too small to run Emacs. You can run `makeinfo` in any one of three ways: from an operating system shell, from a shell inside Emacs, or by typing the `C-c C-m C-r` or the `C-c C-m C-b` command in Texinfo mode in Emacs.

The `texinfo-format-region` and the `texinfo-format-buffer` commands are useful if you cannot run `makeinfo`. Also, in some circumstances, they format short regions or buffers more quickly than `makeinfo`.

20.1.2 Running `makeinfo` from a Shell

To create an Info file from a Texinfo file, type `makeinfo` followed by the name of the Texinfo file. Thus, to create the Info file for Bison, type the following to the shell:

```
makeinfo bison.texinfo
```

(You can run a shell inside Emacs by typing `M-x shell`.)

20.1.3 Options for `makeinfo`

The `makeinfo` command takes a number of options. Most often, options are used to set the value of the fill column and specify the footnote style. Each command line option is a word preceded by '--' or a letter preceded by '-'. You can use abbreviations for the long option names as long as they are unique.

For example, you could use the following shell command to create an Info file for 'bison.texinfo' in which each line is filled to only 68 columns:

```
makeinfo --fill-column=68 bison.texinfo
```

You can write two or more options in sequence, like this:

```
makeinfo --no-split --fill-column=70 ...
```
This would keep the Info file together as one possibly very long file and would also set the fill column to 70.

The options are:

-D *var* Cause the variable *var* to be defined. This is equivalent to @set *var* in the Texinfo file (see Section 16.4 [set clear value], page 141).

--commands-in-node-names

Allow @-commands in node names. This is not recommended, as it can probably never be implemented in TeX. It also makes makeinfo much slower. Also, this option is ignored when '--no-validate' is used. See Section 20.1.4 [Pointer Validation], page 168, for more details.

--error-limit=*limit*

-e *limit* Set the maximum number of errors that makeinfo will report before exiting (on the assumption that continuing would be useless); default 100.

--fill-column=*width*

-f *width* Specify the maximum number of columns in a line; this is the right-hand edge of a line. Paragraphs that are filled will be filled to this width. (Filling is the process of breaking up and connecting lines so that lines are the same length as or shorter than the number specified as the fill column. Lines are broken between words.) The default value is 72. Ignored with '--html'.

--footnote-style=*style*

-s *style* Set the footnote style to *style*, either 'end' for the end node style (the default) or 'separate' for the separate node style. The value set by this option overrides the value set in a Texinfo file by an @footnotestyle command (see Section 13.10 [Footnotes], page 118). When the footnote style is 'separate', makeinfo makes a new node containing the footnotes found in the current node. When the footnote style is 'end', makeinfo places the footnote references at the end of the current node. Ignored with '--html'.

--force

-F Ordinarily, if the input file has errors, the output files are not created. With this option, they are preserved.

--help

-h Print a usage message listing all available options, then exit successfully.

--html Generate HTML output rather than Info. See Section 20.1.9 [makeinfo html], page 173.

-I *dir* Append *dir* to the directory search list for finding files that are included using the @include command. By default, makeinfo searches only the current directory. If *dir* is not given, the current directory '.' is appended. Note that *dir* can actually be a list of several directories separated by the usual path separator character (':' on Unix, ';' on MS-DOS/MS-Windows).

`--macro-expand=`*file*
`-E` *file*   Output the Texinfo source with all the macros expanded to the named file. Normally, the results of macro expansion are used internally by `makeinfo` and then discarded. This option is used by `texi2dvi` if you are using an old version of 'texinfo.tex' that does not support `@macro`.

`--no-headers`
           For Info output, do not include menus or node lines in the output and write to standard output (unless '`--output`' is specified). This results in an ASCII file that you cannot read in Info since it does not contain the requisite nodes or menus. It is primarily useful to extract certain pieces of a manual into separate files to be included in a distribution, such as 'INSTALL' files.

           For HTML output, if '`--no-split`' is also specified, do not include a navigation links at the top of each node. See Section 20.1.9 [makeinfo html], page 173.

`--no-split` Suppress the splitting stage of `makeinfo`. By default, large output files (where the size is greater than 70k bytes) are split into smaller subfiles. For Info output, each one is approximately 50k bytes. For HTML output, each file contains one node (see Section 20.1.9 [makeinfo html], page 173).

`--no-pointer-validate`
`--no-validate`
           Suppress the pointer-validation phase of `makeinfo`. This can also be done with the `@novalidate` command (see Section 19.1 [Use TeX], page 153). Normally, after a Texinfo file is processed, some consistency checks are made to ensure that cross references can be resolved, etc. See Section 20.1.4 [Pointer Validation], page 168.

`--no-warn` Suppress warning messages (but *not* error messages). You might want this if the file you are creating has examples of Texinfo cross references within it, and the nodes that are referenced do not actually exist.

`--number-sections`
           Output chapter, section, and appendix numbers as in printed manuals.

`--no-number-footnotes`
           Suppress automatic footnote numbering. By default, `makeinfo` numbers each footnote sequentially in a single node, resetting the current footnote number to 1 at the start of each node.

`--output=`*file*
`-o` *file*   Specify that the output should be directed to *file* and not to the file name specified in the `@setfilename` command found in the Texinfo source (see Section 3.2.3 [setfilename], page 33). If *file* is

'-', output goes to standard output and '--no-split' is implied. For split HTML output, *file* is the name of the output file for the top node (see Section 20.1.9 [makeinfo html], page 173).

-P *dir*   Prepend *dir* to the directory search list for @include. If *dir* is not given, the current directory '.' is prepended. See '-I' for more details.

--paragraph-indent=*indent*
-p *indent*   Set the paragraph indentation style to *indent*. The value set by this option overrides the value set in a Texinfo file by an @paragraphindent command (see Section 3.2.6 [paragraphindent], page 35). The value of *indent* is interpreted as follows:

      'asis'   Preserve any existing indentation at the starts of paragraphs.

      '0' or 'none'
            Delete any existing indentation.

      num   Indent each paragraph by *num* spaces.

--reference-limit=*limit*
-r *limit*   Set the value of the number of references to a node that makeinfo will make without reporting a warning. If a node has more than this number of references in it, makeinfo will make the references but also report a warning. The default is 1000.

-U *var*   Cause *var* to be undefined. This is equivalent to @clear *var* in the Texinfo file (see Section 16.4 [set clear value], page 141).

--verbose   Cause makeinfo to display messages saying what it is doing. Normally, makeinfo only outputs messages if there are errors or warnings.

--version
-V   Print the version number, then exit successfully.

20.1.4 Pointer Validation

If you do not suppress pointer validation with the '--no-validate' option or the @novalidate command in the source file (see Section 19.1 [Use TEX], page 153), makeinfo will check the validity of the final Info file. Mostly, this means ensuring that nodes you have referenced really exist. Here is a complete list of what is checked:

1. If a 'Next', 'Previous', or 'Up' node reference is a reference to a node in the current file and is not an external reference such as to '(dir)', then the referenced node must exist.

2. In every node, if the 'Previous' node is different from the 'Up' node, then the node pointed to by the 'Previous' field must have a 'Next' field which points back to this node.

3. Every node except the 'Top' node must have an 'Up' pointer.

4. The node referenced by an 'Up' pointer must itself reference the current node through a menu item, unless the node referenced by 'Up' has the form '(*file*)'.

5. If the 'Next' reference of a node is not the same as the 'Next' reference of the 'Up' reference, then the node referenced by the 'Next' pointer must have a 'Previous' pointer that points back to the current node. This rule allows the last node in a section to point to the first node of the next chapter.

6. Every node except 'Top' should be referenced by at least one other node, either via the 'Previous' or 'Next' links, or via a menu or a cross-reference.

Some Texinfo documents might fail during the validation phase because they use commands like `@value` and `@definfoenclose` in node definitions and cross-references inconsistently. Consider the following example:

```
@set nodename Node 1

@node @value{nodename}, Node 2, Top, Top

This is node 1.

@node Node 2, , Node 1, Top

This is node 2.
```

Here, the node "Node 1" was referenced both verbatim and through `@value`.

By default, `makeinfo` fails such cases, because node names are not fully expanded until they are written to the output file. You should always try to reference nodes consistently; e.g., in the above example, the second `@node` line should have also used `@value`. However, if, for some reason, you *must* reference node names inconsistently, and `makeinfo` fails to validate the file, you can use the '`--commands-in-node-names`' option to force `makeinfo` to perform the expensive expansion of all node names it finds in the document. This might considerably slow down the program, though; twofold increase in conversion time was measured for large documents such as the Jargon file.

The support for `@`-commands in `@node` directives is not general enough to be freely used. For example, if the example above redefined `nodename` somewhere in the document, `makeinfo` will fail to convert it, even if invoked with the '`--commands-in-node-names`' option.

'`--commands-in-node-names`' has no effect if the '`--no-validate`' option is given.

20.1.5 Running `makeinfo` inside Emacs

You can run `makeinfo` in GNU Emacs Texinfo mode by using either the `makeinfo-region` or the `makeinfo-buffer` commands. In Texinfo mode, the commands are bound to `C-c C-m C-r` and `C-c C-m C-b` by default.

```
C-c C-m C-r
M-x makeinfo-region
```
> Format the current region for Info.

```
C-c C-m C-b
M-x makeinfo-buffer
```
> Format the current buffer for Info.

When you invoke either `makeinfo-region` or `makeinfo-buffer`, Emacs prompts for a file name, offering the name of the visited file as the default. You can edit the default file name in the minibuffer if you wish, before pressing (RET) to start the `makeinfo` process.

The Emacs `makeinfo-region` and `makeinfo-buffer` commands run the `makeinfo` program in a temporary shell buffer. If `makeinfo` finds any errors, Emacs displays the error messages in the temporary buffer.

You can parse the error messages by typing `C-x ‘` (`next-error`). This causes Emacs to go to and position the cursor on the line in the Texinfo source that `makeinfo` thinks caused the error. See section "Running `make` or Compilers Generally" in *The GNU Emacs Manual*, for more information about using the `next-error` command.

In addition, you can kill the shell in which the `makeinfo` command is running or make the shell buffer display its most recent output.

```
C-c C-m C-k
M-x makeinfo-kill-job
```
> Kill the current running `makeinfo` job (from `makeinfo-region` or `makeinfo-buffer`).

```
C-c C-m C-l
M-x makeinfo-recenter-output-buffer
```
> Redisplay the `makeinfo` shell buffer to display its most recent output.

(Note that the parallel commands for killing and recentering a TeX job are `C-c C-t C-k` and `C-c C-t C-l`. See Section 19.6 [Texinfo Mode Printing], page 156.)

You can specify options for `makeinfo` by setting the `makeinfo-options` variable with either the `M-x edit-options` or the `M-x set-variable` command, or by setting the variable in your '`.emacs`' initialization file.

For example, you could write the following in your '`.emacs`' file:

```
(setq makeinfo-options
      "--paragraph-indent=0 --no-split
      --fill-column=70 --verbose")
```

For more information, see Section 20.1.3 [Options for `makeinfo`], page 165, as well as "Editing Variable Values," "Examining and Setting Variables," and "Init File" in *The GNU Emacs Manual*.

20.1.6 The `texinfo-format...` Commands

In GNU Emacs in Texinfo mode, you can format part or all of a Texinfo file with the `texinfo-format-region` command. This formats the current region and displays the formatted text in a temporary buffer called '`*Info Region*`'.

Similarly, you can format a buffer with the `texinfo-format-buffer` command. This command creates a new buffer and generates the Info file in it. Typing `C-x C-s` will save the Info file under the name specified by the `@setfilename` line which must be near the beginning of the Texinfo file.

`C-c C-e C-r`
`texinfo-format-region`
>   Format the current region for Info.

`C-c C-e C-b`
`texinfo-format-buffer`
>   Format the current buffer for Info.

The `texinfo-format-region` and `texinfo-format-buffer` commands provide you with some error checking, and other functions can provide you with further help in finding formatting errors. These procedures are described in an appendix; see Appendix G [Catching Mistakes], page 218. However, the `makeinfo` program is often faster and provides better error checking (see Section 20.1.5 [makeinfo in Emacs], page 169).

20.1.7 Batch Formatting

You can format Texinfo files for Info using `batch-texinfo-format` and Emacs Batch mode. You can run Emacs in Batch mode from any shell, including a shell inside of Emacs. (See section "Command Line Switches and Arguments" in *The GNU Emacs Manual*.)

Here is a shell command to format all the files that end in '`.texinfo`' in the current directory:

```
emacs -batch -funcall batch-texinfo-format *.texinfo
```

Emacs processes all the files listed on the command line, even if an error occurs while attempting to format some of them.

Run `batch-texinfo-format` only with Emacs in Batch mode as shown; it is not interactive. It kills the Batch mode Emacs on completion.

`batch-texinfo-format` is convenient if you lack `makeinfo` and want to format several Texinfo files at once. When you use Batch mode, you create a new Emacs process. This frees your current Emacs, so you can continue working in it. (When you run `texinfo-format-region` or `texinfo-format-buffer`, you cannot use that Emacs for anything else until the command finishes.)

20.1.8 Tag Files and Split Files

If a Texinfo file has more than 30,000 bytes, `texinfo-format-buffer` automatically creates a tag table for its Info file; `makeinfo` always creates a tag table. With a *tag table*, Info can jump to new nodes more quickly than it can otherwise.

In addition, if the Texinfo file contains more than about 70,000 bytes, `texinfo-format-buffer` and `makeinfo` split the large Info file into shorter *indirect* subfiles of about 50,000 bytes each. Big files are split into smaller files so that Emacs does not need to make a large buffer to hold the whole of a large Info file; instead, Emacs allocates just enough memory for the small, split-off file that is needed at the time. This way, Emacs avoids wasting memory when you run Info. (Before splitting was implemented, Info files were always kept short and *include files* were designed as a way to create a single, large printed manual out of the smaller Info files. See Appendix E [Include Files], page 209, for more information. Include files are still used for very large documents, such as *The Emacs Lisp Reference Manual*, in which each chapter is a separate file.)

When a file is split, Info itself makes use of a shortened version of the original file that contains just the tag table and references to the files that were split off. The split-off files are called *indirect* files.

The split-off files have names that are created by appending '-1', '-2', '-3' and so on to the file name specified by the `@setfilename` command. The shortened version of the original file continues to have the name specified by `@setfilename`.

At one stage in writing this document, for example, the Info file was saved as the file '`test-texinfo`' and that file looked like this:

```
Info file: test-texinfo,    -*-Text-*-
produced by texinfo-format-buffer
from file: new-texinfo-manual.texinfo


^_
Indirect:
test-texinfo-1: 102
test-texinfo-2: 50422
test-texinfo-3: 101300
^_^L
Tag table:
(Indirect)
Node: overview^?104
Node: info file^?1271
Node: printed manual^?4853
Node: conventions^?6855

...
```

(But '`test-texinfo`' had far more nodes than are shown here.) Each of the split-off, indirect files, '`test-texinfo-1`', '`test-texinfo-2`', and '`test-texinfo-3`', is listed in this file after the line that says '`Indirect:`'. The tag table is listed after the line that says '`Tag table:`'.

In the list of indirect files, the number following the file name records the cumulative number of bytes in the preceding indirect files, not counting the file list itself, the tag table, or the permissions text in each file. In the tag table, the number following the node name records the location of the beginning of the node, in bytes from the beginning of the (unsplit) output.

If you are using `texinfo-format-buffer` to create Info files, you may want to run the `Info-validate` command. (The `makeinfo` command does such a good job on its own, you do not need `Info-validate`.) However, you cannot run the `M-x Info-validate` node-checking command on indirect files. For information on how to prevent files from being split and how to validate the structure of the nodes, see Section G.5.1 [Using Info-validate], page 223.

20.1.9 Generating HTML

As an alternative to the normal Info format output you can use the '`--html`' option to generate output in HTML format, for installation on a web site (for example). In this release, HTML output from `makeinfo` is monolithic, splitting the output by chapter or node is not supported. We hope to implement this feature soon.

The HTML output file is named according to `@setfilename`, but with any '`.info`' extension replaced with '`.html`'.

Texinfo input marked up with the `@ifhtml` command will produce output only with the '`--html`' option supplied. Input marked up with the `@html` is passed literally to the output (suppressing the normal escaping of input '`<`', '`>`' and '`&`' characters which have special significance in HTML).

The '`--footnote-style`' option is currently ignored for HTML output; footnotes are hyperlinked at the end of the output file.

The HTML generated is mostly standard (i.e., HTML 2.0, RFC1866). The exception is that HTML 3.2 tables are generated from the `@multitable` command, but tagged to degrade as well as possible in browsers without table support. Please report output from an error-free run of `makeinfo` which violates the HTML 3.2 DTD as a bug.

Navigation bars are inserted at the start of nodes, similarly to Info output. The '`--no-headers`' option will suppress this if used with '`--no-split`'. Header `<link>` elements in split output can support info-like navigation with browsers like Lynx and Emacs W3 which implement this HTML 1.0 feature. You still won't normally get the multi-file regexp and index search facilities provided by Info readers. Otherwise, hyperlinks are generated from Texinfo commands where appropriate. '`@xref`' commands to other documents are generated assuming the other document is available in HTML form too, and '`.html`' is appended to the '`@xref`' Info file name. This presumably will often not work.

20.2 Installing an Info File

Info files are usually kept in the '`info`' directory. You can read Info files using the standalone Info program or the Info reader built into Emacs. (See Info file '`info`', node '`Top`', for an introduction to Info.)

20.2.1 The Directory File 'dir'

For Info to work, the 'info' directory must contain a file that serves as a top level directory for the Info system. By convention, this file is called 'dir'. (You can find the location of this file within Emacs by typing `C-h i` to enter Info and then typing `C-x C-f` to see the pathname to the 'info' directory.)

The 'dir' file is itself an Info file. It contains the top level menu for all the Info files in the system. The menu looks like this:

```
* Menu:
* Info:    (info).     Documentation browsing system.
* Emacs:   (emacs).    The extensible, self-documenting
                       text editor.
* Texinfo: (texinfo).  With one source file, make
                       either a printed manual using
                       TeX or an Info file.
...
```

Each of these menu entries points to the 'Top' node of the Info file that is named in parentheses. (The menu entry does not need to specify the 'Top' node, since Info goes to the 'Top' node if no node name is mentioned. See Section 7.5 [Nodes in Other Info Files], page 67.)

Thus, the 'Info' entry points to the 'Top' node of the 'info' file and the 'Emacs' entry points to the 'Top' node of the 'emacs' file.

In each of the Info files, the 'Up' pointer of the 'Top' node refers back to the dir file. For example, the line for the 'Top' node of the Emacs manual looks like this in Info:

```
File: emacs  Node: Top, Up: (DIR), Next: Distrib
```

In this case, the 'dir' file name is written in upper case letters—it can be written in either upper or lower case. This is not true in general, it is a special case for 'dir'.

20.2.2 Listing a New Info File

To add a new Info file to your system, you must write a menu entry to add to the menu in the 'dir' file in the 'info' directory. For example, if you were adding documentation for GDB, you would write the following new entry:

```
* GDB: (gdb).         The source-level C debugger.
```

The first part of the menu entry is the menu entry name, followed by a colon. The second part is the name of the Info file, in parentheses, followed by a period. The third part is the description.

The name of an Info file often has a '.info' extension. Thus, the Info file for GDB might be called either 'gdb' or 'gdb.info'. The Info reader programs automatically try the file name both with and without '.info'[1]; so it is better to avoid clutter and not to write '.info' explicitly in the menu entry. For

---

[1] On MS-DOS/MS-Windows systems, Info will try the '.inf' extension as well.

example, the GDB menu entry should use just 'gdb' for the file name, not
'gdb.info'.

20.2.3 Info Files in Other Directories

If an Info file is not in the 'info' directory, there are three ways to specify
its location:

1. Write the pathname in the 'dir' file as the second part of the menu.

2. If you are using Emacs, list the name of the file in a second 'dir' file,
   in its directory; and then add the name of that directory to the Info-
   directory-list variable in your personal or site initialization file.

   This variable tells Emacs where to look for 'dir' files (the files must
   be named 'dir'). Emacs merges the files named 'dir' from each of the
   listed directories. (In Emacs version 18, you can set the Info-directory
   variable to the name of only one directory.)

3. Specify the Info directory name in the INFOPATH environment variable
   in your '.profile' or '.cshrc' initialization file. (Only you and others
   who set this environment variable will be able to find Info files whose
   location is specified this way.)

For example, to reach a test file in the '/home/bob/info' directory, you
could add an entry like this to the menu in the standard 'dir' file:

```
* Test: (/home/bob/info/info-test).   Bob's own test file.
```

In this case, the absolute file name of the 'info-test' file is written as the
second part of the menu entry.

Alternatively, you could write the following in your '.emacs' file:

```
(require 'info)
(setq Info-directory-list
      (cons (expand-file-name "/home/bob/info") Info-directory-list))
```

This tells Emacs to merge the 'dir' file from the '/home/bob/info' directory
with the system 'dir' file. Info will list the '/home/bob/info/info-test' file
as a menu entry in the '/home/bob/info/dir' file. Emacs does the merging
only when M-x info is first run, so if you want to set Info-directory-list in
an Emacs session where you've already run info, you must (setq Info-dir-
contents nil) to force Emacs to recompose the 'dir' file.

Finally, you can tell Info where to look by setting the INFOPATH environment variable in your shell startup file, such as '.cshrc', '.profile' or
'autoexec.bat'. If you use a Bourne-compatible shell such as sh or bash for
your shell command interpreter, you set the INFOPATH environment variable
in the '.profile' initialization file; but if you use csh or tcsh, you set the variable in the '.cshrc' initialization file. On MS-DOS/MS-Windows systems,
you must set INFOPATH in your 'autoexec.bat' file or in the Registry. Each type
of shell uses a different syntax.

- In a '.cshrc' file, you could set the INFOPATH variable as follows:

```
setenv INFOPATH .:~/info:/usr/local/emacs/info
```

- In a '.profile' file, you would achieve the same effect by writing:

```
INFOPATH=.:$HOME/info:/usr/local/emacs/info
export INFOPATH
```

- In a 'autoexec.bat' file, you write this command[2]:

```
set INFOPATH=.;%HOME%/info;c:/usr/local/emacs/info
```

The '.' indicates the current directory as usual. Emacs uses the INFOPATH environment variable to initialize the value of Emacs's own Info-directory-list variable. The stand-alone Info reader merges any files named 'dir' in any directory listed in the INFOPATH variable into a single menu presented to you in the node called '(dir)Top'.

However you set INFOPATH, if its last character is a colon[3], this is replaced by the default (compiled-in) path. This gives you a way to augment the default path with new directories without having to list all the standard places. For example (using sh syntax):

```
INFOPATH=/local/info:
export INFOPATH
```

will search '/local/info' first, then the standard directories. Leading or doubled colons are not treated specially.

When you create your own 'dir' file for use with Info-directory-list or INFOPATH, it's easiest to start by copying an existing 'dir' file and replace all the text after the '* Menu:' with your desired entries. That way, the punctuation and special CTRL-_ characters that Info needs will be present.

20.2.4 Installing Info Directory Files

When you install an Info file onto your system, you can use the program install-info to update the Info directory file 'dir'. Normally the makefile for the package runs install-info, just after copying the Info file into its proper installed location.

In order for the Info file to work with install-info, you should use the commands @dircategory and @direntry...@end direntry in the Texinfo source file. Use @direntry to specify the menu entries to add to the Info directory file, and use @dircategory to specify which part of the Info directory to put it in. Here is how these commands are used in this manual:

```
@dircategory Texinfo documentation system
@direntry
* Texinfo: (texinfo).            The GNU documentation format.
* install-info: (texinfo)Invoking install-info. ...

...

@end direntry
```

Here's what this produces in the Info file:

```
INFO-DIR-SECTION Texinfo documentation system
START-INFO-DIR-ENTRY
```

---

[2] Note the use of ';' as the directory separator, and a different syntax for using values of other environment variables.

[3] On MS-DOS/MS-Windows systems, use semi-colon instead.

```
* Texinfo: (texinfo).          The GNU documentation format.
* install-info: (texinfo)Invoking install-info. ...
  ...
  END-INFO-DIR-ENTRY
```

The `install-info` program sees these lines in the Info file, and that is how it knows what to do.

Always use the `@direntry` and `@dircategory` commands near the beginning of the Texinfo input, before the first `@node` command. If you use them later on in the input, `install-info` will not notice them.

If you use `@dircategory` more than once in the Texinfo source, each usage specifies the 'current' category; any subsequent `@direntry` commands will add to that category.

Here are some recommended `@dircategory` categories: 'GNU packages', 'GNU programming tools', 'GNU programming documentation', 'GNU Emacs Lisp', 'GNU libraries', 'Linux', 'TeX', 'Individual utilities'. The idea is to include the 'invoking' node for every program installed by a package under 'Individual utilities', and an entry for the manual as a whole in the appropriate other category.

20.2.5 Invoking install-info

`install-info` inserts menu entries from an Info file into the top-level 'dir' file in the Info system (see the previous sections for an explanation of how the 'dir' file works). It's most often run as part of software installation, or when constructing a 'dir' file for all manuals on a system. Synopsis:

```
install-info [option]... [info-file [dir-file]]
```

If *info-file* or *dir-file* are not specified, the options (described below) that define them must be. There are no compile-time defaults, and standard input is never used. `install-info` can read only one Info file and write only one 'dir' file per invocation.

If *dir-file* (however specified) does not exist, `install-info` creates it if possible (with no entries).

If any input file is compressed with `gzip` (see section "Invoking gzip" in *Gzip*), `install-info` automatically uncompresses it for reading. And if *dir-file* is compressed, `install-info` also automatically leaves it compressed after writing any changes. If *dir-file* itself does not exist, `install-info` tries to open '*dir-file*.gz'.

Options:

`--delete`   Delete the entries in *info-file* from *dir-file*. The file name in the entry in *dir-file* must be *info-file* (except for an optional '.info' in either one). Don't insert any new entries.

`--dir-file=`*name*
`-d` *name*   Specify file name of the Info directory file. This is equivalent to using the *dir-file* argument.

`--entry=`*text*

`-e` *text*   Insert *text* as an Info directory entry; *text* should have the form of an Info menu item line plus zero or more extra lines starting with whitespace. If you specify more than one entry, they are all added. If you don't specify any entries, they are determined from information in the Info file itself.

`--help`

`-h`   Display a usage message listing basic usage and all available options, then exit successfully.

`--info-file=`*file*

`-i` *file*   Specify Info file to install in the directory. Equivalent to using the *info-file* argument.

`--info-dir=`*dir*

`-D` *dir*   Specify the directory where 'dir' resides. Equivalent to '`--dir-file=`*dir*`/dir`'.

`--item=`*text*   Same as '`--entry=`*text*'. An Info directory entry is actually a menu item.

`--quiet`   Suppress warnings.

`--remove`

`-r`   Same as '`--delete`'.

`--section=`*sec*

`-s` *sec*   Put this file's entries in section *sec* of the directory. If you specify more than one section, all the entries are added in each of the sections. If you don't specify any sections, they are determined from information in the Info file itself.

`--version`

`-V`   Display version information and exit successfully.

Appendix A @-Command List

Here is an alphabetical list of the @-commands in Texinfo. Square brackets, [ ], indicate optional arguments; an ellipsis, '...', indicates repeated text.

@*whitespace* An @ followed by a space, tab, or newline produces a normal, stretchable, interword space. See Section 13.2.3 [Multiple Spaces], page 111.

@! Generate an exclamation point that really does end a sentence (usually after an end-of-sentence capital letter). See Section 13.2.2 [Ending a Sentence], page 110.

@"
@' Generate an umlaut or acute accent, respectively, over the next character, as in ö and ó. See Section 13.3 [Inserting Accents], page 112.

@* Force a line break. Do not end a paragraph that uses @* with an @refill command. See Section 14.1 [Line Breaks], page 121.

@,{c} Generate a cedilla accent under c, as in ç. See Section 13.3 [Inserting Accents], page 112.

@- Insert a discretionary hyphenation point. See Section 14.2 [- and hyphenation], page 122.

@. Produce a period that really does end a sentence (usually after an end-of-sentence capital letter). See Section 13.2.2 [Ending a Sentence], page 110.

@: Indicate to TeX that an immediately preceding period, question mark, exclamation mark, or colon does not end a sentence. Prevent TeX from inserting extra whitespace as it does at the end of a sentence. The command has no effect on the Info file output. See Section 13.2.1 [Not Ending a Sentence], page 110.

@= Generate a macron (bar) accent over the next character, as in ō. See Section 13.3 [Inserting Accents], page 112.

@? Generate a question mark that really does end a sentence (usually after an end-of-sentence capital letter). See Section 13.2.2 [Ending a Sentence], page 110.

@@ Stands for an at sign, '@'. See Section 13.1 [Inserting @ and braces], page 109.

@^
@` Generate a circumflex (hat) or grave accent, respectively, over the next character, as in ô. See Section 13.3 [Inserting Accents], page 112.

@{ Stands for a left brace, '{'. See Section 13.1 [Inserting @ and braces], page 109.

`@}`   Stands for a right-hand brace, '}'.
                 See Section 13.1 [Inserting @ and braces], page 109.

`@~`   Generate a tilde accent over the next character, as in Ñ. See
                 Section 13.3 [Inserting Accents], page 112.

`@AA{}`
`@aa{}`   Generate the uppercase and lowercase Scandinavian A-ring let-
                 ters, respectively: Å, å. See Section 13.3 [Inserting Accents],
                 page 112.

`@acronym{`*abbrev*`}`
                 Tag *abbrev* as an acronym, that is, an abbreviation written in
                 all capital letters, such as 'NASA'. See Section 9.1.12 [`acronym`],
                 page 86.

`@AE{}`
`@ae{}`   Generate the uppercase and lowercase AE ligatures, respec-
                 tively: Æ, æ. See Section 13.3 [Inserting Accents], page 112.

`@afourlatex`
`@afourpaper`
`@afourwide`   Change page dimensions for the A4 paper size. See Section 19.12
                 [A4 Paper], page 162.

`@alias` *new=existing*
                 Make the command '@*new*' an alias for the existing command
                 '@*existing*'. See Section 18.4 [alias], page 150.

`@anchor{`*name*`}`
                 Define *name* as the current location for use as a cross-reference
                 target. See Section 6.5 [`@anchor`], page 63.

`@appendix` *title*
                 Begin an appendix. The title appears in the table of contents
                 of a printed manual. In Info, the title is underlined with aster-
                 isks. See Section 5.5 [The `@unnumbered` and `@appendix` Commands],
                 page 51.

`@appendixsec` *title*
`@appendixsection` *title*
                 Begin an appendix section within an appendix. The section title
                 appears in the table of contents of a printed manual. In Info, the
                 title is underlined with equal signs. `@appendixsection` is a longer
                 spelling of the `@appendixsec` command. See Section 5.8 [Section
                 Commands], page 52.

`@appendixsubsec` *title*
                 Begin an appendix subsection within an appendix. The title
                 appears in the table of contents of a printed manual. In Info, the
                 title is underlined with hyphens. See Section 5.10 [Subsection
                 Commands], page 53.

`@appendixsubsubsec` *title*
                 Begin an appendix subsubsection within an appendix subsec-
                 tion. The title appears in the table of contents of a printed

manual. In Info, the title is underlined with periods. See Section 5.11 [The 'subsub' Commands], page 53.

@asis Used following @table, @ftable, and @vtable to print the table's first column without highlighting ("as is"). See Section 11.3 [Making a Two-column Table], page 99.

@author *author*
> Typeset *author* flushleft and underline it. See Section 3.4.3 [The @title and @author Commands], page 39.

@b{*text*} Print *text* in **bold** font. No effect in Info. See Section 9.2.3 [Fonts], page 88.

@bullet{} Generate a large round dot, or the closest possible thing to one. See Section 13.4.2 [@bullet], page 113.

@bye Stop formatting a file. The formatters do not see the contents of a file following an @bye command. See Chapter 4 [Ending a File], page 46.

@c *comment* Begin a comment in Texinfo. The rest of the line does not appear in either the Info file or the printed manual. A synonym for @comment. See Section 1.7 [Comments], page 10.

@cartouche Highlight an example or quotation by drawing a box with rounded corners around it. Pair with @end cartouche. No effect in Info. See Section 10.11 [Drawing Cartouches Around Examples], page 95.)

@center *line-of-text*
> Center the line of text following the command. See Section 3.4.2 [@center], page 38.

@centerchap *line-of-text*
> Like @chapter, but centers the chapter title. See Section 5.4 [@chapter], page 51.

@chapheading *title*
> Print a chapter-like heading in the text, but not in the table of contents of a printed manual. In Info, the title is underlined with asterisks. See Section 5.6 [@majorheading and @chapheading], page 51.

@chapter *title*
> Begin a chapter. The chapter title appears in the table of contents of a printed manual. In Info, the title is underlined with asterisks. See Section 5.4 [@chapter], page 51.

@cindex *entry*
> Add *entry* to the index of concepts. See Section 12.1 [Defining the Entries of an Index], page 104.

@cite{*reference*}
> Highlight the name of a book or other reference that lacks a companion Info file. See Section 9.1.11 [@cite], page 86.

@clear *flag*   Unset *flag*, preventing the Texinfo formatting commands from
formatting text between subsequent pairs of @ifset *flag* and @end
ifset commands, and preventing @value{*flag*} from expanding to
the value to which *flag* is set. See Section 16.4 [@set @clear @value],
page 141.

@code{*sample-code*}
Highlight text that is an expression, a syntactically complete
token of a program, or a program name. See Section 9.1.1 [@code],
page 80.

@command{*command-name*}
Indicate a command name, such as ls. See Section 9.1.8
[@command], page 85.

@comment *comment*
Begin a comment in Texinfo. The rest of the line does not appear
in either the Info file or the printed manual. A synonym for @c.
See Section 1.7 [Comments], page 10.

@contents   Print a complete table of contents. Has no effect in Info, which
uses menus instead. See Section 4.2 [Generating a Table of Con-
tents], page 47.

@copyright{}
Generate a copyright symbol. See Section 13.5.2 [@copyright],
page 113.

@defcodeindex *index-name*
Define a new index and its indexing command. Print entries in
an @code font. See Section 12.5 [Defining New Indices], page 107.

@defcv *category class name*
@defcvx *category class name*
Format a description for a variable associated with a class in
object-oriented programming. Takes three arguments: the category of thing being defined, the class to which it belongs, and
its name. See Chapter 15 [Definition Commands], page 125, and
Section 15.3 [Def Cmds in Detail], page 127.

@deffn *category name arguments*...
@deffnx *category name arguments*...
Format a description for a function, interactive command, or
similar entity that may take arguments. @deffn takes as arguments the category of entity being described, the name of this
particular entity, and its arguments, if any. See Chapter 15
[Definition Commands], page 125.

@defindex *index-name*
Define a new index and its indexing command. Print entries in
a roman font. See Section 12.5 [Defining New Indices], page 107.

@definfoenclose *newcmd, before, after,*
Create new @-command *newcmd* for Info that marks text by enclosing it in strings that precede and follow the text. See Section 18.5 [definfoenclose], page 151.

`@defivar` *class instance-variable-name*
`@defivarx` *class instance-variable-name*

> This command formats a description for an instance variable in object-oriented programming. The command is equivalent to '`@defcv {Instance Variable}` ...'. See Chapter 15 [Definition Commands], page 125, and Section 15.3 [Def Cmds in Detail], page 127.

`@defmac` *macroname arguments...*
`@defmacx` *macroname arguments...*

> Format a description for a macro. The command is equivalent to '`@deffn Macro` ...'. See Chapter 15 [Definition Commands], page 125, and Section 15.3 [Def Cmds in Detail], page 127.

`@defmethod` *class method-name arguments...*
`@defmethodx` *class method-name arguments...*

> Format a description for a method in object-oriented programming. The command is equivalent to '`@defop Method` ...'. Takes as arguments the name of the class of the method, the name of the method, and its arguments, if any. See Chapter 15 [Definition Commands], page 125, and Section 15.3 [Def Cmds in Detail], page 127.

`@defop` *category class name arguments...*
`@defopx` *category class name arguments...*

> Format a description for an operation in object-oriented programming. `@defop` takes as arguments the overall name of the category of operation, the name of the class of the operation, the name of the operation, and its arguments, if any. See Chapter 15 [Definition Commands], page 125, and Section 15.4.5 [Abstract Objects], page 133.

`@defopt` *option-name*
`@defoptx` *option-name*

> Format a description for a user option. The command is equivalent to '`@defvr {User Option}` ...'. See Chapter 15 [Definition Commands], page 125, and Section 15.3 [Def Cmds in Detail], page 127.

`@defspec` *special-form-name arguments...*
`@defspecx` *special-form-name arguments...*

> Format a description for a special form. The command is equivalent to '`@deffn {Special Form}` ...'. See Chapter 15 [Definition Commands], page 125, and Section 15.3 [Def Cmds in Detail], page 127.

`@deftp` *category name-of-type attributes...*
`@deftpx` *category name-of-type attributes...*

> Format a description for a data type. `@deftp` takes as arguments the category, the name of the type (which is a word like '`int`' or '`float`'), and then the names of attributes of objects of that type. See Chapter 15 [Definition Commands], page 125, and Section 15.4.6 [Data Types], page 136.

`@deftypefn` *classification data-type name arguments...*
`@deftypefnx` *classification data-type name arguments...*

> Format a description for a function or similar entity that may take arguments and that is typed. `@deftypefn` takes as arguments the classification of entity being described, the type, the name of the entity, and its arguments, if any. See Chapter 15 [Definition Commands], page 125, and Section 15.3 [Def Cmds in Detail], page 127.

`@deftypefun` *data-type function-name arguments...*
`@deftypefunx` *data-type function-name arguments...*

> Format a description for a function in a typed language. The command is equivalent to '`@deftypefn Function ...`'. See Chapter 15 [Definition Commands], page 125, and Section 15.3 [Def Cmds in Detail], page 127.

`@deftypeivar` *class data-type variable-name*
`@deftypeivarx` *class data-type variable-name*

> Format a description for a typed instance variable in object-oriented programming. See Chapter 15 [Definition Commands], page 125, and Section 15.4.5 [Abstract Objects], page 133.

`@deftypemethod` *class data-type method-name arguments...*
`@deftypemethodx` *class data-type method-name arguments...*

> Format a description for a typed method in object-oriented programming. See Chapter 15 [Definition Commands], page 125, and Section 15.3 [Def Cmds in Detail], page 127.

`@deftypeop` *category class data-type name arguments...*
`@deftypeopx` *category class data-type name arguments...*

> Format a description for a typed operation in object-oriented programming. See Chapter 15 [Definition Commands], page 125, and Section 15.4.5 [Abstract Objects], page 133.

`@deftypevar` *data-type variable-name*
`@deftypevarx` *data-type variable-name*

> Format a description for a variable in a typed language. The command is equivalent to '`@deftypevr Variable ...`'. See Chapter 15 [Definition Commands], page 125, and Section 15.3 [Def Cmds in Detail], page 127.

`@deftypevr` *classification data-type name*
`@deftypevrx` *classification data-type name*

> Format a description for something like a variable in a typed language—an entity that records a value. Takes as arguments the classification of entity being described, the type, and the name of the entity. See Chapter 15 [Definition Commands], page 125, and Section 15.3 [Def Cmds in Detail], page 127.

`@defun` *function-name arguments...*
`@defunx` *function-name arguments...*

> Format a description for functions. The command is equivalent to '`@deffn Function ...`'. See Chapter 15 [Definition Commands], page 125, and Section 15.3 [Def Cmds in Detail], page 127.

`@defvar` *variable-name*
`@defvarx` *variable-name*

> Format a description for variables. The command is equivalent to '`@defvr Variable ...`'. See Chapter 15 [Definition Commands], page 125, and Section 15.3 [Def Cmds in Detail], page 127.

`@defvr` *category name*
`@defvrx` *category name*

> Format a description for any kind of variable. `@defvr` takes as arguments the category of the entity and the name of the entity. See Chapter 15 [Definition Commands], page 125, and Section 15.3 [Def Cmds in Detail], page 127.

`@detailmenu`

> Avoid `makeinfo` confusion stemming from the detailed node listing in a master menu. See Section 3.5.2 [Master Menu Parts], page 44.

`@dfn{`*term*`}` Highlight the introductory or defining use of a term. See Section 9.1.10 [`@dfn`], page 85.

`@dircategory` *dirpart*

> Specify a part of the Info directory menu where this file's entry should go. See Section 20.2.4 [Installing Dir Entries], page 176.

`@direntry` Begin the Info directory menu entry for this file. Pair with `@end direntry`. See Section 20.2.4 [Installing Dir Entries], page 176.

`@display` Begin a kind of example. Like `@example` (indent text, do not fill), but do not select a new font. Pair with `@end display`. See Section 10.7 [`@display`], page 93.

`@dmn{`*dimension*`}`

> Format a unit of measure, as in 12 pt. Causes TeX to insert a thin space before *dimension*. No effect in Info. See Section 13.2.4 [`@dmn`], page 111.

`@documentencoding` *enc*

> Declare the input encoding as *enc*. See Section 17.2 [`@documentencoding`], page 147.

`@documentlanguage` *CC*

> Declare the document language as the two-character ISO-639 abbreviation *CC*. See Section 17.1 [`@documentlanguage`], page 145.

`@dotaccent{`*c*`}`

> Generate a dot accent over the character *c*, as in ȯ. See Section 13.3 [Inserting Accents], page 112.

`@dots{}` Insert an ellipsis: '...'. See Section 13.4.1 [`@dots`], page 113.

`@email{`*address*`[, `*displayed-text*`]}`

> Indicate an electronic mail address. See Section 9.1.14 [`@email`], page 86.

`@emph{`*text*`}` Highlight *text*; text is displayed in *italics* in printed output, and surrounded by asterisks in Info. See Section 9.2 [Emphasizing Text], page 86.

@end *environment*

> Ends *environment*, as in '@end example'.   See Section 1.5 [@-commands], page 7.

@env{*environment-variable*}

> Indicate an environment variable name, such as PATH. See Section 9.1.6 [@env], page 84.

@enddots{}   Generate an end-of-sentence of ellipsis, like this .... See Section 13.4.1 [@dots{}], page 113.

@enumerate [*number-or-letter*]

> Begin a numbered list, using @item for each entry. Optionally, start list with *number-or-letter*. Pair with @end enumerate. See Section 11.2 [@enumerate], page 98.

@equiv{}   Indicate to the reader the exact equivalence of two forms with a glyph: '≡'. See Section 13.9.5 [Equivalence], page 116.

@error{}   Indicate to the reader with a glyph that the following text is an error message: ' error '. See Section 13.9.4 [Error Glyph], page 116.

@evenfooting [*left*] @| [*center*] @| [*right*]
@evenheading [*left*] @| [*center*] @| [*right*]

> Specify page footings resp. headings for even-numbered (left-hand) pages. Only allowed inside @iftex. See Section F.3 [How to Make Your Own Headings], page 215.

@everyfooting [*left*] @| [*center*] @| [*right*]
@everyheading [*left*] @| [*center*] @| [*right*]

> Specify page footings resp. headings for every page. Not relevant to Info. See Section F.3 [How to Make Your Own Headings], page 215.

@example   Begin an example. Indent text, do not fill, and select fixed-width font. Pair with @end example. See Section 10.3 [@example], page 90.

@exampleindent *indent*

> Indent example-like environments by *indent* number of spaces (perhaps 0). See Section 3.2.7 [Paragraph Indenting], page 36.

@exclamdown{}

> Produce an upside-down exclamation point. See Section 13.3 [Inserting Accents], page 112.

@exdent *line-of-text*

> Remove any indentation a line might have. See Section 10.9 [Undoing the Indentation of a Line], page 93.

@expansion{}

> Indicate the result of a macro expansion to the reader with a special glyph: '↦'. See Section 13.9.2 [↦ Indicating an Expansion], page 115.

@file{filename**}**

> Highlight the name of a file, buffer, node, or directory. See Section 9.1.7 [@file], page 84.

@finalout   Prevent TEX from printing large black warning rectangles beside
                over-wide lines. See Section 19.10 [Overfull hboxes], page 160.

@findex *entry*

                Add *entry* to the index of functions. See Section 12.1 [Defining
                the Entries of an Index], page 104.

@flushleft
@flushright

                Left justify every line but leave the right end ragged. Leave
                font as is. Pair with @end flushleft. @flushright analogous. See
                Section 10.10 [@flushleft and @flushright], page 94.

@footnote{*text-of-footnote*}

                Enter a footnote. Footnote text is printed at the bottom of the
                page by TEX; Info may format in either 'End' node or 'Separate'
                node style. See Section 13.10 [Footnotes], page 118.

@footnotestyle *style*

                Specify an Info file's footnote style, either 'end' for the end node
                style or 'separate' for the separate node style. See Section 13.10
                [Footnotes], page 118.

@format   Begin a kind of example. Like @display, but do not narrow
                the margins. Pair with @end format. See Section 10.3 [@example],
                page 90.

@ftable *formatting-command*

                Begin a two-column table, using @item for each entry. Automat-
                ically enter each of the items in the first column into the index
                of functions. Pair with @end ftable. The same as @table, except
                for indexing. See Section 11.3.1 [@ftable and @vtable], page 100.

@group   Hold text together that must appear on one printed page. Pair
                with @end group. Not relevant to Info. See Section 14.6 [@group],
                page 123.

@H{*c*}   Generate the long Hungarian umlaut accent over *c*, as in ő.

@heading *title*

                Print an unnumbered section-like heading in the text, but not in
                the table of contents of a printed manual. In Info, the title is un-
                derlined with equal signs. See Section 5.8 [Section Commands],
                page 52.

@headings *on-off-single-double*

                Turn page headings on or off, and/or specify single-sided or
                double-sided page headings for printing. See Section 3.4.6 [The
                @headings Command], page 42.

@html   Enter HTML completely. Pair with @end html. See Section 16.3
                [Raw Formatter Commands], page 140.

@hyphenation{*hy-phen-a-ted words*}

                Explicitly define hyphenation points. See Section 14.2 [@- and
                @hyphenation], page 122.

`@i{`*text*`}`   Print *text* in *italic* font. No effect in Info. See Section 9.2.3 [Fonts], page 88.

`@ifclear` *flag*

If *flag* is cleared, the Texinfo formatting commands format text between `@ifclear` *flag* and the following `@end ifclear` command. See Section 16.4 [`@set @clear @value`], page 141.

`@ifhtml`
`@ifinfo`   Begin a stretch of text that will be ignored by TEX when it typesets the printed manual. The text appears only in the HTML resp. Info file. Pair with `@end ifhtml` resp. `@end ifinfo`. See Chapter 16 [Conditionals], page 139.

`@ifnothtml`
`@ifnotinfo`
`@ifnottex`   Begin a stretch of text that will be ignored in one output format but not the others. The text appears only in the format not specified. Pair with `@end ifnothtml` resp. `@end ifnotinfo` resp. `@end ifnotinfo`. See Chapter 16 [Conditionals], page 139.

`@ifset` *flag*   If *flag* is set, the Texinfo formatting commands format text between `@ifset` *flag* and the following `@end ifset` command. See Section 16.4 [`@set @clear @value`], page 141.

`@iftex`   Begin a stretch of text that will not appear in the Info file, but will be processed only by TEX. Pair with `@end iftex`. See Chapter 16 [Conditionally Visible Text], page 139.

`@ignore`   Begin a stretch of text that will not appear in either the Info file or the printed output. Pair with `@end ignore`. See Section 1.7 [Comments and Ignored Text], page 10.

`@image{`*filename*`, [`*width*`], [`*height*`]}`

Include graphics image in external *filename* scaled to the given *width* and/or *height*. See Section 13.11 [Images], page 119.

`@include` *filename*

Incorporate the contents of the file *filename* into the Info file or printed document. See Appendix E [Include Files], page 209.

`@inforef{`*node-name*`, [`*entry-name*`]`, *info-file-name*`}`

Make a cross reference to an Info file for which there is no printed manual. See Section 8.7 [Cross references using `@inforef`], page 76.

`\input` *macro-definitions-file*

Use the specified macro definitions file. This command is used only in the first line of a Texinfo file to cause TEX to make use of the 'texinfo' macro definitions file. The backslash in `\input` is used instead of an `@` because TEX does not recognize `@` until after it has read the definitions file. See Section 3.2 [The Texinfo File Header], page 31.

`@item`   Indicate the beginning of a marked paragraph for `@itemize` and `@enumerate`; indicate the beginning of the text of a first column entry for `@table`, `@ftable`, and `@vtable`. See Chapter 11 [Lists and Tables], page 96.

`@itemize` *mark-generating-character-or-command*

Produce a sequence of indented paragraphs, with a mark inside the left margin at the beginning of each paragraph. Pair with `@end itemize`. See Section 11.1 [`@itemize`], page 96.

`@itemx`   Like `@item` but do not generate extra vertical space above the item text. See Section 11.3.2 [`@itemx`], page 101.

`@kbd{`*keyboard-characters*`}`

Indicate text that is characters of input to be typed by users. See Section 9.1.2 [`@kbd`], page 81.

`@kbdinputstyle` *style*

Specify when `@kbd` should use a font distinct from `@code`. See Section 9.1.2 [`@kbd`], page 81.

`@key{`*key-name*`}`

Indicate a name for a key on a keyboard. See Section 9.1.3 [`@key`], page 82.

`@kindex` *entry*

Add *entry* to the index of keys. See Section 12.1 [Defining the Entries of an Index], page 104.

`@L{}`

`@l{}`   Generate the uppercase and lowercase Polish suppressed-L letters, respectively: L, ł.

`@lisp`   Begin an example of Lisp code. Indent text, do not fill, and select fixed-width font. Pair with `@end lisp`. See Section 10.5 [`@lisp`], page 92.

`@lowersections`

Change subsequent chapters to sections, sections to subsections, and so on. See Section 5.12 [`@raisesections` and `@lowersections`], page 54.

`@macro` *macroname* `{`*params*`}`

Define a new Texinfo command `@`*macroname*`{`*params*`}`. Only supported by `makeinfo` and `texi2dvi`. See Section 18.1 [Defining Macros], page 148.

`@majorheading` *title*

Print a chapter-like heading in the text, but not in the table of contents of a printed manual. Generate more vertical whitespace before the heading than the `@chapheading` command. In Info, the chapter heading line is underlined with asterisks. See Section 5.6 [`@majorheading` and `@chapheading`], page 51.

`@math{`*mathematical-expression*`}`

Format a mathematical expression. See Section 13.8 [`@math`: Inserting Mathematical Expressions], page 114.

@menu   Mark the beginning of a menu of nodes in Info. No effect in a
                   printed manual. Pair with **@end menu**. See Chapter 7 [Menus],
                   page 64.

@minus{}   Generate a minus sign, '−'. See Section 13.7 [@minus], page 114.

@multitable *column-width-spec*
                   Begin a multi-column table. Pair with **@end multitable**. See Sec-
                   tion 11.4.1 [Multitable Column Widths], page 101.

@need *n*   Start a new page in a printed manual if fewer than *n* mils (thou-
                   sandths of an inch) remain on the current page. See Section 14.7
                   [@need], page 124.

@node *name*, *next*, *previous*, *up*
                   Define the beginning of a new node in Info, and serve as a locator
                   for references for TEX. See Section 6.3 [@node], page 58.

@noindent   Prevent text from being indented as if it were a new paragraph.
                   See Section 10.4 [@noindent], page 91.

@novalidate
                   Suppress validation of node references, omit creation of auxil-
                   iary files with TEX. Use before **@setfilename**. See Section 20.1.4
                   [Pointer Validation], page 168.

@O{}
@o{}   Generate the uppercase and lowercase O-with-slash letters, re-
                   spectively: Ø, ø.

@oddfooting [*left*] @| [*center*] @| [*right*]
@oddheading [*left*] @| [*center*] @| [*right*]
                   Specify page footings resp. headings for odd-numbered (right-
                   hand) pages. Only allowed inside **@iftex**. See Section F.3 [How
                   to Make Your Own Headings], page 215.

@OE{}
@oe{}   Generate the uppercase and lowercase OE ligatures, respec-
                   tively: Œ, œ. See Section 13.3 [Inserting Accents], page 112.

@option{option-name**}**
                   Indicate a command-line option, such as '-l' or '--help'. See
                   Section 9.1.9 [@option], page 85.

@page   Start a new page in a printed manual. No effect in Info. See
                   Section 14.5 [@page], page 123.

@pagesizes [*width*][, *height*]
                   Change page dimensions. See Section 19.13 [pagesizes],
                   page 162.

@paragraphindent *indent*
                   Indent paragraphs by *indent* number of spaces (perhaps 0); pre-
                   serve source file indentation if *indent* is **asis**. See Section 3.2.6
                   [Paragraph Indenting], page 35.

`@pindex` *entry*

Add *entry* to the index of programs. See Section 12.1 [Defining the Entries of an Index], page 104.

`@point{}`   Indicate the position of point in a buffer to the reader with a glyph: '⋆'. See Section 13.9.6 [Indicating Point in a Buffer], page 117.

`@pounds{}`   Generate the pounds sterling currency sign. See Section 13.6 [`@pounds{}`], page 113.

`@print{}`   Indicate printed output to the reader with a glyph: ' ⊣ '. See Section 13.9.3 [Print Glyph], page 115.

`@printindex` *index-name*

Print an alphabetized two-column index in a printed manual or generate an alphabetized menu of index entries for Info. See Section 4.1 [Printing Indices & Menus], page 46.

`@pxref{`*node-name*, [*entry*], [*topic-or-title*], [*info-file*], [*manual*]`}`

Make a reference that starts with a lower case 'see' in a printed manual. Use within parentheses only. Do not follow command with a punctuation mark—the Info formatting commands automatically insert terminating punctuation as needed. Only the first argument is mandatory. See Section 8.6 [`@pxref`], page 75.

`@questiondown{}`

Generate an upside-down question mark. See Section 13.3 [Inserting Accents], page 112.

`@quotation`   Narrow the margins to indicate text that is quoted from another real or imaginary work. Write command on a line of its own. Pair with `@end quotation`. See Section 10.2 [`@quotation`], page 90.

`@r{`*text*`}`   Print *text* in roman font. No effect in Info. See Section 9.2.3 [Fonts], page 88.

`@raisesections`

Change subsequent sections to chapters, subsections to sections, and so on. See Section 5.12 [`@raisesections` and `@lowersections`], page 54.

`@ref{`*node-name*, [*entry*], [*topic-or-title*], [*info-file*], [*manual*]`}`

Make a reference. In a printed manual, the reference does not start with a 'See'. Follow command with a punctuation mark. Only the first argument is mandatory. See Section 8.5 [`@ref`], page 74.

`@refill`   In Info, refill and indent the paragraph after all the other processing has been done. No effect on TeX, which always refills. This command is no longer needed, since all formatters now automatically refill. See Appendix H [Refilling Paragraphs], page 226.

`@result{}`   Indicate the result of an expression to the reader with a special glyph: '⇒'. See Section 13.9.1 [`@result`], page 115.

@ringaccent{*c***}**

Generate a ring accent over the next character, as in o̊. See Section 13.3 [Inserting Accents], page 112.

@samp{*text***}** Highlight *text* that is a literal example of a sequence of characters. Used for single characters, for statements, and often for entire shell commands. See Section 9.1.4 [@samp], page 83.

@sc{*text***}** Set *text* in a printed output in THE SMALL CAPS FONT and set text in the Info file in uppercase letters. See Section 9.2.2 [Smallcaps], page 87.

@section *title*

Begin a section within a chapter. In a printed manual, the section title is numbered and appears in the table of contents. In Info, the title is underlined with equal signs. See Section 5.7 [@section], page 52.

@set *flag* [*string*]

Make *flag* active, causing the Texinfo formatting commands to format text between subsequent pairs of @ifset *flag* and @end ifset commands. Optionally, set value of *flag* to *string*. See Section 16.4 [@set @clear @value], page 141.

@setchapternewpage *on-off-odd*

Specify whether chapters start on new pages, and if so, whether on odd-numbered (right-hand) new pages. See Section 3.2.5 [@setchapternewpage], page 34.

@setcontentsaftertitlepage

Put the table of contents after the '@end titlepage' even if the @contents command is not there. See Section 4.2 [Contents], page 47.

@setfilename *info-file-name*

Provide a name to be used by the Info file. This command is essential for TeX formatting as well, even though it produces no output. See Section 3.2.3 [@setfilename], page 33.

@setshortcontentsaftertitlepage

Place the short table of contents after the '@end titlepage' command even if the @shortcontents command is not there. See Section 4.2 [Contents], page 47.

@settitle *title*

Provide a title for page headers in a printed manual. See Section 3.2.4 [@settitle], page 33.

@shortcontents

Print a short table of contents. Not relevant to Info, which uses menus rather than tables of contents. A synonym for @summarycontents. See Section 4.2 [Generating a Table of Contents], page 47.

@shorttitlepage *title*

Generate a minimal title page. See Section 3.4.1 [@titlepage], page 37.

@smallbook   Cause TeX to produce a printed manual in a 7 by 9.25 inch
format rather than the regular 8.5 by 11 inch format. See
Section 19.11 [Printing Small Books], page 161. Also, see Section 10.6 [small], page 92.

@smalldisplay

Begin a kind of example. Like @smallexample (indent text, no
filling), but do not select the fixed-width font. In @smallbook
format, print text in a smaller font than with @display. Pair
with @end smalldisplay. See Section 10.6 [small], page 92.

@smallexample

Indent text to indicate an example. Do not fill, select fixed-width
font. In @smallbook format, print text in a smaller font than with
@example. Pair with @end smallexample. See Section 10.6 [small],
page 92.

@smallformat

Begin a kind of example. Like @smalldisplay, but do not narrow
the margins and do not select the fixed-width font. In @smallbook
format, print text in a smaller font than with @format. Pair with
@end smallformat. See Section 10.6 [small], page 92.

@smalllisp   Begin an example of Lisp code. Indent text, do not fill, select
fixed-width font. In @smallbook format, print text in a smaller
font. Pair with @end smalllisp. See Section 10.6 [small], page 92.

@sp n   Skip n blank lines. See Section 14.4 [@sp], page 123.

@ss{}   Generate the German sharp-S es-zet letter, ß. See Section 13.3
[Inserting Accents], page 112.

@strong {text}

Emphasize text by typesetting it in a **bold** font for the printed
manual and by surrounding it with asterisks for Info. See Section 9.2.1 [Emphasizing Text], page 87.

@subheading title

Print an unnumbered subsection-like heading in the text, but not
in the table of contents of a printed manual. In Info, the title
is underlined with hyphens. See Section 5.10 [@unnumberedsubsec
@appendixsubsec @subheading], page 53.

@subsection title

Begin a subsection within a section. In a printed manual, the
subsection title is numbered and appears in the table of contents.
In Info, the title is underlined with hyphens. See Section 5.9
[@subsection], page 53.

@subsubheading title

Print an unnumbered subsubsection-like heading in the text, but
not in the table of contents of a printed manual. In Info, the
title is underlined with periods. See Section 5.11 [The 'subsub'
Commands], page 53.

@subsubsection *title*

Begin a subsubsection within a subsection. In a printed manual, the subsubsection title is numbered and appears in the table of contents. In Info, the title is underlined with periods. See Section 5.11 [The 'subsub' Commands], page 53.

@subtitle *title*

In a printed manual, set a subtitle in a normal sized font flush to the right-hand side of the page. Not relevant to Info, which does not have title pages. See Section 3.4.3 [@title @subtitle and @author Commands], page 39.

@summarycontents

Print a short table of contents. Not relevant to Info, which uses menus rather than tables of contents. A synonym for @shortcontents. See Section 4.2 [Generating a Table of Contents], page 47.

@syncodeindex *from-index into-index*

Merge the index named in the first argument into the index named in the second argument, printing the entries from the first index in @code font. See Section 12.4 [Combining Indices], page 106.

@synindex *from-index into-index*

Merge the index named in the first argument into the index named in the second argument. Do not change the font of *from-index* entries. See Section 12.4 [Combining Indices], page 106.

@t{_text_**}**   Print *text* in a fixed-width, typewriter-like font. No effect in Info. See Section 9.2.3 [Fonts], page 88.

@tab   Separate columns in a multitable. See Section 11.4.2 [Multitable Rows], page 102.

@table *formatting-command*

Begin a two-column table, using @item for each entry. Write each first column entry on the same line as @item. First column entries are printed in the font resulting from *formatting-command*. Pair with @end table. See Section 11.3 [Making a Two-column Table], page 99. Also see Section 11.3.1 [@ftable and @vtable], page 100, and Section 11.3.2 [@itemx], page 101.

@TeX{}   Insert the logo TEX. See Section 13.5 [Inserting TEX and ©], page 113.

@tex   Enter TEX completely. Pair with @end tex. See Section 16.3 [Raw Formatter Commands], page 140.

@thischapter
@thischaptername
@thisfile
@thispage
@thistitle   Only allowed in a heading or footing. Stands for the number and name of the current chapter (in the format 'Chapter 1: Title'),

the chapter name only, the filename, the current page number, and the title of the document, respectively. See Section F.3 [How to Make Your Own Headings], page 215.

`@tieaccent{cc}`

Generate a tie-after accent over the next two characters cc, as in 'o͡o'. See Section 13.3 [Inserting Accents], page 112.

`@tindex` *entry*

Add *entry* to the index of data types. See Section 12.1 [Defining the Entries of an Index], page 104.

`@title` *title*   In a printed manual, set a title flush to the left-hand side of the page in a larger than normal font and underline it with a black rule. Not relevant to Info, which does not have title pages. See Section 3.4.3 [The `@title` `@subtitle` and `@author` Commands], page 39.

`@titlefont{text}`

In a printed manual, print *text* in a larger than normal font. Not relevant to Info, which does not have title pages. See Section 3.4.2 [The `@titlefont` `@center` and `@sp` Commands], page 38.

`@titlepage`   Indicate to Texinfo the beginning of the title page. Write command on a line of its own. Pair with `@end titlepage`. Nothing between `@titlepage` and `@end titlepage` appears in Info. See Section 3.4.1 [`@titlepage`], page 37.

`@today{}`   Insert the current date, in '1 Jan 1900' style. See Section F.3 [How to Make Your Own Headings], page 215.

`@top` *title*   In a Texinfo file to be formatted with `makeinfo`, identify the topmost `@node` line in the file, which must be written on the line immediately preceding the `@top` command. Used for `makeinfo`'s node pointer insertion feature. The title is underlined with asterisks. Both the `@node` line and the `@top` line normally should be enclosed by `@ifinfo` and `@end ifinfo`. In TEX and `texinfo-format-buffer`, the `@top` command is merely a synonym for `@unnumbered`. See Section 6.4 [Creating Pointers with `makeinfo`], page 62.

`@u{c}`
`@ubaraccent{c}`
`@udotaccent{c}`

Generate a breve, underbar, or underdot accent, respectively, over or under the character c, as in ŏ, o̱, ọ. See Section 13.3 [Inserting Accents], page 112.

`@unnumbered` *title*

In a printed manual, begin a chapter that appears without chapter numbers of any kind. The title appears in the table of contents of a printed manual. In Info, the title is underlined with asterisks. See Section 5.5 [`@unnumbered` and `@appendix`], page 51.

`@unnumberedsec` *title*

In a printed manual, begin a section that appears without section numbers of any kind. The title appears in the table of contents of a printed manual. In Info, the title is underlined with equal signs. See Section 5.8 [Section Commands], page 52.

@unnumberedsubsec *title*

In a printed manual, begin an unnumbered subsection within a chapter. The title appears in the table of contents of a printed manual. In Info, the title is underlined with hyphens. See Section 5.10 [**@unnumberedsubsec @appendixsubsec @subheading**], page 53.

@unnumberedsubsubsec *title*

In a printed manual, begin an unnumbered subsubsection within a chapter. The title appears in the table of contents of a printed manual. In Info, the title is underlined with periods. See Section 5.11 [The 'subsub' Commands], page 53.

@uref{*url***[, ***displayed-text***][, ***replacement***}**

Define a cross reference to an external uniform resource locator for the World Wide Web. See Section 8.8 [**@uref**], page 77.

@url{*url***}**

Indicate text that is a uniform resource locator for the World Wide Web. See Section 9.1.13 [**@url**], page 86.

@v{*c***}**

Generate check accent over the character *c*, as in ŏ. See Section 13.3 [Inserting Accents], page 112.

@value{*flag***}**

Replace *flag* with the value to which it is set by **@set** *flag*. See Section 16.4 [**@set @clear @value**], page 141.

@var{*metasyntactic-variable***}**

Highlight a metasyntactic variable, which is something that stands for another piece of text. See Section 9.1.5 [Indicating Metasyntactic Variables], page 83.

@vindex *entry*

Add *entry* to the index of variables. See Section 12.1 [Defining the Entries of an Index], page 104.

@vskip *amount*

In a printed manual, insert whitespace so as to push text on the remainder of the page towards the bottom of the page. Used in formatting the copyright page with the argument '**0pt plus 1filll**'. (Note spelling of '**filll**'.) **@vskip** may be used only in contexts ignored for Info. See Section 3.4.4 [The Copyright Page and Printed Permissions], page 40.

@vtable *formatting-command*

Begin a two-column table, using **@item** for each entry. Automatically enter each of the items in the first column into the index of variables. Pair with **@end vtable**. The same as **@table**, except for indexing. See Section 11.3.1 [**@ftable** and **@vtable**], page 100.

@w{*text***}**

Prevent *text* from being split across two lines. Do not end a paragraph that uses **@w** with an **@refill** command. See Section 14.3 [**@w**], page 122.

`@xref{`*node-name*`, [`*entry*`], [`*topic-or-title*`], [`*info-file*`], [`*manual*`]}`

Make a reference that starts with 'See' in a printed manual. Follow command with a punctuation mark. Only the first argument is mandatory. See Section 8.3 [`@xref`], page 70.

Appendix B Tips and Hints

Here are some tips for writing Texinfo documentation:

- Write in the present tense, not in the past or the future.
- Write actively! For example, write "We recommend that ..." rather than "It is recommended that ...".
- Use 70 or 72 as your fill column. Longer lines are hard to read.
- Include a copyright notice and copying permissions.

Index, Index, Index!

Write many index entries, in different ways. Readers like indices; they are helpful and convenient.

Although it is easiest to write index entries as you write the body of the text, some people prefer to write entries afterwards. In either case, write an entry before the paragraph to which it applies. This way, an index entry points to the first page of a paragraph that is split across pages.

Here are more hints we have found valuable:

- Write each index entry differently, so each entry refers to a different place in the document.
- Write index entries only where a topic is discussed significantly. For example, it is not useful to index "debugging information" in a chapter on reporting bugs. Someone who wants to know about debugging information will certainly not find it in that chapter.
- Consistently capitalize the first word of every concept index entry, or else consistently use lower case. Terse entries often call for lower case; longer entries for capitalization. Whichever case convention you use, please use one or the other consistently! Mixing the two styles looks bad.
- Always capitalize or use upper case for those words in an index for which this is proper, such as names of countries or acronyms. Always use the appropriate case for case-sensitive names, such as those in C or Lisp.
- Write the indexing commands that refer to a whole section immediately after the section command, and write the indexing commands that refer to a paragraph before that paragraph.

In the example that follows, a blank line comes after the index entry for "Leaping":

```
@section The Dog and the Fox
@cindex Jumping, in general
@cindex Leaping

@cindex Dog, lazy, jumped over
@cindex Lazy dog jumped over
@cindex Fox, jumps over dog
@cindex Quick fox jumps over dog
The quick brown fox jumps over the lazy dog.
```

(Note that the example shows entries for the same concept that are
written in different ways—'Lazy dog', and 'Dog, lazy'—so readers can look
up the concept in different ways.)

Blank Lines

- Insert a blank line between a sectioning command and the first following
  sentence or paragraph, or between the indexing commands associated
  with the sectioning command and the first following sentence or paragraph, as shown in the tip on indexing. Otherwise, a formatter may
  fold title and paragraph together.

- Always insert a blank line before an @table command and after an @end
  table command; but never insert a blank line after an @table command
  or before an @end table command.

  For example,

  ```
  Types of fox:

  @table @samp
  @item Quick
  Jump over lazy dogs.

  @item Brown
  Also jump over lazy dogs.
  @end table


  @noindent
  On the other hand, ...
  ```

  Insert blank lines before and after @itemize ... @end itemize and
  @enumerate ... @end enumerate in the same way.

Complete Phrases

  Complete phrases are easier to read than ...

- Write entries in an itemized list as complete sentences; or at least, as
  complete phrases. Incomplete expressions ... awkward ... like this.

- Write the prefatory sentence or phrase for a multi-item list or table as a
  complete expression. Do not write "You can set:"; instead, write "You
  can set these variables:". The former expression sounds cut off.

Editions, Dates and Versions

  Write the edition and version numbers and date in three places in every
manual:

1. In the first @ifinfo section, for people reading the Texinfo file.
2. In the @titlepage section, for people reading the printed manual.
3. In the 'Top' node, for people reading the Info file.

Also, it helps to write a note before the first @ifinfo section to explain what you are doing.

For example:

```
@c ===> NOTE! <==
@c Specify the edition and version numbers and date
@c in *three* places:
@c    1. First ifinfo section  2. title page  3. top node
@c To find the locations, search for !!set

@ifinfo
@c !!set edition, date, version
This is Edition 4.03, January 1992,
of the @cite{GDB Manual} for GDB Version 4.3.
...
```

—or use @set and @value (see Section 16.4.3 [@value Example], page 143).

Definition Commands

Definition commands are @deffn, @defun, @defmac, and the like, and enable you to write descriptions in a uniform format.

- Write just one definition command for each entity you define with a definition command. The automatic indexing feature creates an index entry that leads the reader to the definition.

- Use @table ... @end table in an appendix that contains a summary of functions, not @deffn or other definition commands.

Capitalization

- Capitalize "Texinfo"; it is a name. Do not write the 'x' or 'i' in upper case.

- Capitalize "Info"; it is a name.

- Write TEX using the @TeX{} command. Note the uppercase 'T' and 'X'. This command causes the formatters to typeset the name according to the wishes of Donald Knuth, who wrote TEX.

Spaces

Do not use spaces to format a Texinfo file, except inside of @example ... @end example and similar commands.

For example, TEX fills the following:

```
@kbd{C-x v}
@kbd{M-x vc-next-action}
    Perform the next logical operation
    on the version-controlled file
    corresponding to the current buffer.
```

so it looks like this:

> `C-x v M-x vc-next-action` Perform the next logical operation on the version-controlled file corresponding to the current buffer.

In this case, the text should be formatted with `@table`, `@item`, and `@itemx`, to create a table.

@code, @samp, @var, and '---'

- Use `@code` around Lisp symbols, including command names. For example,

  ```
  The main function is @code{vc-next-action}, ...
  ```

- Avoid putting letters such as 's' immediately after an '`@code`'. Such letters look bad.

- Use `@var` around meta-variables. Do not write angle brackets around them.

- Use three hyphens in a row, '`---`', to indicate a long dash. TeX typesets these as a long dash and the Info formatters reduce three hyphens to two.

Periods Outside of Quotes

Place periods and other punctuation marks *outside* of quotations, unless the punctuation is part of the quotation. This practice goes against publishing conventions in the United States, but enables the reader to distinguish between the contents of the quotation and the whole passage.

For example, you should write the following sentence with the period outside the end quotation marks:

```
Evidently, 'au' is an abbreviation for ''author''.
```

since 'au' does *not* serve as an abbreviation for '`author.`' (with a period following the word).

Introducing New Terms

- Introduce new terms so that a reader who does not know them can understand them from context; or write a definition for the term.

  For example, in the following, the terms "check in", "register" and "delta" are all appearing for the first time; the example sentence should be rewritten so they are understandable.

  > The major function assists you in checking in a file to your version control system and registering successive sets of changes to it as deltas.

- Use the `@dfn` command around a word being introduced, to indicate that the reader should not expect to know the meaning already, and should expect to learn the meaning from this passage.

@pxref

Absolutely never use `@pxref` except in the special context for which it is designed: inside parentheses, with the closing parenthesis following immediately after the closing brace. One formatter automatically inserts closing punctuation and the other does not. This means that the output looks right both in printed output and in an Info file, but only when the command is used inside parentheses.

Invoking from a Shell

You can invoke programs such as Emacs, GCC, and `gawk` from a shell. The documentation for each program should contain a section that describes this. Unfortunately, if the node names and titles for these sections are all different, readers find it hard to search for the section.

Name such sections with a phrase beginning with the word 'Invoking . . .', as in 'Invoking Emacs'; this way users can find the section easily.

ANSI C Syntax

When you use `@example` to describe a C function's calling conventions, use the ANSI C syntax, like this:

```
void dld_init (char *@var{path});
```

And in the subsequent discussion, refer to the argument values by writing the same argument names, again highlighted with `@var`.

Avoid the obsolete style that looks like this:

```
#include <dld.h>
```

```
dld_init (path)
char *path;
```

Also, it is best to avoid writing `#include` above the declaration just to indicate that the function is declared in a header file. The practice may give the misimpression that the `#include` belongs near the declaration of the function. Either state explicitly which header file holds the declaration or, better yet, name the header file used for a group of functions at the beginning of the section that describes the functions.

Bad Examples

Here are several examples of bad writing to avoid:

In this example, say, " . . . you must `@dfn{check in}` the new version." That flows better.

When you are done editing the file, you must perform a `@dfn{check in}`.

In the following example, say, ". . . makes a unified interface such as VC mode possible."

SCCS, RCS and other version-control systems all perform similar functions in broadly similar ways (it is this resemblance which makes a unified control mode like this possible).

And in this example, you should specify what 'it' refers to:

If you are working with other people, it assists in coordinating everyone's changes so they do not step on each other.

And Finally . . .

- Pronounce TEX as if the 'x' were a Greek 'chi', as the last sound in the name 'Bach'. But pronounce Texinfo as in 'speck': "teckinfo".
- Write notes for yourself at the very end of a Texinfo file after the `@bye`. None of the formatters process text after the `@bye`; it is as if the text were within `@ignore` . . . `@end ignore`.

Appendix C A Sample Texinfo File

Here is a complete, short sample Texinfo file, without any commentary. You can see this file, with comments, in the first chapter. See Section 1.10 [A Short Sample Texinfo File], page 12.

```
\input texinfo   @c -*-texinfo-*-
@c %**start of header
@setfilename sample.info
@settitle Sample Document
@c %**end of header


@setchapternewpage odd


@ifinfo
This is a short example of a complete Texinfo file.

Copyright 1990 Free Software Foundation, Inc.
@end ifinfo


@titlepage
@sp 10
@comment The title is printed in a large font.
@center @titlefont{Sample Title}


@c The following two commands start the copyright page.
@page
@vskip 0pt plus 1filll
Copyright @copyright{} 1990 Free Software Foundation, Inc.
@end titlepage


@node    Top,       First Chapter,         , (dir)
@comment node-name, next,          previous, up


@menu
* First Chapter::    The first chapter is the
                     only chapter in this sample.
* Concept Index::    This index has two entries.
@end menu


@node    First Chapter, Concept Index, Top,    Top
@comment node-name,      next,         previous, up
@chapter First Chapter
@cindex Sample index entry
```

```
This is the contents of the first chapter.
@cindex Another sample index entry

Here is a numbered list.

@enumerate
@item
This is the first item.

@item
This is the second item.
@end enumerate

The @code{makeinfo} and @code{texinfo-format-buffer}
commands transform a Texinfo file such as this into
an Info file; and @TeX{} typesets it for a printed
manual.

@node    Concept Index,    , First Chapter, Top
@comment node-name,    next,  previous,      up
@unnumbered Concept Index

@printindex cp

@contents
@bye
```

Appendix D Sample Permissions

Texinfo files should contain sections that tell the readers that they have the right to copy and distribute the Texinfo file, the Info file, and the printed manual.

Also, if you are writing a manual about software, you should explain that the software is free and either include the GNU General Public License (GPL) or provide a reference to it. See section "Distribution" in *The GNU Emacs Manual*, for an example of the text that could be used in the software "Distribution", "General Public License", and "NO WARRANTY" sections of a document. See [Texinfo Copying Conditions], page 2, for an example of a brief explanation of how the copying conditions provide you with rights.

In a Texinfo file, the first @ifinfo section usually begins with a line that says what the file documents. This is what a person reading the unprocessed Texinfo file or using the advanced Info command g * sees first. See Info file 'info', node 'Expert', for more information. (A reader using the regular Info commands usually starts reading at the first node and skips this first section, which is not in a node.)

In the @ifinfo section, the summary sentence is followed by a copyright notice and then by the copying permission notice. One of the copying permission paragraphs is enclosed in @ignore and @end ignore commands. This paragraph states that the Texinfo file can be processed through TeX and printed, provided the printed manual carries the proper copying permission notice. This paragraph is not made part of the Info file since it is not relevant to the Info file; but it is a mandatory part of the Texinfo file since it permits people to process the Texinfo file in TeX and print the results.

In the printed manual, the Free Software Foundation copying permission notice follows the copyright notice and publishing information and is located within the region delineated by the @titlepage and @end titlepage commands. The copying permission notice is exactly the same as the notice in the @ifinfo section except that the paragraph enclosed in @ignore and @end ignore commands is not part of the notice.

To make it simple to insert a permission notice into each section of the Texinfo file, sample permission notices for each section are reproduced in full below.

You may need to specify the correct name of a section mentioned in the permission notice. For example, in *The GDB Manual*, the name of the section referring to the General Public License is called the "GDB General Public License", but in the sample shown below, that section is referred to generically as the "GNU General Public License". If the Texinfo file does not carry a copy of the General Public License, leave out the reference to it, but be sure to include the rest of the sentence.

D.1 'ifinfo' Copying Permissions

In the @ifinfo section of a Texinfo file, the standard Free Software Foundation permission notice reads as follows:

```
This file documents ...
```

```
Copyright 1999 Free Software Foundation, Inc.
```

```
Permission is granted to make and distribute verbatim
copies of this manual provided the copyright notice and
this permission notice are preserved on all copies.
```

```
@ignore
Permission is granted to process this file through TeX
and print the results, provided the printed document
carries a copying permission notice identical to this
one except for the removal of this paragraph (this
paragraph not being relevant to the printed manual).
```

```
@end ignore
Permission is granted to copy and distribute modified
versions of this manual under the conditions for
verbatim copying, provided also that the sections
entitled ''Copying'' and ''GNU General Public License''
are included exactly as in the original, and provided
that the entire resulting derived work is distributed
under the terms of a permission notice identical to this
one.
```

```
Permission is granted to copy and distribute
translations of this manual into another language,
under the above conditions for modified versions,
except that this permission notice may be stated in a
translation approved by the Free Software Foundation.
```

D.2 Titlepage Copying Permissions

In the @titlepage section of a Texinfo file, the standard Free Software Foundation copying permission notice follows the copyright notice and publishing information. The standard phrasing is as follows:

```
Permission is granted to make and distribute verbatim
copies of this manual provided the copyright notice and
this permission notice are preserved on all copies.
```

```
Permission is granted to copy and distribute modified
versions of this manual under the conditions for
verbatim copying, provided also that the sections
entitled ''Copying'' and ''GNU General Public License''
are included exactly as in the original, and provided
```

```
that the entire resulting derived work is distributed
under the terms of a permission notice identical to this
one.
```

```
Permission is granted to copy and distribute
translations of this manual into another language,
under the above conditions for modified versions,
except that this permission notice may be stated in a
translation approved by the Free Software Foundation.
```

Appendix E Include Files

When TEX or an Info formatting command sees an @include command in a Texinfo file, it processes the contents of the file named by the command and incorporates them into the DVI or Info file being created. Index entries from the included file are incorporated into the indices of the output file.

Include files let you keep a single large document as a collection of conveniently small parts.

E.1 How to Use Include Files

To include another file within a Texinfo file, write the @include command at the beginning of a line and follow it on the same line by the name of a file to be included. For example:

```
@include buffers.texi
```

An included file should simply be a segment of text that you expect to be included as is into the overall or *outer* Texinfo file; it should not contain the standard beginning and end parts of a Texinfo file. In particular, you should not start an included file with a line saying '\input texinfo'; if you do, that phrase is inserted into the output file as is. Likewise, you should not end an included file with an @bye command; nothing after @bye is formatted.

In the past, you were required to write an @setfilename line at the beginning of an included file, but no longer. Now, it does not matter whether you write such a line. If an @setfilename line exists in an included file, it is ignored.

Conventionally, an included file begins with an @node line that is followed by an @chapter line. Each included file is one chapter. This makes it easy to use the regular node and menu creating and updating commands to create the node pointers and menus within the included file. However, the simple Emacs node and menu creating and updating commands do not work with multiple Texinfo files. Thus you cannot use these commands to fill in the 'Next', 'Previous', and 'Up' pointers of the @node line that begins the included file. Also, you cannot use the regular commands to create a master menu for the whole file. Either you must insert the menus and the 'Next', 'Previous', and 'Up' pointers by hand, or you must use the GNU Emacs Texinfo mode command, texinfo-multiple-files-update, that is designed for @include files.

E.2 texinfo-multiple-files-update

GNU Emacs Texinfo mode provides the texinfo-multiple-files-update command. This command creates or updates 'Next', 'Previous', and 'Up' pointers of included files as well as those in the outer or overall Texinfo file, and it creates or updates a main menu in the outer file. Depending whether you call it with optional arguments, the command updates only the pointers in the first @node line of the included files or all of them:

M-x texinfo-multiple-files-update
Called without any arguments:

- Create or update the 'Next', 'Previous', and 'Up' pointers of the first @node line in each file included in an outer or overall Texinfo file.

- Create or update the 'Top' level node pointers of the outer or overall file.

- Create or update a main menu in the outer file.

`C-u M-x texinfo-multiple-files-update`
Called with `C-u` as a prefix argument:

- Create or update pointers in the first @node line in each included file.

- Create or update the 'Top' level node pointers of the outer file.

- Create and insert a master menu in the outer file. The master menu is made from all the menus in all the included files.

`C-u 8 M-x texinfo-multiple-files-update`
Called with a numeric prefix argument, such as `C-u 8`:

- Create or update all the 'Next', 'Previous', and 'Up' pointers of all the included files.

- Create or update all the menus of all the included files.

- Create or update the 'Top' level node pointers of the outer or overall file.

- And then create a master menu in the outer file. This is similar to invoking `texinfo-master-menu` with an argument when you are working with just one file.

Note the use of the prefix argument in interactive use: with a regular prefix argument, just `C-u`, the `texinfo-multiple-files-update` command inserts a master menu; with a numeric prefix argument, such as `C-u 8`, the command updates every pointer and menu in all the files and then inserts a master menu.

E.3 Include File Requirements

If you plan to use the `texinfo-multiple-files-update` command, the outer Texinfo file that lists included files within it should contain nothing but the beginning and end parts of a Texinfo file, and a number of @include commands listing the included files. It should not even include indices, which should be listed in an included file of their own.

Moreover, each of the included files must contain exactly one highest level node (conventionally, @chapter or equivalent), and this node must be the first node in the included file. Furthermore, each of these highest level nodes in each included file must be at the same hierarchical level in the file structure. Usually, each is an @chapter, an @appendix, or an @unnumbered node. Thus, normally, each included file contains one, and only one, chapter or equivalent-level node.

The outer file should contain only *one* node, the 'Top' node. It should *not* contain any nodes besides the single 'Top' node. The `texinfo-multiple-files-update` command will not process them.

E.4 Sample File with `@include`

Here is an example of a complete outer Texinfo file with `@include` files within it before running `texinfo-multiple-files-update`, which would insert a main or master menu:

```
\input texinfo @c -*-texinfo-*-
@setfilename  include-example.info
@settitle Include Example

@setchapternewpage odd
@titlepage
@sp 12
@center @titlefont{Include Example}
@sp 2
@center by Whom Ever

@page
@vskip 0pt plus 1filll
Copyright @copyright{} 1999 Free Software Foundation, Inc.
@end titlepage

@ifinfo
@node Top, First, , (dir)
@top Master Menu
@end ifinfo

@include foo.texinfo
@include bar.texinfo
@include concept-index.texinfo

@summarycontents
@contents

@bye
```

An included file, such as 'foo.texinfo', might look like this:

```
@node First, Second, , Top
@chapter First Chapter

Contents of first chapter ...
```

The full contents of 'concept-index.texinfo' might be as simple as this:

```
@node Concept Index
@unnumbered Concept Index
```

```
@printindex cp
```

The outer Texinfo source file for *The GNU Emacs Lisp Reference Manual* is named 'elisp.texi'. This outer file contains a master menu with 417 entries and a list of 41 @include files.

E.5 Evolution of Include Files

When Info was first created, it was customary to create many small Info files on one subject. Each Info file was formatted from its own Texinfo source file. This custom meant that Emacs did not need to make a large buffer to hold the whole of a large Info file when someone wanted information; instead, Emacs allocated just enough memory for the small Info file that contained the particular information sought. This way, Emacs could avoid wasting memory.

References from one file to another were made by referring to the file name as well as the node name. (See Section 7.5 [Referring to Other Info Files], page 67. Also, see Section 8.3.4 [@xref with Four and Five Arguments], page 73.)

Include files were designed primarily as a way to create a single, large printed manual out of several smaller Info files. In a printed manual, all the references were within the same document, so TEX could automatically determine the references' page numbers. The Info formatting commands used include files only for creating joint indices; each of the individual Texinfo files had to be formatted for Info individually. (Each, therefore, required its own @setfilename line.)

However, because large Info files are now split automatically, it is no longer necessary to keep them small.

Nowadays, multiple Texinfo files are used mostly for large documents, such as *The GNU Emacs Lisp Reference Manual*, and for projects in which several different people write different sections of a document simultaneously.

In addition, the Info formatting commands have been extended to work with the @include command so as to create a single large Info file that is split into smaller files if necessary. This means that you can write menus and cross references without naming the different Texinfo files.

Appendix F Page Headings

Most printed manuals contain headings along the top of every page except the title and copyright pages. Some manuals also contain footings. (Headings and footings have no meaning to Info, which is not paginated.)

Texinfo provides standard page heading formats for manuals that are printed on one side of each sheet of paper and for manuals that are printed on both sides of the paper. Typically, you will use these formats, but you can specify your own format if you wish.

In addition, you can specify whether chapters should begin on a new page, or merely continue the same page as the previous chapter; and if chapters begin on new pages, you can specify whether they must be odd-numbered pages.

By convention, a book is printed on both sides of each sheet of paper. When you open a book, the right-hand page is odd-numbered, and chapters begin on right-hand pages—a preceding left-hand page is left blank if necessary. Reports, however, are often printed on just one side of paper, and chapters begin on a fresh page immediately following the end of the preceding chapter. In short or informal reports, chapters often do not begin on a new page at all, but are separated from the preceding text by a small amount of whitespace.

The `@setchapternewpage` command controls whether chapters begin on new pages, and whether one of the standard heading formats is used. In addition, Texinfo has several heading and footing commands that you can use to generate your own heading and footing formats.

In Texinfo, headings and footings are single lines at the tops and bottoms of pages; you cannot create multiline headings or footings. Each header or footer line is divided into three parts: a left part, a middle part, and a right part. Any part, or a whole line, may be left blank. Text for the left part of a header or footer line is set flushleft; text for the middle part is centered; and, text for the right part is set flushright.

F.1 Standard Heading Formats

Texinfo provides two standard heading formats, one for manuals printed on one side of each sheet of paper, and the other for manuals printed on both sides of the paper.

By default, nothing is specified for the footing of a Texinfo file, so the footing remains blank.

The standard format for single-sided printing consists of a header line in which the left-hand part contains the name of the chapter, the central part is blank, and the right-hand part contains the page number.

A single-sided page looks like this:

```
------------------------
|                      |
| chapter    page number |
|                      |
| Start of text ...    |
| ...                  |
|                      |
```

The standard format for two-sided printing depends on whether the page number is even or odd. By convention, even-numbered pages are on the left and odd-numbered pages are on the right. (TeX will adjust the widths of the left- and right-hand margins. Usually, widths are correct, but during double-sided printing, it is wise to check that pages will bind properly— sometimes a printer will produce output in which the even-numbered pages have a larger right-hand margin than the odd-numbered pages.)

In the standard double-sided format, the left part of the left-hand (even-numbered) page contains the page number, the central part is blank, and the right part contains the title (specified by the @settitle command). The left part of the right-hand (odd-numbered) page contains the name of the chapter, the central part is blank, and the right part contains the page number.

Two pages, side by side as in an open book, look like this:

```
------------------------      ------------------------
|                      |      |                      |
| page number    title |      | chapter    page number |
|                      |      |                      |
| Start of text ...    |      | More   text ...      |
| ...                  |      | ...                  |
|                      |      |                      |
```

The chapter name is preceded by the word "Chapter", the chapter number and a colon. This makes it easier to keep track of where you are in the manual.

F.2 Specifying the Type of Heading

TeX does not begin to generate page headings for a standard Texinfo file until it reaches the @end titlepage command. Thus, the title and copyright pages are not numbered. The @end titlepage command causes TeX to begin to generate page headings according to a standard format specified by the @setchapternewpage command that precedes the @titlepage section.

There are four possibilities:

No `@setchapternewpage` command

> Cause TEX to specify the single-sided heading format, with chapters on new pages. This is the same as `@setchapternewpage on`.

`@setchapternewpage on`

> Specify the single-sided heading format, with chapters on new pages.

`@setchapternewpage off`

> Cause TEX to start a new chapter on the same page as the last page of the preceding chapter, after skipping some vertical whitespace. Also cause TEX to typeset for single-sided printing. (You can override the headers format with the `@headings double` command; see Section 3.4.6 [The `@headings` Command], page 42.)

`@setchapternewpage odd`

> Specify the double-sided heading format, with chapters on new pages.

Texinfo lacks an `@setchapternewpage even` command.

F.3 How to Make Your Own Headings

You can use the standard headings provided with Texinfo or specify your own. By default, Texinfo has no footers, so if you specify them, the available page size for the main text will be slightly reduced.

Texinfo provides six commands for specifying headings and footings:

- `@everyheading @everyfooting` generate page headers and footers that are the same for both even- and odd-numbered pages.

- `@evenheading` and `@evenfooting` command generate headers and footers for even-numbered (left-hand) pages.

- `@oddheading` and `@oddfooting` generate headers and footers for odd-numbered (right-hand) pages.

Write custom heading specifications in the Texinfo file immediately after the `@end titlepage` command. Enclose your specifications between `@iftex` and `@end iftex` commands since the `texinfo-format-buffer` command may not recognize them. Also, you must cancel the predefined heading commands with the `@headings off` command before defining your own specifications.

Here is how to tell TEX to place the chapter name at the left, the page number in the center, and the date at the right of every header for both even- and odd-numbered pages:

```
@iftex

@headings off

@everyheading @thischapter @| @thispage @| @today{}

@end iftex
```

You need to divide the left part from the central part and the central part from the right part by inserting '`@|`' between parts. Otherwise, the specifica-

tion command will not be able to tell where the text for one part ends and
the next part begins.

Each part can contain text or @-commands. The text is printed as if
the part were within an ordinary paragraph in the body of the page. The
@-commands replace themselves with the page number, date, chapter name,
or whatever.

Here are the six heading and footing commands:

`@everyheading` *left* `@|` *center* `@|` *right*
`@everyfooting` *left* `@|` *center* `@|` *right*

> The 'every' commands specify the format for both even- and
> odd-numbered pages. These commands are for documents that
> are printed on one side of each sheet of paper, or for documents
> in which you want symmetrical headers or footers.

`@evenheading` *left* `@|` *center* `@|` *right*
`@oddheading` *left* `@|` *center* `@|` *right*
`@evenfooting` *left* `@|` *center* `@|` *right*
`@oddfooting` *left* `@|` *center* `@|` *right*

> The 'even' and 'odd' commands specify the format for even-
> numbered pages and odd-numbered pages. These commands
> are for books and manuals that are printed on both sides of
> each sheet of paper.

Use the '`@this`...' series of @-commands to provide the names of chapters
and sections and the page number. You can use the '`@this`...' commands in
the left, center, or right portions of headers and footers, or anywhere else in
a Texinfo file so long as they are between `@iftex` and `@end iftex` commands.

Here are the '`@this`...' commands:

`@thispage`   Expands to the current page number.

`@thischaptername`

> Expands to the name of the current chapter.

`@thischapter`

> Expands to the number and name of the current chapter, in the
> format 'Chapter 1: Title'.

`@thistitle`   Expands to the name of the document, as specified by the
                 `@settitle` command.

`@thisfile`   For `@include` files only: expands to the name of the current
                 `@include` file. If the current Texinfo source file is not an `@include`
                 file, this command has no effect. This command does *not* pro-
                 vide the name of the current Texinfo source file unless it is an
                 `@include` file. (See Appendix E [Include Files], page 209, for more
                 information about `@include` files.)

You can also use the `@today{}` command, which expands to the current date,
in '1 Jan 1900' format.

Other @-commands and text are printed in a header or footer just as if
they were in the body of a page. It is useful to incorporate text, particularly
when you are writing drafts:

```
@iftex
@headings off
@everyheading @emph{Draft!} @| @thispage @| @thischapter
@everyfooting @| @| Version: 0.27: @today{}
@end iftex
```

Beware of overlong titles: they may overlap another part of the header or footer and blot it out.

Appendix G Formatting Mistakes

Besides mistakes in the content of your documentation, there are two kinds of mistake you can make with Texinfo: you can make mistakes with @-commands, and you can make mistakes with the structure of the nodes and chapters.

Emacs has two tools for catching the @-command mistakes and two for catching structuring mistakes.

For finding problems with @-commands, you can run TEX or a region formatting command on the region that has a problem; indeed, you can run these commands on each region as you write it.

For finding problems with the structure of nodes and chapters, you can use `C-c C-s` (`texinfo-show-structure`) and the related `occur` command and you can use the `M-x Info-validate` command.

The `makeinfo` program does an excellent job of catching errors and reporting them—far better than `texinfo-format-region` or `texinfo-format-buffer`. In addition, the various functions for automatically creating and updating node pointers and menus remove many opportunities for human error.

If you can, use the updating commands to create and insert pointers and menus. These prevent many errors. Then use `makeinfo` (or its Texinfo mode manifestations, `makeinfo-region` and `makeinfo-buffer`) to format your file and check for other errors. This is the best way to work with Texinfo. But if you cannot use `makeinfo`, or your problem is very puzzling, then you may want to use the tools described in this appendix.

G.1 Catching Errors with Info Formatting

After you have written part of a Texinfo file, you can use the `texinfo-format-region` or the `makeinfo-region` command to see whether the region formats properly.

Most likely, however, you are reading this section because for some reason you cannot use the `makeinfo-region` command; therefore, the rest of this section presumes that you are using `texinfo-format-region`.

If you have made a mistake with an @-command, `texinfo-format-region` will stop processing at or after the error and display an error message. To see where in the buffer the error occurred, switch to the '`*Info Region*`' buffer; the cursor will be in a position that is after the location of the error. Also, the text will not be formatted after the place where the error occurred (or more precisely, where it was detected).

For example, if you accidentally end a menu with the command `@end menus` with an 's' on the end, instead of with `@end menu`, you will see an error message that says:

```
@end menus is not handled by texinfo
```

The cursor will stop at the point in the buffer where the error occurs, or not long after it. The buffer will look like this:

```
---------- Buffer: *Info Region* ----------
* Menu:

* Using texinfo-show-structure::   How to use
                                   'texinfo-show-structure'
                                   to catch mistakes.
* Running Info-Validate::          How to check for
                                   unreferenced nodes.
@end menus

*
---------- Buffer: *Info Region* ----------
```

The `texinfo-format-region` command sometimes provides slightly odd error messages. For example, the following cross reference fails to format:

```
(@xref{Catching Mistakes, for more info.)
```

In this case, `texinfo-format-region` detects the missing closing brace but displays a message that says 'Unbalanced parentheses' rather than 'Unbalanced braces'. This is because the formatting command looks for mismatches between braces as if they were parentheses.

Sometimes `texinfo-format-region` fails to detect mistakes. For example, in the following, the closing brace is swapped with the closing parenthesis:

```
(@xref{Catching Mistakes), for more info.}
```

Formatting produces:

```
(*Note for more info.: Catching Mistakes)
```

The only way for you to detect this error is to realize that the reference should have looked like this:

```
(*Note Catching Mistakes::, for more info.)
```

Incidentally, if you are reading this node in Info and type f (RET) (Info-follow-reference), you will generate an error message that says:

```
No such node: "Catching Mistakes) The only way ...
```

This is because Info perceives the example of the error as the first cross reference in this node and if you type a (RET) immediately after typing the Info f command, Info will attempt to go to the referenced node. If you type f catch (TAB) (RET), Info will complete the node name of the correctly written example and take you to the 'Catching Mistakes' node. (If you try this, you can return from the 'Catching Mistakes' node by typing l (Info-last).)

G.2 Catching Errors with TeX Formatting

You can also catch mistakes when you format a file with TeX.

Usually, you will want to do this after you have run `texinfo-format-buffer` (or, better, `makeinfo-buffer`) on the same file, because `texinfo-format-buffer` sometimes displays error messages that make more sense than TeX. (See Section G.1 [Debugging with Info], page 218, for more information.)

For example, TeX was run on a Texinfo file, part of which is shown here:

```
---------- Buffer: texinfo.texi ----------
name of the Texinfo file as an extension.  The
@samp{??} are 'wildcards' that cause the shell to
substitute all the raw index files.  (@xref{sorting
indices, for more information about sorting
indices.)@refill
---------- Buffer: texinfo.texi ----------
```

(The cross reference lacks a closing brace.) TEX produced the following output, after which it stopped:

```
---------- Buffer: *tex-shell* ----------
Runaway argument?
{sorting indices, for more information about sorting
indices.) @refill @ETC.
! Paragraph ended before @xref was complete.
<to be read again>
                  @par
1.27


?
---------- Buffer: *tex-shell* ----------
```

In this case, TEX produced an accurate and understandable error message:

Paragraph ended before @xref was complete.

'@par' is an internal TEX command of no relevance to Texinfo. '1.27' means that TEX detected the problem on line 27 of the Texinfo file. The '?' is the prompt TEX uses in this circumstance.

Unfortunately, TEX is not always so helpful, and sometimes you must truly be a Sherlock Holmes to discover what went wrong.

In any case, if you run into a problem like this, you can do one of three things.

1. You can tell TEX to continue running and ignore just this error by typing ⟨RET⟩ at the '?' prompt.

2. You can tell TEX to continue running and to ignore all errors as best it can by typing r ⟨RET⟩ at the '?' prompt.

   This is often the best thing to do. However, beware: the one error may produce a cascade of additional error messages as its consequences are felt through the rest of the file. To stop TEX when it is producing such an avalanche of error messages, type C-c (or C-c C-c, if you are running a shell inside Emacs).

3. You can tell TEX to stop this run by typing x ⟨RET⟩ at the '?' prompt.

If you are running TEX inside Emacs, you need to switch to the shell buffer and line at which TEX offers the '?' prompt.

Sometimes TEX will format a file without producing error messages even though there is a problem. This usually occurs if a command is not ended but TEX is able to continue processing anyhow. For example, if you fail to end an itemized list with the @end itemize command, TEX will write a DVI file that you can print out. The only error message that TEX will give you is the somewhat mysterious comment that

```
(@end occurred inside a group at level 1)
```

However, if you print the DVI file, you will find that the text of the file that follows the itemized list is entirely indented as if it were part of the last item in the itemized list. The error message is the way TEX says that it expected to find an @end command somewhere in the file; but that it could not determine where it was needed.

Another source of notoriously hard-to-find errors is a missing @end group command. If you ever are stumped by incomprehensible errors, look for a missing @end group command first.

If the Texinfo file lacks header lines, TEX may stop in the beginning of its run and display output that looks like the following. The '*' indicates that TEX is waiting for input.

```
This is TeX, Version 3.14159 (Web2c 7.0)
(test.texinfo [1])
*
```

In this case, simply type \end (RET) after the asterisk. Then write the header lines in the Texinfo file and run the TEX command again. (Note the use of the backslash, '\'. TEX uses '\' instead of '@'; and in this circumstance, you are working directly with TEX, not with Texinfo.)

G.3 Using `texinfo-show-structure`

It is not always easy to keep track of the nodes, chapters, sections, and subsections of a Texinfo file. This is especially true if you are revising or adding to a Texinfo file that someone else has written.

In GNU Emacs, in Texinfo mode, the `texinfo-show-structure` command lists all the lines that begin with the @-commands that specify the structure: @chapter, @section, @appendix, and so on. With an argument (C-u as prefix argument, if interactive), the command also shows the @node lines. The `texinfo-show-structure` command is bound to C-c C-s in Texinfo mode, by default.

The lines are displayed in a buffer called the '*Occur*' buffer, indented by hierarchical level. For example, here is a part of what was produced by running `texinfo-show-structure` on this manual:

```
Lines matching "^@\\(chapter \\|sect\\|subs\\|subh\\|
unnum\\|major\\|chapheading \\|heading \\|appendix\\)"
in buffer texinfo.texi.

...

4177:@chapter Nodes
4198:    @heading Two Paths
4231:    @section Node and Menu Illustration
4337:    @section The @code{@@node} Command
4393:        @subheading Choosing Node and Pointer Names
4417:        @subsection How to Write an @code{@@node} Line
4469:        @subsection @code{@@node} Line Tips

...
```

This says that lines 4337, 4393, and 4417 of ‘texinfo.texi’ begin with the @section, @subheading, and @subsection commands respectively. If you move your cursor into the ‘*Occur*’ window, you can position the cursor over one of the lines and use the C-c C-c command (occur-mode-goto-occurrence), to jump to the corresponding spot in the Texinfo file. See section "Using Occur" in *The GNU Emacs Manual*, for more information about occur-mode-goto-occurrence.

The first line in the ‘*Occur*’ window describes the *regular expression* specified by *texinfo-heading-pattern*. This regular expression is the pattern that texinfo-show-structure looks for. See section "Using Regular Expressions" in *The GNU Emacs Manual*, for more information.

When you invoke the texinfo-show-structure command, Emacs will display the structure of the whole buffer. If you want to see the structure of just a part of the buffer, of one chapter, for example, use the C-x n n (narrow-to-region) command to mark the region. (See section "Narrowing" in *The GNU Emacs Manual*.) This is how the example used above was generated. (To see the whole buffer again, use C-x n w (widen).)

If you call texinfo-show-structure with a prefix argument by typing C-u C-c C-s, it will list lines beginning with @node as well as the lines beginning with the @-sign commands for @chapter, @section, and the like.

You can remind yourself of the structure of a Texinfo file by looking at the list in the ‘*Occur*’ window; and if you have mis-named a node or left out a section, you can correct the mistake.

G.4 Using occur

Sometimes the texinfo-show-structure command produces too much information. Perhaps you want to remind yourself of the overall structure of a Texinfo file, and are overwhelmed by the detailed list produced by texinfo-show-structure. In this case, you can use the occur command directly. To do this, type

    M-x occur

and then, when prompted, type a *regexp*, a regular expression for the pattern you want to match. (See section "Regular Expressions" in *The GNU Emacs*

Manual.) The `occur` command works from the current location of the cursor in the buffer to the end of the buffer. If you want to run `occur` on the whole buffer, place the cursor at the beginning of the buffer.

For example, to see all the lines that contain the word '`@chapter`' in them, just type '`@chapter`'. This will produce a list of the chapters. It will also list all the sentences with '`@chapter`' in the middle of the line.

If you want to see only those lines that start with the word '`@chapter`', type '`^@chapter`' when prompted by `occur`. If you want to see all the lines that end with a word or phrase, end the last word with a '`$`'; for example, '`catching mistakes$`'. This can be helpful when you want to see all the nodes that are part of the same chapter or section and therefore have the same 'Up' pointer.

See section "Using Occur" in *The GNU Emacs Manual*, for more information.

G.5 Finding Badly Referenced Nodes

You can use the `Info-validate` command to check whether any of the 'Next', 'Previous', 'Up' or other node pointers fail to point to a node. This command checks that every node pointer points to an existing node. The `Info-validate` command works only on Info files, not on Texinfo files.

The `makeinfo` program validates pointers automatically, so you do not need to use the `Info-validate` command if you are using `makeinfo`. You only may need to use `Info-validate` if you are unable to run `makeinfo` and instead must create an Info file using `texinfo-format-region` or `texinfo-format-buffer`, or if you write an Info file from scratch.

G.5.1 Running `Info-validate`

To use `Info-validate`, visit the Info file you wish to check and type:

```
M-x Info-validate
```

Note that the `Info-validate` command requires an upper case 'I'. You may also need to create a tag table before running `Info-validate`. See Section G.5.3 [Tagifying], page 224.

If your file is valid, you will receive a message that says "File appears valid". However, if you have a pointer that does not point to a node, error messages will be displayed in a buffer called '`*problems in info file*`'.

For example, `Info-validate` was run on a test file that contained only the first node of this manual. One of the messages said:

```
In node "Overview", invalid Next: Texinfo Mode
```

This meant that the node called '`Overview`' had a 'Next' pointer that did not point to anything (which was true in this case, since the test file had only one node in it).

Now suppose we add a node named '`Texinfo Mode`' to our test case but we do not specify a 'Previous' for this node. Then we will get the following error message:

```
In node "Texinfo Mode", should have Previous: Overview
```

This is because every 'Next' pointer should be matched by a 'Previous' (in the node where the 'Next' points) which points back.

Info-validate also checks that all menu entries and cross references point to actual nodes.

Info-validate requires a tag table and does not work with files that have been split. (The texinfo-format-buffer command automatically splits large files.) In order to use Info-validate on a large file, you must run texinfo-format-buffer with an argument so that it does not split the Info file; and you must create a tag table for the unsplit file.

G.5.2 Creating an Unsplit File

You can run Info-validate only on a single Info file that has a tag table. The command will not work on the indirect subfiles that are generated when a master file is split. If you have a large file (longer than 70,000 bytes or so), you need to run the texinfo-format-buffer or makeinfo-buffer command in such a way that it does not create indirect subfiles. You will also need to create a tag table for the Info file. After you have done this, you can run Info-validate and look for badly referenced nodes.

The first step is to create an unsplit Info file. To prevent texinfo-format-buffer from splitting a Texinfo file into smaller Info files, give a prefix to the M-x texinfo-format-buffer command:

```
C-u M-x texinfo-format-buffer
```

or else

```
C-u C-c C-e C-b
```

When you do this, Texinfo will not split the file and will not create a tag table for it.

G.5.3 Tagifying a File

After creating an unsplit Info file, you must create a tag table for it. Visit the Info file you wish to tagify and type:

```
M-x Info-tagify
```

(Note the upper case 'I' in Info-tagify.) This creates an Info file with a tag table that you can validate.

The third step is to validate the Info file:

```
M-x Info-validate
```

(Note the upper case 'I' in Info-validate.) In brief, the steps are:

```
C-u M-x texinfo-format-buffer
M-x Info-tagify
M-x Info-validate
```

After you have validated the node structure, you can rerun texinfo-format-buffer in the normal way so it will construct a tag table and split the file automatically, or you can make the tag table and split the file manually.

G.5.4 Splitting a File Manually

You should split a large file or else let the `texinfo-format-buffer` or `makeinfo-buffer` command do it for you automatically. (Generally you will let one of the formatting commands do this job for you. See Section 20.1 [Creating an Info File], page 165.)

The split-off files are called the indirect subfiles.

Info files are split to save memory. With smaller files, Emacs does not have make such a large buffer to hold the information.

If an Info file has more than 30 nodes, you should also make a tag table for it. See Section G.5.1 [Using Info-validate], page 223, for information about creating a tag table. (Again, tag tables are usually created automatically by the formatting command; you only need to create a tag table yourself if you are doing the job manually. Most likely, you will do this for a large, unsplit file on which you have run `Info-validate`.)

Visit the Info file you wish to tagify and split and type the two commands:

```
M-x Info-tagify
M-x Info-split
```

(Note that the 'I' in 'Info' is upper case.)

When you use the `Info-split` command, the buffer is modified into a (small) Info file which lists the indirect subfiles. This file should be saved in place of the original visited file. The indirect subfiles are written in the same directory the original file is in, with names generated by appending '-' and a number to the original file name.

The primary file still functions as an Info file, but it contains just the tag table and a directory of subfiles.

Appendix H Refilling Paragraphs

The `@refill` command refills and, optionally, indents the first line of a paragraph.[1] The `@refill` command is no longer important, but we describe it here because you once needed it. You will see it in many old Texinfo files.

Without refilling, paragraphs containing long `@`-constructs may look bad after formatting because the formatter removes `@`-commands and shortens some lines more than others. In the past, neither the `texinfo-format-region` command nor the `texinfo-format-buffer` command refilled paragraphs automatically. The `@refill` command had to be written at the end of every paragraph to cause these formatters to fill them. (Both TeX and `makeinfo` have always refilled paragraphs automatically.) Now, all the Info formatters automatically fill and indent those paragraphs that need to be filled and indented.

The `@refill` command causes `texinfo-format-region` and `texinfo-format-buffer` to refill a paragraph in the Info file *after* all the other processing has been done. For this reason, you can not use `@refill` with a paragraph containing either `@*` or `@w{ ... }` since the refilling action will override those two commands.

The `texinfo-format-region` and `texinfo-format-buffer` commands now automatically append `@refill` to the end of each paragraph that should be filled. They do not append `@refill` to the ends of paragraphs that contain `@*` or `@w{ ...}` and therefore do not refill or indent them.

---

[1] Perhaps the command should have been called the `@refillandindent` command, but `@refill` is shorter and the name was chosen before indenting was possible.

Appendix I @-Command Syntax

The character '@' is used to start special Texinfo commands. (It has the same meaning that '\' has in plain TEX.) Texinfo has four types of @-command:

1. Non-alphabetic commands.

These commands consist of an @ followed by a punctuation mark or other character that is not part of the alphabet. Non-alphabetic commands are almost always part of the text within a paragraph, and never take any argument. The two characters (@ and the other one) are complete in themselves; none is followed by braces. The non-alphabetic commands are: @., @:, @*, @SPACE, @TAB, @NL, @@, @{, and @}.

2. Alphabetic commands that do not require arguments.

These commands start with @ followed by a word followed by left- and right-hand braces. These commands insert special symbols in the document; they do not require arguments. For example, @dots{} ⇒ '...', @equiv{} ⇒ '≡', @TeX{} ⇒ 'TEX', and @bullet{} ⇒ '•'.

3. Alphabetic commands that require arguments within braces.

These commands start with @ followed by a letter or a word, followed by an argument within braces. For example, the command @dfn indicates the introductory or defining use of a term; it is used as follows: 'In Texinfo, @@-commands are @dfn{mark-up} commands.'

4. Alphabetic commands that occupy an entire line.

These commands occupy an entire line. The line starts with @, followed by the name of the command (a word); for example, @center or @cindex. If no argument is needed, the word is followed by the end of the line. If there is an argument, it is separated from the command name by a space. Braces are not used.

Thus, the alphabetic commands fall into classes that have different argument syntaxes. You cannot tell to which class a command belongs by the appearance of its name, but you can tell by the command's meaning: if the command stands for a glyph, it is in class 2 and does not require an argument; if it makes sense to use the command together with other text as part of a paragraph, the command is in class 3 and must be followed by an argument in braces; otherwise, it is in class 4 and uses the rest of the line as its argument.

The purpose of having a different syntax for commands of classes 3 and 4 is to make Texinfo files easier to read, and also to help the GNU Emacs paragraph and filling commands work properly. There is only one exception to this rule: the command @refill, which is always used at the end of a paragraph immediately following the final period or other punctuation character. @refill takes no argument and does *not* require braces. @refill never confuses the Emacs paragraph commands because it cannot appear at the beginning of a line.

Appendix J How to Obtain TeX

TeX is freely redistributable. You can obtain TeX for Unix systems via anonymous ftp or on physical media. The core material consists of the Web2c TeX distribution (`http://tug.org/web2c`).

Instructions for retrieval by anonymous ftp and information on other available distributions:

`ftp://tug.org/tex/unixtex.ftp`

`http://tug.org/unixtex.ftp`

The Free Software Foundation provides a core distribution on its Source Code CD-ROM suitable for printing Texinfo manuals. To order it, contact:

Free Software Foundation, Inc.
59 Temple Place Suite 330
Boston, MA   02111-1307
USA
Telephone: +1-617-542-5942
Fax: (including Japan) +1-617-542-2652
Free Dial Fax (in Japan):
    0031-13-2473 (KDD)
    0066-3382-0158 (IDC)
Electronic mail: `gnu@gnu.org`

Many other TeX distributions are available; see `http://tug.org/`.

Command and Variable Index

This is an alphabetical list of all the @-commands, assorted Emacs Lisp functions, and several variables. To make the list easier to use, the commands are listed without their preceding '@'.

A

B

C

D

E

F

G

H

I

K

Concept Index

L

M

N